Breach of Faith

Breach of Faith

A CRISIS OF COVERAGE IN THE AGE
OF CORPORATE NEWSPAPERING

Gene Roberts
Editor in Chief

Thomas Kunkel
General Editor

THE UNIVERSITY OF ARKANSAS PRESS
FAYETTEVILLE
2002

Copyright © 2002 by The University of Arkansas Press

All rights reserved
Manufactured in the United States of America

06   05   04   03   02   5   4   3   2   1

TEXT DESIGN BY ELLEN BEELER

☺ The paper used in this publication meets the minimum requirements of the
American National Standard for Permanence of Paper for Printed Library Materials
Z39.48-1984.

Library of Congress Cataloging-in-Publication Data

Breach of faith : a crisis of coverage in the age of corporate newspapering / Gene
Roberts, editor in chief ; Thomas Kunkel, general editor.
    p. cm.
  ISBN 1-55728-728-7 (cloth : alk. paper)
  1. Journalism—United States. 2. Journalism—Economic aspects—United States.
  I. Roberts, Gene. II. Kunkel, Thomas, 1955–
  PN4867 .B674 2002
  071'.3—dc21   2002009732

COVER ILLUSTRATION BY BOB DAHM.

Acknowledgments

Once again the editors must express their appreciation to the people most responsible for bringing about the original Project on the State of the American Newspaper series, which comprised the pieces in this volume and its companion, *Leaving Readers Behind*. Foremost among these visionary people are Rebecca W. Rimel, president and chief executive officer of the Pew Charitable Trusts; Donald Kimelman, director of Pew's Venture Fund; and Tom Rosenstiel, director of the Project for Excellence in Journalism.

At *American Journalism Review*, we'd again like to thank editor Rem Rieder, art director Lissa Cronin, and Lissa's predecessor, Jann Alexander. And at the University of Maryland's Philip Merrill College of Journalism, we gratefully acknowledge the help and support of longtime Dean Reese Cleghorn and Assistant Dean Frank Quine.

Kevin Galvin expertly re-edited and updated much of the original material for this volume. Carolyn White and Charles Layton first edited some of these pieces, and researchers Rachel Powers Kelson, David Allan, and Penny Bender Fuchs made countless contributions to the series. Thanks as well to our friends at the University of Arkansas Press, especially Lawrence Malley, Brian King, John Coghlan, and Carol Sickman-Garner, for their hard work and support in pulling together both books.

Finally, we would again thank the writers, who worked so long and so well, and for such a good cause.

Contents

Introduction

In the months after the terrorist attacks of September 11, 2001, it became a cliché that this infamous act had "changed everything." Yet as with any cliché, there was a fair amount of truth underlying it. One year later it was evident how much of American life *had* changed, be it getting frisked at the airport, watching your 401K disappear in the plummeting stock market, or simply wondering whether you were still safe in your own living room.

The news media changed, too. They demonstrated a commitment to overseas coverage from abroad that hadn't been seen since the Persian Gulf War—for a while. But as the war on terror settled in and the horrific images from New York and Washington began to recede into memory, most of those legions of reporters came home and, in the main, the news went back to its discouraging norm.

This is the second volume in a project that reprints, with updates, eighteen articles that assessed the state of the American newspaper industry. The articles appeared originally in *American Journalism Review;* the eight contained here ran between July 1998 and November 1999. The first volume, *Leaving Readers Behind,* detailed the economic changes sweeping through the industry. *Breach of Faith* shows in graphic relief how the increased focus on the bottom line has led many newspapers to shrink from their civic mission.

The articles in the series were, by definition, snapshots in time. Taken together, however, they documented an industry at a crossroads. The war on terrorism and the other major news stories that have occurred since the series concluded early in 2000—suicide bombings in Israel, the bursting of the high-tech bubble, the presidential election deadlock, the falling stock market, and the corporate accounting scandals—only reinforce why public-affairs reporting is so essential to the functioning of democracy. But as the pieces here demonstrate, all signs indicate an industry moving away from that essential obligation. If anything, the situation is even worse than when these stories first were reported.

As shareholder concerns supplanted concern for the public, government coverage slipped and international coverage all but vanished from the pages of most American dailies. Narrow reporting on local issues and shallow coverage of lifestyle and entertainment topics gained the upper hand in the fight over the newshole. Downsized news budgets combined with increased productivity demands to yield more errors in the paper and less enthusiasm in the newsroom.

Statehouse coverage was diminished and even disparaged, despite the fact that state capitals were becoming more powerful than ever. Washington bureaus pulled back from closely monitoring the machinations of the federal bureaucracy in favor of thematic coverage of the environment, health care, defense, and finance. Only the wires and the most prestigious papers consistently produced an original foreign report.

This was all considered acceptable because newspapers were responding to what their readers expected. Or were they? Extensive market research had told newspaper executives exactly what readers wanted. Or had it? There was a convincing case to be made that readers don't expect more movie reviews, slash-and-grab crime stories, and sex tips *instead* of comprehensive coverage of national and international affairs, but *in addition to* the coverage they have come to expect. When they ask for more, readers are assuming that they'll get the news first.

The industry's penchant for navel-gazing had an upside, though, and there was some cause for hope that news managers might remember what it was that made their "products" strong.

At the dawn of the twenty-first century, newspapers were better written than they were even a decade earlier, and they presented hard news more clearly and often more comprehensively then they ever did before. Coverage of sports and business grew dramatically. Reporters were better educated than ever before, and increased specialization helped make them smarter about the subjects that they covered.

Many periodicals were well established on the World Wide Web, and even if it was fear of lost profits more than any pioneering spirit that drove them there, at least they were aggressive about finding new ways to connect with readers. After the virtual gold rush ended with the crash of the dotcoms, the future of online newspapers was far from clear. But as executives and analysts contemplated the fate of a pulp-based medium in the digital age, they were led toward an ironic conclusion.

It turned out that the keys to success in the online world were the very same traits that had built successful newspapers in the first place: Quick and comprehensive information-gathering meant fresh content. Close ties to the community translated into brand-name identification. Like radio and TV before it, the Internet had caused much hand-wringing over the fate of the American newspaper. But it may very well be that the two can use each other to grow into the future.

Contributors

CHARLES LAYTON and **MARY WALTON**, husband and wife, met at the *Philadelphia Inquirer.* Layton was an editor there for twenty years, and as a reporter he has covered legislatures in Louisiana and Delaware. He has contributed two pieces to this volume. Walton, a longtime *Inquirer* reporter and magazine writer, has written four books. Her article "The Selling of Small-Town America" appeared in *Leaving Readers Behind.*

JOHN HERBERS was the *New York Times'* deputy Washington bureau chief and for many years covered the White House and other capital beats. **JAMES MCCARTNEY** was a national security correspondent and columnist for Knight Ridder's Washington bureau. He has written about network news, *USA Today,* and politics for *American Journalism Review.*

PETER ARNETT was for two decades the chief international correspondent for CNN, for which he covered the Persian Gulf War and numerous other major stories. For ten years he covered the Vietnam War for the Associated Press, winning a Pulitzer Prize in 1966.

CARL SESSIONS STEPP teaches at the University of Maryland's Philip Merrill College of Journalism and is a senior editor of *American Journalism Review.* He worked as a reporter and as an editor for twelve years and has done newspaper consulting for more than a decade. His most recent book is *Writing as Craft and Magic.*

LEWIS M. SIMONS's work appears regularly in *National Geographic, Smithsonian,* and other publications. A longtime Asia-based correspondent for the Associated Press, *Washington Post,* and Knight Ridder Newspapers, he has won the Pulitzer Prize and many other awards.

CHIP BROWN, a former reporter for the *Washington Post* and contributing editor of *Esquire,* has written for more than two dozen national magazines. He has won the National Magazine Award and is the author of *Afterwards, You're a Genius: Faith, Medicine, and the Metaphysics of Healing.*

WINNIE HU is a reporter for the *New York Times*. She researched and wrote her contribution to this series while finishing a master's degree program at the University of Maryland. She has also reported for the *Pensacola News Journal* and *Dallas Morning News*.

1 | Missing the Story at the Statehouse

By Mary Walton and Charles Layton
ORIGINALLY PUBLISHED IN JULY 1998

W HEN JIM MITZELFELD started work at the *Detroit News,* he begged to cover the legislature. That had been his beat with the Associated Press, and he loved it. But his Detroit editors discouraged him: It would take him out of the loop; he wouldn't get much support off in Lansing. "They made it sound," Mitzelfeld recalls today, "like it's not a great move if you want to make your name at the *Detroit News.*" But he persisted, and finally they gave in.

Still in his twenties and full of enthusiasm, Mitzelfeld made a strong impression on Charles Cain, the capital bureau chief. "He was driven," Cain remembers. "He was persistent beyond compare. . . . When he was on a story he could just be incredible." One time, Mitzelfeld heard that some lobbyists were taking legislators on a retreat to Gulf Shores, Alabama. He shaved his beard, cut his hair, put on a baseball cap and shades so he wouldn't be recognized—and turned up uninvited. He also took pictures, one of which showed a powerful Michigan lobbyist rubbing sunscreen on a legislator's shoulders and back. Mitzelfeld thought it was "the quintessential lube job."

But this was the early 1990s—a difficult time. With the economy in recession, newsholes shriveling, and editors seeking ways to cut costs, government coverage had become a target at newspapers around the country. There was growing disenchantment with state-government news in particular, and Gannett, which owned the *Detroit News,* was taking the knife to statehouse coverage.

"They were having us crank out a daily story or two every day," Mitzelfeld recalls. "They wanted them short—six, eight inches, twelve if we were lucky—and then a lot of them didn't run." He argued that it took more space to tell both sides of a complex issue. "There were times when they'd say, 'We don't have room for both sides, pick one side.'" Sometimes the desk made him rewrite the top of an AP story so it could run with a staff byline. This might have made sense to an editor trying to pad his daily news budget, but to Mitzelfeld it was "a ridiculous waste of manpower," especially when he was fighting for the time to do enterprise stories.

One day he heard that the governor had frozen the legislature's check-writing authority. It pricked his curiosity. "I was sort of skeptical it would even get in the paper. But I thought, 'Well, I'll ask somebody in the administration about this.' And it was in the course of working on this story that a source, in a phone interview—after failing to answer several questions clearly—said, 'Well, there are rumors.'

"I said, 'What rumors?'

"'Well, there are rumors that someone in the legislature is writing checks out to cash.'

"So immediately I said, Whoa! That's a big story if that's true."

After two weeks of digging into state computer records, scrutinizing lists of processed checks, and chasing other leads, he established that staff people in the House Fiscal Agency, an arm of the legislature, had been writing fat checks to themselves and their colleagues. The fraudulent checks totaled $1.8 million.

Only hours after the story broke, the governor called for a criminal investigation. It was front-page news for the next two weeks. Five people eventually went to prison.

For a while, Mitzelfeld was golden. But Detroit's enthusiasm did not last. He would propose an enterprise story that might take two weeks' work, and editors would turn it down. In time, he says, they even seemed bored with the follow-ups on the bogus checks. "At two months out, we were having to fight the battle all over again."

In 1994, Mitzelfeld was awarded the Pulitzer Prize for beat reporting. But by then he was no longer a newspaper reporter. "I got a sense that a lot of what I didn't like about my job at that paper was happening at other papers," he says, "and that's part of why I got out." He enrolled in the University of Michigan Law School. In October 1997, he began a new career as an attorney for the U.S. Department of Justice in Washington, D.C.

COVERAGE OF STATE GOVERNMENT is in steep decline. In capital pressrooms around the country, there are more and more empty desks and silent phones. Bureaus are shrinking, reporters are younger and less experienced, stories get less space and poorer play, and all too frequently editors just don't care. At the same time, state governments have more power and more money than ever before. Their tentacles reach into every household and business. Everyone—political parties, academics, trade organizations, labor unions, corporations—has discovered this. Everyone, that is, except the press.

With some notable exceptions, newspapers are risking their credibility by failing to provide news that readers have demonstrated time and again they care about. But what may be most imperiled without a watchdog press is democracy.

After Jim Mitzelfeld's departure, the *Detroit News'* statehouse bureau shrank from six reporters to four. The *Detroit Free Press* went from three full-time reporters to two. Altogether, a capital press corps that had as many as twenty-five newspaper reporters in the mid-1980s was down to fifteen by 1998. Other states have had similar declines. When we surveyed all fifty capitals in 1998, we found that the number of full-time statehouse reporters had decreased in twenty-seven states over the past decade, while increasing in only fourteen.

We also found that today's statehouse reporters have less experience, as a group, than their predecessors. And that turnover is faster. For instance, when Lesley Stedman began covering the Indiana statehouse for Fort Wayne's *Journal Gazette* in 1996, she was twenty-six. "It's young in terms of experience and all the things that make you a good reporter," she said, "and there were a lot of other people here just like me." Two years later she had "gone from being the one who was asking everybody else how things work, to being one of the people who answers those questions."

Furthermore, the gulf between reporters and editors seems to have widened. There is often a sense that editors do not understand how state government works and don't much care to learn. Peter Nicholas, who worked for five years in New Orleans's *Times-Picayune* statehouse bureau before coming to the *Philadelphia Inquirer*, tells of an editor who wanted only stories about bills that were reported out of committees. This made no sense to Nicholas. He knew that the best stories were often about why bills got killed in committee.

Things are not all bad. In the 1990s, computers and databases created reporting possibilities no one could have imagined a generation ago, and reporters have moved to exploit these new tools. The current crop of statehouse reporters is as bright and motivated as any previous group. And whereas in the past much of the writing about state government was undeniably dull, everyone's gotten the message now that state stories must be interesting and relevant to readers.

The *New York Times* has made reporting on state government a priority for its national correspondents. "In the '60s and '70s you could stay on top of a lot of American politics and government by having a great Washington bureau," says Robin Toner, chief of correspondents. "You can't do that anymore."

Two of the brightest spots on the map are California and Florida. In Sacramento, in 1998, forty-four newspaper and ten wire-service reporters competed on a daily basis. The most powerful players were the *Los Angeles Times,* with twelve reporters, and the *Sacramento Bee,* with ten. The *Bee's* longtime executive editor, Gregory Favre, said he believed that readers love in-depth news and that government beats "are at the very heart of what the hell we do." The *Bee's* statehouse reporters know that management understands their problems, because some of the paper's top editors started in government news. William Endicott was the *Bee's* capital bureau chief for ten years before becoming an assistant managing editor.

Even with the *Bee's* large bureau, Endicott thought that some state agencies weren't getting the coverage they deserved, so he struck a deal with the metro desk to help out. "There was just no way to do it with a ten- or eleven-person bureau," he says. Endicott wants stories held to forty inches. "I tell them if they can't tell it in forty inches, then they probably can't tell it at all."

In Tallahassee, Florida, where a press corps of thirty newspaper and three wire-service reporters is large enough to stage a sell-out Gridiron-style show each year, competition is intense. The *St. Petersburg Times* and the *Tampa Tribune,* whose circulation areas overlap, are arch-rivals. But they must also contend with the *Orlando Sentinel, Miami Herald, Palm Beach Post,* and some smaller papers. Lucy Morgan, bureau chief of the *St. Petersburg Times,* says, "You can't know something a day or so and not put it in the paper without somebody else getting it."

Yet even Florida and California have had cutbacks. The *San Francisco Chronicle* has gone from three reporters to two, and the *San Francisco Examiner* has gone from two reporters to one. The *Miami Herald* is down to three reporters from five (although one was an education reporter who was moved to Miami), and the Orlando and Fort Lauderdale papers have all dropped from three reporters to two. "I've been immersed in daily stuff," says Miami's statehouse bureau chief, Mark Silva. "We're not doing as much investigative reporting as we should be doing, not looking as much as we could at who's profiting from things."

NATIONWIDE, only 513 newspaper reporters—plus 113 wire-service reporters, most of them with the AP—were covering state government full-time in 1998. By comparison, more than three thousand media credentials were issued for that year's Super Bowl.

In most states, TV reporters have become an endangered species, rarely glimpsed except for a major speech or press conference. Sacramento, which once had a half-dozen TV reporters covering state government full-time, now has none. Californians complained during their last gubernatorial primaries that the only information on TV about those races came from the candidates' paid ads.

Fewer reporters means fewer stories. In the daily crush, state news loses out to crime stories, lighthearted features, and lifestyle reporting—all of which many editors insist readers prefer, even though research shows otherwise.

The biggest round of statehouse cutbacks came between 1989 and 1994, when, according to the American Society of Newspaper Editors (ASNE), the combined editorial workforce of U.S. newspapers fell from 56,900 to 53,800. Today's smaller newsroom staffs have been stretched even thinner by the demands of increased zoning, pagination, Web sites, computer-assisted reporting, civic journalism, new features sections, and new beats. Beefing up statehouse bureaus is simply not a priority.

Even before the recession of the early 1990s, statehouse coverage was under attack. In 1989, Raleigh's *News & Observer* bumped its state-government column, "Under the Dome," from the front page to the Metro section. Ferrel Guillory was the government-affairs editor at the time. After he'd budgeted a long list of stories one day, Guillory heard an editor grumble, "Who wants to read all this government stuff?" Another editor encouraged Guillory to press on, saying, "It's good to have some dinosaurs around."

That same year the CEO of Knight Ridder, James Batten, made a speech that became famous in newspaper circles for its endorsement of "customer-driven" journalism. As a former statehouse reporter, Batten found the implications for government news regrettable. "Most of the best journalists I know were drawn to their careers by an intense interest in public affairs," Batten said. "They saw newspapers as indispensable instruments of American self-government. And they tended—we tended, to be more precise—to assume that ordinary Americans, all good newspaper readers, of course, shared—or at least should share—our voracious appetite for news of government and politics. That was a little naive. But today, that high-minded assumption is hopelessly inaccurate."

In 1990, the *Washington Journalism Review* quoted a Gannett editor, James Gannon, as saying there were "pressures on editors to think more

like marketers. If readers aren't interested in government and foreign policy, then figure out what they are interested in."

In March 1992, *WJR* ran an article entitled "Of the People, By the
People, Bore the People," in which Carl Sessions Stepp reported that "newspapers nationwide have begun pepping up or cutting back government
news, calling into question the *raison d'etre* of journalism." Stepp quoted
then–*Wichita Eagle* editor Davis "Buzz" Merritt Jr. as saying, "We're covering a great deal less of the turn-of-the-wheel kind of thing. Nobody gives
a damn."

That article, which read almost like an obituary, contained one of the
last serious discussions of state-government coverage to appear in the
trade press. *Columbia Journalism Review, Nieman Reports,* and *Media
Studies Journal* largely ignored the subject after that, as did *WJR*'s successor publication, *American Journalism Review.*

IRONICALLY, THE LAST article *Nieman Reports* ran on state government,
in 1991, predicted a bright future. In "Choice Assignment: State House,"
Dall W. Forsythe of the Kennedy School of Government argued that the
"New Federalism"—the Reagan-era name for the shifting of power out of
Washington—would generate more news in state capitals.

Forsythe's prediction may have been wrong, but his reasoning was right
on the money. In what is now seen as the most historic governmental
change in half a century, the feds have been surrendering authority to the
states in almost every vital area of domestic policy. Welfare reform may be
the most dramatic example, but it's not the only one. While Washington
wrings its hands over the decline of education, the states spend four to five
times more money than the feds to improve schools—building and reno-
vating, reducing class sizes, putting computers in the classroom, and trying to compensate for inequities between rich and poor districts. State
education departments have been hatching initiatives such as school
vouchers, charter schools, and single-sex classrooms. And the national
debates over the best ways to teach math and reading will be decided not
in Washington but in the fifty states.

After Congress rejected President Clinton's national health-care plan,
the states took the initiative. In 1998, more than 26,000 health-care bills
were introduced in the various states, and 3,400 became law. In 2000, state
lawmakers considered 29,000 health-care bills. Today, we have state laws
regulating insurance rates and hospital takeovers, banning "drive-through"
child deliveries and mastectomies, expanding children's health insurance,

and forcing insurers to cover preexisting conditions. Regulating HMOs has been a priority. Thirty-eight states have passed laws authorizing independent or external reviews of health-plan decisions, and seven states have allowed patients to sue HMOs for medical malpractice—something Congress could not bring itself to do during the Clinton administration.

"We are building a national health-care system piece by piece out in the states," says William Pound, executive director of the National Conference of State Legislatures. In fact, he says, "It seems to me that almost all of our domestic-policy initiatives begin at the state level today."

Vermont, Maine, Massachusetts, and Arizona have overhauled their campaign-finance laws in major ways. Vermont has also approved civil unions for gay couples. Hawaii recently became the eighth state to endorse the medical use of marijuana. Maine has enacted a law requiring that the state's prescription-drug prices be no higher than those in Canada.

On the conservative side, state officials in Kansas, Kentucky, Oklahoma, Alabama, New Mexico, and elsewhere have been fighting tooth and claw over whether to teach "creationism" alongside evolution in the public schools.

"The cry used to be, 'We don't need state government, we'll go to Washington.' Not anymore," says Alan Rosenthal of Rutgers University, an expert on state governments and lobbying. "Groups today have to make their appeals state by state."

What happens in the corridors and committee rooms of state government determines whether customers can smoke in restaurants and bars, whether children can be tried as adults, where nuclear wastes can be stored, how many prison inmates will be paroled, how many minority students will be admitted to state universities, how difficult it will be for women to get abortions, how many mental patients and autistic children will live in neighborhood group homes, and how much pollution a hospital, dry cleaner, print shop, bakery, auto body shop, wood refinisher, or asphalt manufacturer can release into the environment.

The state capitol is where legislators sort out every screwy, Solomonic dispute imaginable—disputes between dog groomers and veterinarians over the right to brush a dog's teeth, and between orthopedic surgeons and podiatrists as to who has jurisdiction over the ankle, a question that turns on the legislative definition of where the foot stops and the leg begins.

The states determine how much you will pay to get your car insured, how fast you can drive it, how much alcohol can be in your blood at the time, whether you can legally talk on a cell phone while driving, and under what conditions you can lose your license. They regulate foster care for children and nursing-home care for the elderly, and they determine whether your ten-year-old child can legally buy an assault weapon (yes in Arkansas, no in Texas), whether you can hunt alligators in Florida (yes) or bears in New Jersey (no), whether you can keep your home if you declare bankruptcy (yes in Iowa, no in Oklahoma), and whether a doctor can prescribe lethal drugs if you are terminally ill (yes in Oregon, no everywhere else). Twenty-five states have begun their own meat- and poultry-inspection programs. The states even participate in foreign relations to the extent that they promote and market their products abroad.

States hold veto power over much of what local government can do. Albany decides whether New York City subway trains will have one crew member or two. Harrisburg decides whether Philadelphia and Pittsburgh can ban assault weapons within their city limits. When those two cities passed gun-control measures several years ago, the legislature overturned them. The legislature in Indiana did likewise when some municipalities restricted the sale and promotion of cigarettes. And when the scholastic achievement of students in Newark, Jersey City, and Paterson fell into severe decline, the state of New Jersey seized those school systems and began running them itself. In some states, a county, city, or town can't even give its elected officials a pay raise without the legislature's approval. This year, a sheriff in Georgia turned down a $6,650 raise to protest that arrangement.

Everyone knows how the state attorneys general exposed the marketing practices of the tobacco companies and finally brought real pressure upon that industry. But since the 1980s, when President Reagan reined in the consumer-fraud activities of the Federal Trade Commission, state attorneys general have been going after other big game. In 1998 they forced American Family Publishers and its spokesmen, Dick Clark and Ed McMahon, to stop their "you are a winner" come-ons for selling magazines. They have also reached consumer settlements with America Online, American Cyanamid, Bausch & Lomb, General Motors, Mazda, Packard Bell, and Sears. Several activist attorneys general have mounted an antitrust investigation of the gun industry.

"The reversal of roles in American government has taken place gradually and without much fanfare, but it has been dramatic," says *Governing* magazine's Alan Ehrenhalt, who has written about state and local government for more than a decade. "It has reached the point where few of us bother even looking to Congress as the primary instrument for resolving the contradictions and challenges of modern capitalism. We look to Congress to make noise and entertain us. By and large, that is what it does."

Partly because state government is where the action is, political parties have had trouble finding people to run for Congress. The *New York Times* reported in 1998 that it had found a number of politicians who "said they could make more of a difference serving in their state legislatures."

"I think that state-government reporting is the best job in the country," says James Salzer, Atlanta bureau chief for the Morris News Service. He notes that news happens faster in the capitals. "When a bill goes to Congress, it takes four or five years to enact," he says. "It's a long process. Here, someone gets run over by a rampaging truck, someone puts in a bill, 'Bigger penalties for rampaging trucks,' two weeks later it can be on the governor's desk."

Supporters of what's known as "devolution"—the shift of power from the federal government to the states—say the fifty states offer boundless opportunities to test ideas. This is the "laboratories of democracy" argument. As one political scientist expressed it, a home run is more likely with fifty batters swinging.

But so is a foul ball. Columnist Molly Ivins offered her home state as "a national laboratory for bad government." She wrote, "Having a bad idea in your state? Come to Texas and see how it works out in practice. Three strikes and you're out? Watch Texas spend more on prisons than it does on schools. Thinking of making your tax structure more regressive? Come to the Lone Star State and see how it's done."

But even bad ideas make good copy, as Ivins has continued to demonstrate.

WHILE NEWSPAPER EDITORS were losing interest, the rising power of the states did not go unnoticed by the thousands of corporations and organizations that stand to gain or lose. Former Georgia governor Zell Miller remembers that when he became a state senator in 1961, the only lobbyists were from Georgia Power, the teachers' union, the telephone company, the savings and loan industry and perhaps the railroads. "You could count the number of lobbyists on your fingers," he says. "Now you need a computer." Georgia has more than one thousand registered lobbyists.

An AP survey in 1990 found more than 42,500 lobbyists registered in the fifty states, which was an increase of 20 percent in four years. Today that number is almost certainly higher. "Some estimates," according to the National Lobbyist Directory, "list as many as 100,000 persons involved in legislative advocacy nationwide." Dick Miller, an Illinois lobbyist, says he would not trade places with legislators today, considering how besieged they are by lobbyists. "They don't have a minute," Miller told Bloomington's *Pantagraph*. "They can't go to the restroom. They can be standing there, excuse me, whizzing, and there will be a lobbyist next to them saying, 'Hey, Pete, I have this bill coming, can you help me?'"

The amount of money spent lobbying the Connecticut legislature quadrupled in the 1990s. In New York, where lobbyists more than doubled their numbers in twenty years, their spending has increased eighteen years in a row. In 1986 they spent $15 million; in 1997 it was $51 million.

For every lobbyist there is a special-interest group, picking up the tab. California has the most—some two thousand companies, unions, professional groups, and assorted others. The Californians for Ferret Legalization have a paid lobbyist in Sacramento. So do the Los Angeles County Lifeguards, the California Check Cashers Association, Californians United against Rice Burning, the California Motorcyclist Association, the California Native Plant Society, the California Asparagus Commission, the Mountain Lion Foundation, the California Dump Truck Owners Association, the Jockeys' Guild, the Hawaiian Gardens Card Club, and the California Swap Meet Owners Association.

In most states, every election cycle sets new records for fundraising and spending, as special interests pour more money into state races. In New Jersey, spending in the last governor's race and for 120 legislative seats exceeded $70 million. That was about $29 per vote, or as the AP observed, enough to treat every voter to a steak, a beer and a movie. In California, $1 million for a single legislative seat is no longer considered rare. One unsuccessful gubernatorial candidate, Al Checchi, spent some $40 million in the last Democratic primary.

Much of the money state politicians raise—sometimes most of it—comes from outside their districts, even outside their states. But while newspapers have played up the contributions that national parties accept from foreign sources, most don't seem to care that their governors and legislators are obligating themselves to out-of-state interests.

On the Bureau of Labor Statistics' list of growth industries for the 1990s, state government ranked eighth. The states spend $854 billion a year—nearly $9,000 for every American household. State legislatures consider 185,000 bills a year and pass 25 percent of them. And all of it—the money, the bills, the lobbyists, the elections, the bureaucrats—is covered by fewer reporters than in the past. Carolyn Russell, a state representative from Goldsboro, North Carolina, says, "One of the first things I was told when I came to Raleigh was, 'You can vote any way you want to up here because the folks back home will never know.'"

HOW DID IT BECOME common wisdom that government stories bore readers? The answer, at least in part, goes back two decades to an influential research program conducted by newspaper executives worried about the steady decline in readership across the country.

Sponsored by the Newspaper Advertising Bureau (NAB) and the American Newspaper Publishers Association, the Newspaper Readership Project drew editors into the alien world of market research. They were clearly in over their heads. Their own papers, reporting on public-opinion surveys, often failed to differentiate between legitimate surveys and straw polls, or between significant and insignificant research findings. Some papers presented man-in-the-street reaction stories as true reflections of public opinion.

For expert advice, the project had the help of Leo Bogart, a former head of research for Revlon Inc. who was general manager of the NAB. Bogart later told the story of the project in a 1991 book, *Preserving the Press.*

Bogart was commissioned to do a three-thousand-sample telephone survey of newspaper readers. But newspaper editors were also intrigued by focus groups. Both Michael O'Neill of the *New York Daily News,* who co-chaired a committee of the Readership Project, and ASNE President Eugene Patterson of the *St. Petersburg Times* recommended a focus-group researcher named Ruth Clark, who had worked for both their papers. Clark had done door-to-door interviews for Trix cereal before joining the Lou Harris organization in 1959, around the time Harris became John F. Kennedy's pollster. By the 1970s she was working for Daniel Yankelovich Inc.

Bogart cautioned the editors that focus groups were highly subjective, that they were easily manipulated by the person running them, and that their samples were far too small to be valid. Bogart couldn't get the editors to see it that way. "To a journalist," he wrote, "the main question was not whether what respondents said was typical or projectable to a larger population; it was whether or not the quotations were accurate. Had they actually said it?"

A focus group was not, after all, so different from the traditional man-in-the-street interviews. It was ten or twelve people talking, usually in a room with a one-way mirror so the editors themselves could sit and watch. Editors were fascinated to hear these people go on about their newspapers. The editors could even join in at the end and ask questions. It was fun. In contrast, Bogart's surveys seemed sterile, abstract, and incomprehensible.

Bogart was not opposed to focus groups per se. They could supplement hard data gathered by other, more reliable methods, but they were not a substitute for that data. Ruth Clark, however, apparently saw Bogart as a competitor. "Ruth is critical of the massive 3,000-sample survey which Leo Bogart . . . is plunging into," Patterson wrote in a memo that Bogart quotes in his book. According to the memo, Clark thought Bogart's approach was "mechanistic and demographic" but that her focus-group findings could "complement Bogart's undertaking and give meaning to the figures he'll produce." ASNE paid her for twelve focus groups, one in each of a dozen cities. The groups contained about 10 people each—about 120 people in all.

In October 1978, at a gathering of ASNE board members on Cape Cod, Bogart and Clark presented their findings. As expected, Bogart's survey produced a daunting array of statistics, all of which, however, pointed to a straightforward conclusion. People read newspapers primarily for hard news.

Clark could not have disagreed more. As later summarized by ASNE, her report said readers wanted "more attention paid to their personal needs, help in understanding and dealing with their own problems in an increasingly complex world, news about their neighborhood, not just the big city and Washington, and advice on what to buy, where to play, how to cope." They also wanted "more help in handling emotional problems, understanding others, feeling good and eating well, having fun, and in general fulfilling oneself," as well as "news about personally helpful subjects like health rather than just the usual heavy fare of politics and government." Besides all that, they wanted more "good news," more "human drama with a happy ending."

Although Clark did not say so, these were also things many advertisers wanted.

Where Bogart's presentation had been dry, Clark's was peppered with lively quotes from the focus groups. And her conclusions struck a responsive chord: Editors were not helpless in the face of declining readership; there was a lot they could do.

In what amounted to an endorsement, ASNE distributed Clark's report, titled "Changing Needs of Changing Readers," far and wide. An initial five thousand copies were mailed to newspaper executives. "The report contained no forbidding statistics," Bogart observed. "It was short enough"—at fifty-one pages—"to be read by every editor and publisher in the country."

ASNE's foreword to the Clark report suggested that the focus group conclusions were compatible with Bogart's survey results. It called the Clark report "an effort to deepen our understanding of findings that have been emerging from major reader surveys of the Newspaper Readership

Project." The truth was, of course, that it didn't "deepen" anyone's under-standing of the other findings; in many respects, it contradicted them.

As Bogart later wrote, "By proclaiming the message that the public wanted fun rather than facts about the world's grim realities, [the Clark report] legitimized the movement to turn newspapers into daily magazines with the pelletized, palatable characteristics of TV news."

In fairness to Clark, her report never advised editors to run softer, lifestyle content in place of basic news, but rather in addition to it. It also said that all the focus groups "recognized that editors have a responsibility to inform and educate the public and not merely to provide the public with what is popular or wanted." In fact, Clark's first fans—O'Neill of the *Daily News* and Patterson of the *St. Pete Times*—never budged from their commitment to hard news.

But in the years that followed, most papers moved toward the softer kinds of news Clark had advocated—and then some. In 1985, Bogart pub-lished a study of changes in newspaper content between 1979 (the year Clark's report was published) and 1983. The study was based on responses from executives at 1,310 daily newspapers. Two-thirds said they had wit-nessed "substantial changes" in their papers. Among the most common were new lifestyle sections and a higher ratio of features to hard news. Bogart argued that the changes were "in direct contradiction" to what readers had been telling his researchers they wanted.

By that time, even Ruth Clark had serious regrets. *New York Times Magazine* editor Jack Rosenthal knew Clark—who died in 1997—and describes her as "startled and perhaps chagrined by how many papers took her advice to extremes."

Clark tried to undo the damage. In 1983, she declared that readers had developed an entirely new attitude since her 1979 study. "The big change," she said, "is that today the main reason for buying and reading newspapers is hard news. . . .

"Readers want to know what the state is doing in highways, crime, edu-cation, taxation, attracting industry, and what cuts can be anticipated in their areas," she said. "People also want to know how their state is doing compared with others. The sense of regional interest and pride is growing rapidly."

Clark's new research was published the following year by ASNE. Titled "Relating to Readers in the '80s," it did not rely solely on focus groups, but included a telephone survey of 1,202 people.

"According to readers, it's back to basics in newspapers in 1984," the report began. "They are saying: Give us the news—hard news, real news, whether it's national, state, regional or local. Tell us the facts about health, science, technology, diet and nutrition, child-rearing—and we'll do the coping ourselves." It said that lifestyle features, human-interest stories, gossip and advice columns, and big murder stories "are perceived as add-on benefits."

The new report sank like a stone. Others since then have been similarly ignored, including a 1991 ASNE survey, "Keys to Our Survival," which asked 1,264 people to rate their interest in a long list of news topics. Not only did hard news triumph over features in this exercise, but state news did very well. It came in fifth—behind city news, neighborhood news, national news, and regional news but ahead of twenty-eight other categories that included crime news, health news, TV program information, and a Clark-like category labeled "news that's helpful with everyday living."

But by then, it seemed, nothing could stop the flight from government coverage and hard news.

N O NEWSPAPER REFLECTED Ruth Clark's original vision more than USA Today. Launched by Gannett in 1982, the paper became a model and an inspiration for the industry. As Gannett grew and spawned imitators, the model was imposed on cities and towns across America. Editors and publishers answerable to corporate bosses outside the state often lost their commitment to statehouse coverage. This happened in a dramatic way after Gannett bought the *Great Falls Tribune* in Montana.

The *Tribune* had been known for its independence in a state where the other major papers were hardly trusted. Until purchased by Lee Enterprises in 1959, the *Billings Gazette,* Butte's *Montana Standard,* the *Helena Independent Record,* and the *Missoulian* had been owned by Anaconda Mining Company and used to protect and promote its copper and timber interests. Anaconda was notorious for its stranglehold on the state—the "copper collar," it was called—and for using its papers to do favors for the powerful. In 1950, the state's governor, John Bonner, was arrested for public drunkenness in New Orleans and held in a drunk tank for six hours. "He cussed me some," the desk sergeant said, "but I didn't pay any attention to him. He said he was the governor of Montana." When stories moved on the AP and UPI wires the next day, the *Great Falls Tribune* ran them. The Anaconda papers spiked them. Two days later, the papers ran short accounts of Bonner's denial.

Reporter Charles Johnson personified the *Tribune's* strong tradition of state reporting. In 1972, as a graduate student, he had covered Montana's constitutional convention for the AP. When he was twenty-nine, the *Tribune* hired him for its state bureau, and he continued to write about the sweeping changes in Montana government. As head of a two-man bureau, he became known for his meaty analyses of complex issues and was in demand as a speaker at civic clubs throughout the state.

But the *Tribune*'s new president and publisher, a veteran Gannett executive named Chris Jensen, was not impressed with the bureau's accomplishments. In April 1991, about a year after Gannett bought the paper, two editors drove the ninety miles down to Helena to inform Johnson's colleague, Steve Shirley, that he was being transferred back to Great Falls. Johnson was told that Shirley would not be replaced in the capital. In fact, the editors said, Johnson was lucky to be staying there himself: Jensen had wanted to shut down the whole bureau and just rely on AP. The editors said they'd had a hard time talking Jensen out of that.

In the months ahead, Jensen continued to make known his low opinion of government news. Johnson heard that tearsheets with big "G's" scrawled on them were being found on editors' desks. The publisher was going through the paper with a felt-tipped pen, marking a "G" on any story he considered too governmental.

Johnson's copy was being cut as never before. So was his budget. "We always got a new set of law books after every session," Johnson says. "They were vital to the work. And he cut that out." Johnson subscribed to newspapers, including the *Wall Street Journal,* which he clipped and filed for background and story ideas. "I used to send the subscription notice up there [to Great Falls] and usually somebody would okay them. But Jensen had all these expenses go to him, even the little ones, you know, $100. And then I'd notice the papers weren't coming. He was just chucking them." Eventually, Johnson did get his law books back, but he ended up paying for the *Wall Street Journal* out of his own pocket.

Johnson and his editors tried to resist. "We tried to say, 'You do a story on electric rates, is that a government story or is that a consumer story?' I don't know how you draw the line. We don't sit down and say we're going to cover government stories. We're just covering issues."

One day Johnson got a call from the publisher. Jensen sounded irritated. He said he wanted to see Johnson in Great Falls the next day to discuss a letter from Danny Oberg, a member of the Montana Public Service Commission, complaining about the lack of coverage in Helena. Oberg wrote that he had been reading the *Tribune* since he was a kid and couldn't believe the changes he was seeing.

As Johnson recalls the meeting, "Jensen showed me the letter, said it was a bunch of nonsense, and wanted to know who Oberg was." Johnson told him.

"He said, 'Well, this is all just a bunch of junk. We don't need this.'

"I said, 'Well, I think a lot of people feel that way.'" The reporter restated his case for state-government news. Jensen repeated that the paper could just as well use AP. They talked more, "but it was clear we weren't going to get anywhere. . . . There was no convincing him."

The capital press corps in Montana was quite small. Besides Johnson, there was one full-time AP reporter and a two-person bureau that served the Lee chain's Montana papers. While Johnson was struggling with Gannett, the Lee bureau was in even worse shape. It had always been a difficult bureau to work in, partly because it served four different masters. The editors in Butte wanted stories on mining and gambling. Missoula, home of the state university, wanted higher-education news. Helena, the capital-city paper, wanted all the government news it could get. And Billings was more of an agricultural city. "They all had different opinions, and they all were pulling in different directions," says a reporter who had worked for Lee.

Soon after Johnson's bureau was cut, both Lee reporters resigned, and the chain couldn't fill the vacancies. At one point Lee was in such disarray that it closed the bureau entirely, leaving Johnson and the AP's Bob Anez as the only reporters in the statehouse.

By then the problem was so dire that the *Bozeman Chronicle,* a 14,000-circulation paper in southern Montana, ran a three-story, front-page Sunday package about the dearth of political news statewide.

"In this election year, voters looking for solid news stories about Montana candidates and issues are likely to be shortchanged," reporter Joan Haines wrote. "Some critics charge the media is feeding the public a junk food diet of fancy color graphics and skimpy stories—short takes and sound bites—while downplaying coverage of state government that people need to make informed decisions."

In one of her two sidebars, Haines quoted from the debut issue of a sharp-tongued journal, the *Treasure State Review,* published by Nathaniel Blumberg, a retired professor and former journalism dean at the University of Montana. Blumberg described the situation as "horrendous" and "indefensible."

He blamed the problem on the two out-of-state chains that now controlled all of Montana's major papers. "The Gannett chain, famed for its innovative typographical devices, skim-the-surface reporting and slippery sense of journalistic ethics, has taken over the *Great Falls Tribune,* once a splendid locally owned daily, and the Lee chain has abandoned the excellent performance and high promise that peaked in the 1970s."

The *Chronicle*'s story ran on May 24, 1992. Jensen had been transferred by then to run a larger Gannett paper, the *El Paso Times*, so Haines interviewed his successor as publisher, Barbara Henry, as well as Richard Wesnick, the editor of Lee's *Billings Gazette*. "Executives of the *Tribune* and the *Gazette* say they are not giving state government reporting short shrift, but rather giving readers what they want," she wrote. The story quoted Montana speaker of the house Hal Harper as saying he had told Henry that the media were falling down on the job in Helena. "More and more," Harper said, "newspapers are at the mercy of spin doctors. It's easier to crank out a press release. Reporters who do not have time to dig won't do it."

The *Tribune*'s Barbara Henry was, by all accounts, a more personable boss than her predecessor—Blumberg called her "the good cop"—but she was no more responsive to Charles Johnson's pleas than Jensen had been. And so, soon after the *Chronicle*'s report, when Lee Enterprises asked Johnson to rebuild its capital bureau, he accepted.

Today Johnson runs a three-person bureau that is free from many of the old frustrations, thanks to an extraordinary arrangement in which he reports directly to the publisher of the *Billings Gazette*, the largest of the four Lee papers. He is on an equal footing with the top editors in Billings, Helena, Butte, and Missoula. "We meet with the editors and some of the publishers every so often and say what we've got coming and get feedback on ideas on what to cover. And they give us quite a bit of freedom."

Life still isn't perfect. The Lee papers often cut Johnson's stories severely, or omit them, as they see fit. But Johnson and his reporters have been given an assistant who clips and files for them, and there's a $900-a-month travel budget. One of Johnson's reporters went to Texas to investigate a private prison where Montana sends the convicts that its own small system can't handle. The bureau has made environmental reporting a priority. One of Johnson's reporters spent two months preparing a series on Montana's water problems.

The Great Falls paper, meanwhile, continues to make do with a one-man bureau.

As for Chris Jensen, he ended up as publisher of the *Times* of Gainesville, Georgia. Reached there by telephone, he said he could not remember any controversy over government news. He could not recall cutting the statehouse bureau from two reporters to one. He could not remember Charles Johnson's name. Neither could he remember scrawling those big "G's" on government stories.

"When I got there the bureau was in full operation," he said. "I don't recall any of what you're talking about." He said Barbara Henry succeeded him—maybe she had done this. Asked a final time about the cutback in the bureau, he said maybe "somebody's got me confused with somebody else."

Back in Montana, the *Tribune* was a long time in living down the controversy. In 1997, at a celebration of the twenty-fifth anniversary of the Montana Constitutional Convention, the curmudgeonly press critic Blumberg delivered a speech titled "The Role of the Press: Then and Now." He made the most of his opportunity, charging that "the out-of-state corporations that control the primary sources of our news and editorial opinion no longer even claim to serve the public interest." Publishers with no training in journalism, he said, "regard their newsroom employees as little more than cogs in a money machine" and deny them the resources to do investigative stories on such things as the prison system, nursing-home conditions, health care, and the tax system.

Blumberg delivered the speech in the chamber of the House of Representatives. Afterward, he received a standing ovation. The AP filed a story containing the above quotes. The *Great Falls Tribune* edited them out.

IN ARKANSAS, as in Montana, Gannett purchased a paper with a distinguished history and set about tailoring it to the Gannett philosophy. But in this case there was a crucial difference. Gannett had strong competition in Arkansas. And events took a turn the company had never anticipated.

The *Arkansas Gazette* of Little Rock was the state's dominant newspaper when Gannett took over in 1986. Ponderous and old-fashioned in style but liberal in its politics, the *Gazette* reached every county and crossroads. People still remembered its courage during the civil-rights era, when it stood firmly for integration despite being attacked by the governor and boycotted by advertisers. Its coverage of school desegregation in Little Rock won two Pulitzers.

Max Brantley, the paper's city editor, says he believed a newspaper's duty "was to have the best people you could have covering the city and the courthouse and the state, and have them write their fingers off every night. I loved nothing more than courthouse agate. And I think that people liked all that. I mean, your planning commissions and your courts and your governments are what determines how life is lived."

The new Gannett "overlords," as Brantley calls them, thought otherwise. Soon after taking over, they circulated a critique of the *Gazette*, written at Gannett headquarters in Virginia, which said, among other things,

that the paper carried too much inconsequential news—stories on plan-
ning-commission meetings and the like.

"What they were looking for," says Brantley, "were the boy-howdy stories, in features and fashion and food." Color, charts, beauty queens—these
became the new order.

The new editor Gannett brought in was Walker Lundy, who struck
Brantley as "one of those everybody-hates-government brand of editors.
He just didn't care about government coverage. It just put him to sleep. It
didn't make any difference how you wrote it. He liked movies. He'd go to
three movies a week."

Brantley's feelings about the new regime were shared by John Reed, one
of his three state-capital reporters. Lundy didn't cut the size of the statehouse bureau, but he did reduce story lengths. Twenty-inch stories shrank
to ten. Ten-inch stories were held to seven. And while traditional news stories were being downplayed, the stories of certain feature writers—mere
kids, some of them, and from out of state—got more space than they
needed, or so it seemed to Reed. "They would have a twenty-three-year-old
girl from California writing a fluffy piece about hillbillies," he says. "Well,
people in Arkansas aren't interested in this."

Lundy didn't see it that way. He recalls that when he first arrived, much
of the paper's government news "didn't seem to me to connect with our
readers. And a number of us pushed to make all of our government coverage more reader-focused. I'm not sure many readers have a fascination
with the processes of government. I think they're interested in how it
affects them."

To the extent that Lundy and his people updated the *Gazette* and gave
it more personality, both Brantley and Reed thought the paper was the better for it. "I didn't totally discount everything they said," says Brantley. "I
thought some of it was good. I saw ways that I could accommodate what
they wanted without selling my soul." And Reed, looking back on it now,
praises some of the legislative packaging. Instead of publishing long
"roundup" stories that combined the day's unrelated events, the paper
broke out individual stories, jazzed up the graphics, and made the whole
package more lively and accessible.

Before long, though, loyal readers of the old *Gazette* were writing out-
raged letters asking why the paper was being trivialized. And they were discovering they could go elsewhere for news. The city's afternoon paper, the
Arkansas Democrat, had started filling the void—emphasizing hard news,
serious issues, government coverage. The *Democrat* greatly expanded its

newshole, consistently printing more pages than the *Gazette*. As part of the strategy, it increased its statehouse bureau from one reporter to three, matching the *Gazette*. "The more fluff they put in the paper, the more we moved into harder content," Walter Hussman, the *Democrat*'s owner, told a reporter. Readership and advertising surged.

By 1990, both papers were fighting as hard as they could—cutting ad and subscription rates to record-low levels—and both were losing money. The *Gazette* thought it could win in a war of attrition. Although Hussman was a multimillionaire, his staying power was surely no match for a multi-billion-dollar company like Gannett. The question was only how long Hussman could hang on.

"It was a newspaper war the likes of which you will never see again," says Brantley, gleeful at the memory. On a given day as many as eight *Gazette* reporters would descend on the capitol, he says, and that didn't count the four political columnists, which included himself. Brantley was both editor and writer now. During the 1991 legislative session he and his people produced a daily eight-page tabloid section on state government. The *Gazette* was running every wire story that moved, every scrap of news it could lay its hands on. The newshole was so large that some days the editors were hard-pressed to fill it.

The *Democrat* was doing the same. The *Wall Street Journal* wrote that the people of Little Rock were "probably the best-served readership—per subscription dollar, anyway—in the nation."

"It was a wonderful and a terrible time," Brantley says. "It was the best year of my life.

"I'd say, 'I want to go to Des Moines and cover the health-care conference' and they'd say, 'Go to Des Moines.'

"I'd say, 'I want to go cover the national convention' and they'd say, 'Go to the convention, take somebody with you, get a nice hotel, rent a car.' This was unheard of in Arkansas." It was also unusual for Gannett. The company's losses in Little Rock amounted to more than $25 million a year in 1990 and 1991, according to company statements.

And then the war ended.

In October 1991, after nearly six years in Little Rock, Gannett surrendered. It sold its facilities to the *Democrat* for $69 million, and the paper was closed. Reflecting on what happened, Walker Lundy, now editor of Knight Ridder's *Philadelphia Inquirer*, said, "Our slogan when I got there was, 'Quality makes a difference.' Their slogan was, 'Arkansas' newspaper.' They won. The last year I was there, I remember we swept all thirteen categories of the Associated Press journalism contest in Arkansas, and I'm not sure that counted for much with the readers."

Hussman renamed his paper the *Arkansas Democrat-Gazette.* Hundreds of *Gazette* employees lost their jobs. Today, John Reed works for the state senate and Max Brantley is editor of the *Arkansas Times,* a Little Rock weekly. But in the *Democrat-Gazette,* Arkansas readers continue to have a paper that emphasizes hard news. The wisdom of that approach, Brantley says, is a legacy of the newspaper war: "It has made for a city and state of newspaper readers."

IN LITTLE ROCK, readers had a choice. In Atlanta, where a founding editor of *USA Today* pushed legislative coverage back with the obits, the *Journal and Constitution* was the only game in town. In the 1990s, this once-distinguished paper lost the respect of the people it covered, from the governor on down.

Even some corporate lobbyists in Georgia yearned for the days when, as one put it, "journalists would get fire in their bellies and a commitment to issues." Said Wayne Reece, a lobbyist for the Georgia Railroad Association and BellSouth Corporation, "I don't perceive that to be the case anymore. They don't have the resources and time to do it."

During our visit to Atlanta, state-government stories were in short supply on page one of the *Journal and Constitution,* the largest of seventeen daily papers owned by Cox Newspapers. A front-page layout with photos, briefs, and "refers" had space for only three or four stories, and one was usually a quirky attention-getter—a feature about couples who renewed their vows en masse, or a ban on keychains dangling from kids' backpacks. The paper's no-jump policy was sometimes relaxed to allow the occasional story to continue inside. *Journal and Constitution* reporters we talked with didn't necessarily consider a front-page byline an achievement. "You almost don't want to mess with the front page," said one statehouse reporter. "It's more trouble than it's worth."

Inexperience was a problem in the state bureau; reporters came and went. "They don't have a long view of the leaders," said then-governor Zell Miller. "They don't have context. There's no historical perspective whatsoever." Miller, who had spent four decades in state government, remembered the paper's fearless reporting in the 1950s and 1960s. "That was the high-water mark," he said. "Now we're at the low-water mark."

"We really covered state government in those days," said Jack Nelson, who won a Pulitzer at the *Constitution* in 1960 for his coverage of a state mental hospital. Looking at the paper now, he said, "it doesn't really feel very good. I spent thirteen years of my life down there and I was always very proud of the papers."

Eugene Patterson, editor emeritus of the *St. Petersburg Times,* came to Atlanta in 1956 as executive editor when civil-rights crusader Ralph McGill was in charge, and he stayed for the next twelve years. Back then, Patterson said, the capital bureau had "much more prestige than even the Washington bureau because that's where the big stories were and where the best people were."

As recently as 1990, when James Salzer went to work at the statehouse for the Morris chain, the *Atlanta Journal and Constitution* had a forceful presence. "You couldn't walk in a door without bumping into someone from the *Journal and Constitution,*" Salzer said. "They were three deep [in the House], two or three deep in the Senate, and they had people running around. They were just kicking butt."

By 1998, the *Journal and Constitution* was down to only three reporters year-round, with a fourth brought in during the legislative session. The Morris chain had two reporters filing copy for papers in Augusta, Athens, Savannah, and Jacksonville, Florida. To cover that year's forty-day session, the *Columbus Ledger-Enquirer* and the *Macon Telegraph* hired freelancers. The *Marietta Daily Journal* assigned one of two county reporters when events warranted. Other papers relied on AP's three-person bureau. This was the press corps charged with following 236 legislators who introduced 1,184 bills and 1,137 resolutions, with analyzing the proposed $12.5 billion state budget, and with covering news of the administration—all in an election year fraught with speculation that Republicans would take over both houses and the governor's office. Lobbyists outnumbered reporters 150 to one.

At the *Journal and Constitution,* "the thinking seems to be that people just aren't that interested," explained Stephen Harvey, a former capital reporter who had become the editor in charge of state-government coverage. If the number of reporters is any measure of what editors think does interest people, television has the edge. Five *Journal and Constitution* staffers were assigned to write stories and columns about TV—four in features, one in sports.

Rick Dent, the governor's press secretary, said he worked with more reporters on a daily basis than probably anyone else in Georgia. "The folks who cover us understand how important it is to cover government," he said. "We make major decisions on a daily basis. But there's a disconnect," he said, between reporters and their "editors and management."

During the 1994 gubernatorial campaign, Dent said, pollsters measuring public awareness of the governor's record discovered a "black hole" in the Atlanta area. The only explanation that made sense to the campaign staff was that the Atlanta newspaper had devoted so little coverage to the governor's first term.

Kevin Sack, who once worked for the *Journal and Constitution* and now covers eight southern states for the *New York Times,* said national reporters like him "rely on newspapers to tell us what's going on. It's hard to pick up [the *Journal and Constitution*] and get a clear feel for what's significant. Everything in the paper is buried. They have completely abdicated the use of their front page to set agendas or to tell readers what's important. . . . They lack a sense of the players—how the governor is doing on a day-to-day basis, how he's getting along with the legislature, what's on his mind. They don't bring you into the political intrigue of the place." Sack himself covered New York state government for the *Times* in Albany.

Sometimes the *Constitution*'s editorial page would take the lead because Jay Bookman, the associate editorial-page editor, had time to do what the paper's reporters didn't—hang out with lobbyists and legislators. "I walk the hallways, make the circuit, till I see everybody or they see me," Bookman said. This occasionally placed him in the awkward position of editorializing about bills that the paper had overlooked in its news coverage. "It means," he said, "only one side of the story is told."

Not everyone was critical of the weak coverage. Said Speaker Thomas B. Murphy, seventy-four, who had been a member of the House since 1961 and its leader since 1974, "It doesn't bother me at all."

The possibility that reporters might be missing stories was the one fear *Journal and Constitution* metro editor Mike King expressed in an interview. The Georgia legislature is "an old-fashioned structure of government," he said. "It has a powerful speaker who can use it to his advantage." Lobbyists themselves actually draw up bills, he said, and legislators don't have the resources for research.

This would seem to argue for more digging by the newspaper, but King said he had developed "a hardened attitude" about "how much time and how much resources to devote to something that has so little impact."

Year-round, King said, two full-time reporters were plenty: "Somebody to pay attention to the governor and somebody who pays attention to everything else." That meant, though, that statehouse reporters seldom had time to pursue promising leads. "If one of us goes off on a big project," said reporter Peter Mantius, "it leaves just one person to cover all of state government. It's not that easy."

King argued that if the bureau needed more manpower, "there are 70 others working in other parts of metro Atlanta who can write state stories whenever we need them." Sometimes these fill-in reporters would call Rick

Dent in the governor's office for help. "They'll get assigned a welfare piece," Dent said. "I'll have to spoon-feed the information to them. . . . But I'm an advocate. I'm not going to give you the whole side of the story. . . . They say, 'Who else should I talk to?' Well, hell, I'm not going to tell them to talk to the people who are on the other side." They'd tell him they didn't have much time for research. They'd say, "I have to get up to speed on this because they want it by 5 P.M."

Usually, Dent said, the reporters captured the fundamentals, but "they traditionally miss the 'why' of most stories. They tell what happened without any context." Dent knew better than anyone how often the paper missed newsworthy administrative snafus. "Most of my day," he said, "is not spent on the media but on crisis management among agencies. . . . Time and time again we fix things before they get out. We fix things before we're embarrassed by it. It wouldn't happen if there were more aggressive coverage."

He grew accustomed to hearing mournful complaints from *Journal and Constitution* reporters. "I have a couch in my office and sometimes I almost feel like a therapist," he said. "They're frustrated, almost embarrassed about it. They tell me, 'We know we should have covered that event, but it snowed in north Georgia and I had to cover it.'"

In some ways the 1997 legislative session marked a low in the *Journal and Constitution*'s coverage. Both statehouse reporters that year—Kathey Pruitt and Peter Mantius—were relatively new to the beat, having replaced two others who were reassigned to the Cox chain's Washington bureau. One of two additional reporters sent to help had little experience. The session generated more news than there was space. Protracted battles raged over welfare, partial-birth abortion, and a bill stiffening penalties on teenage driving violations. James Salzer said *Journal and Constitution* reporters would spend all day listening to heated debate and then joke, "I have a couple briefs to write."

The 1998 session produced less news, so more of it made the paper. And before the session began, the newspaper ran stories on major issues for eight days, devoting more space than in previous years. A Sunday chart gave the status of major legislation, and a new twice-weekly column, "Capitol Insider," allowed coauthors Pruitt and Charles Walston to report from behind-the-scenes.

Editor Ron Martin often had to defend his nine years of changes at the *Journal and Constitution*. Readers in search of anything substantial were forced to thread their way through photos, charts, lists, refers, briefs, Q&As, reader write-in columns, and daily traffic reports. Every day of the week was an alphabet of special sections. On Sundays the sections might run from A to R.

So one day in February of 1998, with CNN flickering soundlessly on his office TV, Martin was ready to defend his newspaper's coverage of state government. "If you measure it by how many angry institutions and public officials and companies there are out there, we've irritated a great many of them by examining what they're doing and asking questions about the way they're operating," he said. "You know, you can set up a straw man and say, why don't you have ninety-one reporters in the state capitol? Well, I wish we had ninety-one reporters, but we also have a lot of turf that we've got to cover in many, many ways." He said the paper had exposed fat in the lottery system and abuses in the justice system.

As the interview drew to a close, Martin declared that he found the criticism of his paper "boring."

And where did that criticism come from?

"Journalists," Martin retorted. "Never readers, never real people."

A FEW DAYS LATER, some 250 miles away, a newspaper with a markedly different approach to statehouse coverage is in the countdown to blastoff: opening day of the fast-paced, big-money 1998 Florida legislature.

It is 9 A.M., March 3, two hours before the governor is to deliver his State of the State address in Tallahassee, and *St. Petersburg Times* bureau chief Lucy Morgan has a small crisis on her hands. The photographer from St. Pete has turned up minus the tie he'll need to get into the House of Representatives. She calls reporter Peter Wallsten and asks him to bring an extra one.

One by one her troops arrive. Morgan has something for everyone: A quip for Julie Hauserman, who'll be handling death penalty bills, by virtue of having once written about an execution. "Did you see all that death-penalty legislation?" Morgan calls. "You are the goddess of death." A source for Adam Smith, who is up from St. Pete to help cover the session: the lobbyist for the League of Cities is an articulate spokesman on an issue Smith is covering. A tip for Diane Rado, the bureau's senior reporter: a troubled legislative committee, where there has been a sexual-harassment case and a recent FBI investigation, has just been abolished and its staff director canned. And for Wallsten, arriving with a fistful of ties, there's a compliment on a story in this morning's paper. "Hi, Peter. Good job on the telephones. Nobody else had it." Wallsten broke the story three weeks earlier that Republican legislators, acting on behalf of several phone companies, were proposing a bill to double local rates. This morning's piece was on the party's efforts to backtrack after a public outcry.

For everyone's benefit, Morgan holds aloft several Florida newspapers. "Here is the competition, if you're interested, who don't seem to know we've got tort reform, the death penalty, and a few other things. Most are advancing abortion."

With Morgan in charge of five reporters, the *St. Petersburg Times* capital bureau sets a standard for state-government coverage. The *Times* is the newspaper most cited by other Tallahassee bureau chiefs as their toughest competitor. Florida has seven newspapers with circulations over one hundred thousand, and they're all fighting for turf, so they all put reporters in the capital. Even chains that scrimp on state-government coverage elsewhere—Knight Ridder, Morris, Cox—maintain a basic level of coverage in Tallahassee, lest a competitor gain an advantage.

Though several reporters for other newspapers have been there longer than Morgan, who arrived in 1986, none has her status as a Pulitzer Prize winner and associate editor. Morgan, in her late fifties, has an arsenal of sources, a rich knowledge of Florida government, and a prescription for covering the statehouse refined by years of experience. When Morgan started, in the mid-1980s, the state bureau had two people. "One of the conditions I set for coming was that we add another person and bring up a session reporter," she says. Back in St. Pete, the state editor, metro editor, and executive editor all once worked in Tallahassee.

"Everybody in my food chain knows government," Morgan says. "It helps us a whole lot in getting space and play for stories." During the session there's usually at least one section-front story or page-one story with a Tallahassee dateline, plus a full page of copy inside.

Morgan's storehouse of knowledge is much on display opening day. From the House gallery on the fifth floor of the capitol, she surveys the legislators' desks, piled high with the largess of lobbyists—baskets of fruit, bouquets of flowers, tropical plants, candy, Girl Scout cookies, caramel popcorn, and, from a company that makes devices for the elderly and disabled, a three-foot wood-handled gripper, the kind grocery-store clerks use to fetch items from high shelves. On each desk sits a pineapple from a firm run by someone named "Pi-a."

But Morgan is more interested in the legislators and their guests, who are taking their seats. "One of the legislators embroiled in an affair with a lobbyist last year married her," she says, "and has her on the floor, holding hands."

Having claimed a chair in the House gallery and filed a story budget "downtown" on her laptop, she decides to track down the attorney general to check out a tip. She knows he'll show up on the fourth-floor rotunda with other members of the administration to wait for the governor. He confirms her tip.

Morgan is also sure that Gov. Lawton Chiles will be late for his address. But will he break his record of twenty minutes? Possibly. Once he was twenty-five minutes late for a ceremony honoring law-enforcement offi- cers who died on duty, even though he was the featured speaker. Morgan wrote a story, and for a week or so he was on time for everything.

As she waits to clock the governor's arrival, Morgan greets Secretary of State Sandra Mortham, who was a Republican candidate for lieutenant governor until a hard-hitting *Tampa Tribune* series embarrassed her into stepping down. Among other questionable activities, the paper caught Mortham raiding the treasury of a state museum for $60,000 to pay for office parties and promotional trinkets such as coffee cups and paper- weights bearing her name and the state seal. Although it was the *Tribune*'s story from beginning to end, the *Times* got in some licks, too. Still, the sec- retary of state seems friendly enough. Says Morgan, "You may piss them off. They don't like the bad stories. But most of them are adult enough not to hold it against you."

Back in the House gallery for the governor's speech—his tardiness fails to set a record—Morgan recognizes that his call for a gun-control measure is a milestone. As he leaves the chamber, she dashes down the stairs to get a quote. In the rotunda, she sees reporter Peter Wallsten and realizes he has left the House, too, while it's still in session—a mistake. Wallsten thought the session was over when the press gallery emptied, but Morgan knows otherwise. "Lucy always knows," Wallsten says.

The next day Florida newspapers are laden with coverage of opening day. Five stories and three editorials in the *Tampa Tribune*. Four stories, an editorial, and a roundup of briefs in the *Miami Herald*. Six stories, a roundup of briefs, and two editorials in the *Tallahassee Democrat*. But the *Times* has even more: seven stories, two columns, a roundup of briefs, and two editorials.

NOTHING CAN REPLACE a bureau of smart, experienced reporters backed by editors who care. But a technological revolution is giving reporters everywhere powerful new investigative tools. Thanks to comput- ers and to campaign-finance disclosure laws in all fifty states, journalists have the power to explore the secret world of money in state politics, something previous generations could only dream of. This is not just an option for powerhouses like the *New York Times,* but for newspapers in places like Carbondale, Illinois, and Newport News, Virginia. As editors seek alternatives to "boring" governmental-process stories, database journalism (despite a name that suggests geeks-at-work) has the power to rivet readers with accounts of how democracy operates.

For five days in February 1996, the *Indianapolis Star* proved the potency of the new electronic tools. The Indiana legislature had been "hijacked" and "plundered," the paper declared in its series opener, by "an extraordinary coalition of about forty big-business interests, led by the Indiana Chamber of Commerce." By pouring millions into the previous year's campaign, this business coalition helped Republicans win control of the General Assembly and then "drew up its own legislative agenda and rammed it through." At the behest of the business coalition, the legislature lowered the wages of construction workers on state projects, gave corporations protection from product-liability suits, and made it more difficult for teachers' unions to raise money for political purposes.

When Republican lawmakers tried to protest or even debate the issues, the paper wrote, "they were reminded in private meetings to stick with the party—and the money that got them elected."

Some of these lawmakers had gotten more than half their funding from the party's legislative leaders, who collected it from special interests and then doled it out as they saw fit. Legislators ended up more obligated to party leaders than to their own constituents. When a few dared to follow their conscience or vote the interests of the people back home, leaders saw to it that none of their bills passed, or warned that mavericks could expect no campaign money in the future.

This was nothing less than the breakdown of democracy, which is exactly how the *Star* characterized it. The series was doubly surprising, considering the source. The *Star* (later bought by Gannett) was then owned by a conservative Republican family, the Pulliams, whose most prominent member is former vice president Dan Quayle. The paper's editorial page had supported some of the legislation highlighted in the stories. "We saw our reputation as being a very conservative paper, very piously Republican," said Mark Rochester, the assistant managing editor for projects. "I think they were very surprised to see us take on the Republican Party in this state." The paper even reported that Quayle had telephoned a legislator who was wavering on a key vote.

Readers responded by bombarding the paper's "InfoLine" with calls. More than two thousand people completed a survey form that ran with the series. Readers sent letters calling the lawmakers "greedy maggots" and "crooks" and demanding that they clean up their act.

In April 1997 the *Star* ran another such series, and then another in August. The following January the paper struck again, this time linking special-interest money to legislative actions on health care, insurance, the environment, education, and liquor. The stories conveyed a vivid sense of legislators' disdain for the average citizen, describing how big donors monopolized lawmakers' time and attention, while a constituent who gave no money was lucky to get a few moments of rushed conversation while walking down a capitol corridor.

One of the bills the tobacco interests pushed into law prevented cities and towns from regulating the sale and promotion of tobacco products. On the day the Senate was to override the governor's veto of this bill, a crowd that included several dozen children, their teachers, and volunteers gathered inside the capitol. They had come to see democracy in action.

"But the children and most of the volunteers saw little," the paper said. "In the middle of the afternoon, when the vote was expected to be taken, senators recessed for nearly two hours so Republicans could caucus. . . . When they returned to the floor, they handled some other matters as the crowd in the hall slowly thinned. By the time the vote was taken at nearly 6 P.M., the children and the volunteers had left."

Only lobbyists remained, and the paper described how, afterward, a senator who had switched sides to cast the deciding vote walked across Capitol Avenue and had drinks at a club with tobacco lobbyists and their allies.

Public interest seemed to grow as the revelations continued. The fourth series drew even more reader responses—about 2,500—than the first one.

While the paper devoted considerable resources—four reporters, an editor and an in-house computer expert—to its investigations, the idea for the project had come from the Center for Public Integrity, a nonprofit organization in Washington, D.C. Backed by a grant from the Joyce Foundation, the center asked eighteen newspapers in Indiana to participate in its project to collect campaign-finance reports on file at the capitol in Indianapolis. After converting the reports into a searchable database, the center mailed a disk to each newspaper in the consortium.

No other paper made such extensive use of the database as did the *Star.* In fact, the only others to run substantial stories were the *Evansville Courier* and the *Fort Wayne Journal Gazette.*

When the center used the same approach in neighboring Illinois, though, it got a broader response. The Illinois papers agreed on an embargo date, allowing time for reporters to flesh out electronic data with original reporting, and on the same day—Sunday, October 5, 1997—a dozen newspapers blanketed the state with powerful page-one stories, giving the people of Illinois more information than they'd ever had before about their legislature.

As in Indiana, the Illinois papers found that a few legislative leaders collected huge stashes of special-interest money and used it to undermine representative government. Candidates in Belleville, Illinois, got two-thirds of their campaign money from party leaders in Springfield. Only after they got to the legislature did the candidates learn exactly where the money came from and what was expected in return.

In recent years, newspapers in Virginia and New York have formed similar consortiums, sharing the costs of building state campaign databases. And in Michigan, Ohio, and other states, individual reporters have assembled databases.

These stories have revealed an important political trend of the 1990s. Across the country, state politicians elected with money from beyond their districts are having to choose between loyalty to constituents and loyalty to outsiders with different agendas. More and more often, politicians are being elected with out-of-state money. Newspapers in New York, for example, reported that for his reelection campaign Gov. George Pataki raised funds in seven other states and Puerto Rico.

To make all of this activity as transparent and useful as possible, the campaign finance databases of various states have been made available on the Internet, enabling reporters and others to see patterns across state lines. The Web site of the Campaign Finance Information Center, posted by Investigative Reporters and Editors (IRE), has clickable maps to each state. One can go online and find out how much money a highway contractor, insurance company, or public utility has given to politicians in each state, and in which states these contributors have received contracts or favorable legislation.

"We're trying to get sort of a one-stop-shopping place," says Brant Houston, IRE's executive director.

Reporters who work with databases often find that the way they look at politics changes forever. "I'd covered the state legislature starting back in '85, and I thought I really knew what it was all about," says David Poole, who, as a reporter for the *Roanoke Times,* helped put together Virginia's campaign-finance database. "Once I got into database journalism, I found out I'd had it wrong all those years. All these big givers, I realized I'd never written about their issues."

Campaign finance, though, does not begin to exhaust the possibilities of database reporting. As public records are computerized, reporters find new and imaginative ways to analyze them. When North Carolina governor Jim Hunt proposed a "Three Strikes and You're Out" law, Raleigh's *News & Observer* applied the proposal to state prison records and found that, if it had been in use over the previous twenty years, the effect would have been negligible. Only ninety-one individuals would have drawn the stronger sentences required under Hunt's bill. (The bill passed anyway.) Also in North Carolina, the *Charlotte Observer* compared two sets of state agency records—one listing everyone who had done time in state prisons, another listing everyone certified to teach in public schools—and discovered eleven ex-convicts working as teachers, including some who had been convicted of rape, assault with a deadly weapon, and child molestation.

FOR ALL ITS PROMISE, however, the database revolution has yet to rescue the coverage of state government from stagnation. Where once the statehouse was a prized assignment, today it can be a difficult slot for editors to fill. Not only are many bureaus understaffed and under pressure to trivialize the news, state capitals are often out-of-the-way cities where reporters don't want to go. "'Oh God, you're gonna send me to Albany!' is a common reaction," says Eric Freedman, a former statehouse reporter who teaches journalism at Michigan State.

The *Sacramento Bee* has trouble filling vacancies in its ten-member bureau even though the capitol is a few blocks from the newsroom, the stories get good play, and the beat is considered a plus for anyone on a career track. "When we post a state-capital job now, we're lucky to get one or two internal applicants," said Gregory Favre, who left as the *Bee*'s editor in July 1998. Today's young people seem disillusioned with government, he says, and journalism schools don't emphasize it. "And also," Favre said, young reporters "see glory coming to people who are doing other things in our business. . . . They want to do the big blowouts, the big projects."

Places like the Poynter Institute for Media Studies and the American Press Institute do not hold seminars for statehouse reporters. Arlene Morgan, a former *Philadelphia Inquirer* editor who has dispatched scores of staffers to education and training programs across the country, says she never sent anyone anywhere to study state government. Ethics, yes. Environment, health care, and business, yes. But not state government. "I swear, I don't remember anybody ever offering anything on how to cover the legislature."

It takes a special breed of reporter to cover a legislature, says St. Pete's Lucy Morgan. Someone can "be the best reporter in the world but look like a deer caught in headlights when you put them in the state capitol." Those who succeed "can write fast, think fast, and can learn an issue fast." And it doesn't happen in a year or even two. When the legislature convenes, she says, "there's a huge village that crops up overnight. It's hard for us to learn who's here, let alone somebody new who's learning the lay of the land."

Lesley Stedman of Fort Wayne's *Journal Gazette* in Indiana certainly agrees. When she came to the beat two years ago, her only state-government experience was a few months with the *Anderson Independent-Mail* in South Carolina.

Stedman is one of 120 reporters nationwide who work in one-person statehouse bureaus. When the legislature is in session, Stedman shuttles between the House and Senate, shadowing members from the Fort Wayne area and watching for stories of local import while trying, at the same time, to keep an eye on the big picture. Her editors have talked about sending in an extra reporter for the session, but that hasn't happened.

"It's so hard being a one-person bureau," she says over lunch at the Indianapolis Press Club, where she goes to mingle with lobbyists, state officials, and other reporters. "I think we should have one person who analyzes things like the budget and what it means to our area, and then someone who covers what some of these issues—like children's issues—mean to people in our area."

Seven of the ten full-time reporters in the Indiana statehouse work in one-person bureaus, and they help each other out. "Sometimes I'll be in the House, at my desk there," Stedman says, "and I'll leave for a while. I'll come back and there'll be a note—'They passed that bill you were watching. I have quotes if you need them.'"

On a typical day when the legislature is in session, she files one story on a bill or an issue plus a roundup of shorter items. She usually files something for Sunday as well. Stedman considers the statehouse AP bureau "an extension of my own organization. A lot of the roundups I do are partly from AP." Her editors, she says, "aren't afraid to use AP" on a story she doesn't have time to cover. She knows of editors who don't like to lead the metro front with an AP story, or who'll overplay a staff-written story while underplaying something more important because it comes from the AP. She appreciates that her paper doesn't do that. Because the *Journal Gazette* is fairly small—with a circulation of 61,000 daily, 133,000 Sunday—she is modestly paid. She stays because she likes her job.

Stedman has it better than Brenda Rios, hired by the *Columbus Ledger-Enquirer* to cover the 1998 session in Georgia. Rios had covered the Kentucky legislature for the *Lexington Herald-Leader,* but she was not prepared for the disorganization and secrecy in Atlanta. Neither the legislators nor the committees had paid staff who could explain legislation. Committee meetings were often scheduled, canceled, or postponed without written notice. She was new to the state, working alone, with no colleagues to show her the ropes. "This is a system where you either have to know someone—a legislator to tell you what's coming up—or you have to have been here long enough to know how it works," says Rios, who has since moved to the *Detroit Free Press.* "You have to rely on lobbyists to tell you certain things."

For all the drawbacks, plenty of today's statehouse reporters love what they do. Mark Silva of the *Miami Herald* believes he's executing a public trust in covering Florida officials. "If the newspapers aren't watching them, nobody else is," Silva says.

And however much the job has been devalued in recent years, reporters like Lawrence Viele of the Morris chain approach it with reverence. One day, as she entered the Georgia House of Representatives, Viele had "an epiphany."

"I walked around the velvet rope and it dawned on me. This is the cut-off point," she says. "We are it between the lobbyists clogging the hallways and the public policy makers. Especially as money continues to more and more affect the process, it's even more important that we are here."

Immediately after the publication of "Missing the Story at the Statehouse" in 1998, the outlook for state news coverage improved somewhat—for a while. Follow-up surveys of statehouse pressrooms by the Project on the State of the American Newspaper in 1999 and again in 2000 showed an increase in the number of full-time state capitol reporters, from 513 to 543.

But then things took a precipitous drop. By the time the project counted noses again, in the spring of 2002, the nation had slipped into recession, and the economic impact had rippled through the newspaper industry. This time only 510 full-time reporters were found in the fifty statehouses, a figure even lower than the original 1998 count. Furthermore, this new survey found that fewer newspapers were sending extra reporters to the capitol to cover legislative sessions. In 1998, the project had counted ninety-nine newspapers sending these session-only reporters. By 2002 the number had fallen to eighty-two.

One sign of progress in 2002 was at the Atlanta Journal and Constitution, *which had nearly doubled the size of its statehouse bureau from three full-time reporters to five. A new editorial management was in place and appeared to be moving the paper toward more comprehensive news coverage.*

Also on the positive side, reporters covering state government all across the country were finding new resources to support their work and broaden the scope of their coverage. The Pew Center on the States, founded in 1998 in Washington, D.C., launched a Web site for statehouse reporters. The site began publishing original reports on state government actions and providing reporters with links to sources, searchable archives, and other services. It also hosted national conferences for state government reporters.

At one of those conferences a group of about twenty reporters banded together to form the Association of Capitol Reporters and Editors (ACRE). The organization established a Web site with a listserv where reporters can swap story ideas and sources, as well as a search engine for information posted by state and local governments nationwide. By 2002 ACRE had held three national conferences, and its membership had reached about 250.

"But while reporters and many of their editors are working to broaden their perspectives and master new skills," Charles Layton and Jennifer Dorroh wrote in American Journalism Review, *"this hardly makes up for the cuts in manpower that their bosses have imposed."*

Canvassing the Capitals

In an effort to gauge the newspaper industry's commitment to covering state issues, the Project on the State of the American Newspaper in 1998 conducted an unprecedented canvass of full-time reporters in all fifty state capitols. The total was 513, or about one for every one hundred or so registered lobbyists in the same statehouses. This original survey also demonstrated that during the decade of the 1990s, a period when state governments were acquiring enormous power and influence over the lives of average citizens, the commitment of resources by the newspaper industry declined precipitously. This was true in some of the nation's most prominent newspaper companies, including the two largest, Gannett and Knight Ridder.

The project repeated its count in subsequent years and found first an increase and then a sudden drop. In 1999 the number of full-time reporters had climbed by nearly 4 percent, to 532. By 2000 the figure had climbed again, to 543. However, in 2002 the number was down to only 510. The following charts break down these numbers state by state and newspaper by newspaper. Where "NA" appears, it stands for "not applicable," which usually means a newspaper has closed its statehouse bureau. Sometimes "NA" indicates that a newspaper has merged its coverage with that of another paper. Newspaper ownership patterns were changing rapidly during these years, as various companies bought, sold, traded, and consolidated their holdings, and sometimes entire papers, such as the *Evansville Press,* in Indiana, or Tennessee's *Chattanooga Free Press,* were folded into their former competitors.

State	FT Staffers in 1998	Trend from Early 1990s	FT Staffers in 1999	FT Staffers in 2000	FT Staffers in 2002
ALABAMA					
Birmingham News	2	flat	2	2	3
Birmingham Post-Herald	0	flat	0	0	0
Montgomery Advertiser	2	down	3	3	2
Huntsville Times	1	flat	1	1	1
New York Times Newspapers	1	flat	1	1	1
Mobile Register	1	flat	1	2	2
Dothan Eagle	0	down	0	0	0
Anniston Star	1	flat	1	1	1
Decatur Daily	1	up	1	1	1

State	FT Staffers in 1998	Trend from Early 1990s	FT Staffers in 1999	FT Staffers in 2000	FT Staffers in 2002
ALASKA					
Anchorage Daily News	0	flat	0	0	1
Juneau Empire	0	flat	0	0	0
Fairbanks Daily News-Miner	0	down	0	NA	0
ARIZONA					
Arizona Republic (Phoenix)	2	down	2	4	3
Arizona Daily Star (Tucson)	0	down	1	1	1
Tribune (Mesa, Scottsdale)	2	flat	2	2	2
Tucson Citizen	0	flat	1	1	0
ARKANSAS					
Democrat-Gazette (Little Rock)	3	flat	4	4	3
Donrey Media Group	3	up	3	3	4
Commercial Appeal (Memphis, TN)	1	flat	1	1	0
CALIFORNIA					
Los Angeles Times	12	flat	11	10	6
San Francisco Chronicle	2	down	3	2	4
Orange County Register	3	flat	3	3	3
San Jose Mercury News	2	down	2	3	4
Sacramento Bee	10	up	9	9	10
Daily News (Los Angeles)	1	flat	NA	NA	NA
San Diego Union-Tribune	2	flat	2	2	2
Contra Costa Times (Walnut Creek)	1	flat	1	1	1
Press-Enterprise (Riverside)	1	flat	1	1	1
Fresno Bee	1	flat	1	1	1
San Francisco Examiner	1	down	1	1	0
Press-Telegram (Long Beach)	0	flat	1	NA	NA
Oakland Tribune	1	flat	1	NA	NA
Record (Stockton)	1	up	1	1	1
Bakersfield Californian	1	flat	1	1	1
Chico Enterprise-Record	1	flat	0	0	0
Ventura County Star	1	up	1	1	1
Modesto Bee	1	flat	1	1	1
Wall Street Journal	2	up	2	2	1
MediaNews Newspapers	NA	NA	3	3	1

State	FT Staffers in 1998	Trend from Early 1990s	FT Staffers in 1999	FT Staffers in 2000	FT Staffers in 2002
Gannett News Service					1
Copley News Service					1

COLORADO

State	FT Staffers in 1998	Trend from Early 1990s	FT Staffers in 1999	FT Staffers in 2000	FT Staffers in 2002
Denver Post	2	flat	3	3	3
Rocky Mountain News (Denver)	2	down	2	2	2
Pueblo Chieftain	1	flat	1	1	1
Lehman Newspapers	1	flat	1	1	1
Daily Camera (Boulder)	0	up	1	1	1
Gazette (Colorado Springs)	2	up	2	2	1

CONNECTICUT

State	FT Staffers in 1998	Trend from Early 1990s	FT Staffers in 1999	FT Staffers in 2000	FT Staffers in 2002
Hartford Courant	3	flat	2	2	2
Connecticut Post (Bridgeport)	1	down	1	1	1
Stamford Advocate	0	down	1	1	1
New Haven Register	1	down	2	2	2
New York (NY) Times	0	down	1	1	1
Journal Inquirer (Manchester)	1	flat	0	2	2
Record-Journal (Meriden)	0	flat	0	0	0
Waterbury Republican-American	0	down	1	1	1
Day (New London)	1	flat	1	1	1
Norwich Bulletin	0	flat	0	0	0
News-Times (Danbury)	0	down	0	0	0
Wall Street Journal	NA	NA	1	1	0

DELAWARE

State	FT Staffers in 1998	Trend from Early 1990s	FT Staffers in 1999	FT Staffers in 2000	FT Staffers in 2002
News Journal (Wilmington)	2	flat	2	2	2
Delaware State News (Dover)	1	flat	1	1	2

FLORIDA

State	FT Staffers in 1998	Trend from Early 1990s	FT Staffers in 1999	FT Staffers in 2000	FT Staffers in 2002
Miami Herald	3	down	3	3	3
St. Petersburg Times	4	up	4	5	5
Sun-Sentinel (Fort Lauderdale)	2	down	2	2	2
Tampa Tribune	5	down	3	3	3
Palm Beach Post	2	flat	2	2	2
Orlando Sentinel	2	down	2	2	2
Florida Times-Union (Jacksonville)	2	down	2	2	2

State	FT Staffers in 1998	Trend from Early 1990s	FT Staffers in 1999	FT Staffers in 2000	FT Staffers in 2002
Daytona Beach News-Journal	0	flat	1	1	1
Bradenton Herald	1	flat	1	1	0
Freedom Newspapers	1	flat	1	1	0
Gannett Newspapers	2	down	2	3	3
Tallahassee Democrat	2	down	2	3	3
New York Times Newspapers	3	up	3	3	2
Wall Street Journal	1	up	1	1	0

GEORGIA

Atlanta Journal and Constitution	3	down	3	3	5
Morris Newspapers	2	down	2	3	4
Columbus Ledger-Enquirer	0	down	0	0	0
Macon Telegraph	0	down	1	1	1
Times (Gainesville)	0	down	0	0	0

HAWAII

Honolulu Advertiser	2	flat	1	2	2
Honolulu Star-Bulletin	1	flat	1	1	3

IDAHO

Idaho Statesman (Boise)	1	flat	1	2	2
Lewiston Morning Tribune	1	flat	1	1	1
Times-News (Twin Falls)	1	flat	0	0	0
Idaho State Journal (Pocatello)	0	down	1	0	0
Post Register (Idaho Falls)	0	flat	0	0	0
Spokesman-Review (Spokane, WA)	NA	NA	1	1	1

ILLINOIS

Chicago Tribune	2	flat	2	2	2
Chicago Sun-Times	1	down	1	1	1
Copley Newspapers	6	up	5	5	5
Lee Enterprises	3	flat	3	2	3
Daily Herald (Chicago)	1	flat	1	1	2
St. Louis (MO) Post-Dispatch	1	flat	1	1	1
Gannett Newspapers	1	flat	1	1	1
Pantagraph (Bloomington)	1	flat	1	1	1
Telegraph (Alton)	0	down	0	NA	NA

State	FT Staffers in 1998	Trend from Early 1990s	FT Staffers in 1999	FT Staffers in 2000	FT Staffers in 2002
News-Gazette (Champagne-Urbana)	0	down	0	1	1
Small Newspapers	NA	NA	NA	2	2

INDIANA

Indianapolis Star and News	3	down	3	3	2
Evansville Courier	1	flat	1	1	1
Evansville Press	0	down	NA	NA	NA
Journal Gazette (Fort Wayne)	1	flat	1	1	1
News-Sentinel (Fort Wayne)	1	flat	1	1	0
Post-Tribune (Gary)	0	down	0	0	0
Times (Munster)	1	flat	1	1	1
South Bend Tribune	1	flat	1	1	1
Gannett Newspapers	1	flat	1	1	1
Herald-Times (Bloomington)	0	up	0	0	0
Tribune-Star (Terre Haute)	0	flat	0	NA	NA
Courier-Journal (Louisville, KY)	1	flat	1	1	1
CNHI Newspapers	NA	NA	NA	1	0

IOWA

Des Moines Register	5	flat	5	5	4
Gazette (Cedar Rapids)	1	flat	1	1	1
Waterloo Courier	0	flat	0	0	0
Sioux City Journal	0	flat	0	0	0
Lee Enterprises	2	up	2	2	2

KANSAS

Wichita Eagle	1	flat	1	1	1
Kansas City (MO) Star	1	flat	1	1	1
Topeka Capital-Journal	1	flat	1	2	1
Harris Newspapers	2	flat	2	2	2
Lawrence Journal-World	NA	NA	1	1	1

KENTUCKY

Courier-Journal (Louisville)	4	down	4	4	3
Lexington Herald-Leader	3	flat	3	3	2
State Journal (Frankfort)	1	flat	1	1	1
Kentucky Post (Covington)	1	flat	1	1	1

State	FT Staffers in 1998	Trend from Early 1990s	FT Staffers in 1999	FT Staffers in 2000	FT Staffers in 2002
Daily Independent (Ashland)	0	flat	0	0	0
Messenger-Inquirer (Owensboro)	0	flat	0	0	0
Paducah Sun	0	flat	0	0	0
LOUISIANA					
Times-Picayune (New Orleans)	4	up	4	4	4
Advocate (Baton Rouge)	6	flat	6	6	6
Lafayette Advertiser	1	flat	1	1	0
Alexandria Daily Town Talk	1	flat	1	1	0
Gannett Newspapers	2	down	1	0	3
Lake Charles American Press	0	flat	0	0	0
New York Times Newspapers	0	up	0	0	0
Times (Shreveport)					1
MAINE					
Portland Press Herald	2	flat	1	1	1
Bangor Daily News	2	up	2	2	1
Sun-Journal (Lewiston)	0	down	1	1	1
Kennebec Journal (Augusta)	1	down	1	1	1
Foster's Daily Democrat (Dover, NH)	1	up	0	0	0
MARYLAND					
Sun (Baltimore)	3	flat	4	4	4
Washington (DC) Post	2	up	2	2	2
Capital (Annapolis)	1	flat	1	1	1
Washington (DC) Times	0	down	0	0	0
Frederick Post					1
MASSACHUSETTS					
Boston Globe	6	up	5	5	4
Boston Herald	3	up	3	4	4
Patriot Ledger (Quincy)	2	up	1	1	1
Enterprise (Brockton)	1	flat	0	0	0
Sun (Lowell)	1	flat	NA	NA	NA
Telegraph & Gazette (Worcester)	2	flat	2	1	1
Springfield Union-News	1	flat	1	1	1
Berkshire Eagle (Pittsfield)	0	down	NA	NA	NA

State	FT Staffers in 1998	Trend from Early 1990s	FT Staffers in 1999	FT Staffers in 2000	FT Staffers in 2002
Community Newspapers	1	down	1	1	1
Eagle-Tribune (Lawrence)	1	flat	1	1	1
Ottaway Newspapers	2	down	2	2	2
MediaNews Newspapers	NA	NA	3	3	3

MICHIGAN

Detroit Free Press	2	down	2	2	2
Detroit News	4	down	4	4	3
Booth Newspapers	7	flat	4	4	4
Lansing State Journal	2	down	3	3	2
Oakland Press (Pontiac)	0	up	1	1	0

MINNESOTA

Star Tribune (Minneapolis)	4	flat	4	4	4
St. Paul Pioneer Press	4	flat	4	4	4
Duluth News Tribune	0	flat	0	0	0
Forum Communications	1	up	1	1	1
Post-Bulletin (Rochester)	NA	NA	1	1	1

MISSISSIPPI

Clarion-Ledger (Jackson)	2	down	2	2	2
Commercial Dispatch (Columbus)	1	flat	1	1	1
Sun Herald (Biloxi)	1	flat	1	1	1
Northeast Mississippi Daily Journal (Tupelo)	1	flat	1	1	1
Commercial Appeal (Memphis, TN)	1	flat	1	1	1
Hattiesburg American	0	down	0	NA	NA

MISSOURI

St. Louis Post-Dispatch	3	up	3	3	3
Kansas City Star	1	flat	2	2	2
Jefferson City Post-Tribune	1	up	1	1	1
Springfield News-Leader	1	flat	0	1	1
Joplin Globe	1	flat	1	1	0
Columbia Daily Tribune	1	flat	1	1	1
Southeast Missourian (Cape Girardeau)	NA	NA	NA	1	1

State	FT Staffers in 1998	Trend from Early 1990s	FT Staffers in 1999	FT Staffers in 2000	FT Staffers in 2002
MONTANA					
Lee Enterprises	3	up	3	3	3
Great Falls Tribune	1	down	1	1	1
Bozeman Daily Chronicle	0	flat	0	0	0
NEBRASKA					
Omaha World-Herald	3	up	4	3	3
Lincoln Journal Star	2	flat	2	2	2
NEVADA					
Las Vegas Review-Journal	2	down	2	2	2
Las Vegas Sun	1	flat	1	1	1
Reno Gazette-Journal	1	flat	1	1	0
Nevada Appeal (Carson City)	1	flat	1	1	1
NEW HAMPSHIRE					
Concord Monitor	2	flat	2	2	2
Foster's Daily Democrat (Dover)	1	flat	1	1	1
Telegraph (Nashua)	1	flat	1	1	1
Union Leader (Manchester)	1	flat	2	2	2
Eagle Tribune (Lawrence, MA)					1
NEW JERSEY					
Star-Ledger (Newark)	10	up	12	12	12
Record (Bergen County)	6	flat	7	7	7
Times (Trenton)	3	down	3	3	4
Gannett Newspapers	6	down	7	7	5
Press of Atlantic City	1	down	1	1	1
Trentonian	1	flat	1	1	1
New Jersey Herald & News (Passaic)	0	down	0	NA	NA
Daily Record (Morristown)	0	down	NA	NA	NA
Jersey Journal	1	flat	1	1	0
New York (NY) Times	2	flat	2	3	3
Philadelphia (PA) Inquirer	2	down	3	3	3
MediaNews Newspapers	NA	NA	1	NA	NA
Newhouse Newspapers	NA	NA	NA	1	1

State	FT Staffers in 1998	Trend from Early 1990s	FT Staffers in 1999	FT Staffers in 2000	FT Staffers in 2002
NEW MEXICO					
Albuquerque Journal	2	down	2	3	3
Santa Fe New Mexican	2	up	2	2	2
Albuquerque Tribune	2	up	1	1	1
NEW YORK					
New York Times	2	flat	2	2	2
New York Daily News	1	flat	1	1	1
Newsday (Long Island)	1	flat	2	2	2
New York Post	2	flat	2	2	2
Buffalo News	1	flat	1	1	1
Watertown Daily Times	2	up	2	2	1
Syracuse Herald-Journal/ Post-Standard	1	down	1	1	1
Staten Island Advance	1	flat	1	0	1
Daily Gazette (Schenectady)	1	down	1	1	1
Times Union (Albany)	3	down	3	3	2
Ottaway News Service	2	flat	2	2	2
Gannett Newspapers	3	flat	3	3	3
Record (Troy)	1	flat	1	1	1
Post-Journal (Jamestown)	NA	NA	1	1	1
New York Sun					1
NORTH CAROLINA					
Charlotte Observer	4	up	3	3	2
News & Observer (Raleigh)	5	flat	5	4	4
Herald-Sun (Durham)	1	flat	1	1	1
Fayetteville Observer-Times	1	up	1	1	1
N.Y. Times Newspapers	1	flat	1	1	0
Winston-Salem Journal	1	down	1	2	2
Asheville Citizen-Times	0	down	NA	NA	1
News & Record (Greensboro)	1	down	1	1	1
Freedom Newspapers	NA	NA	2	2	1
NORTH DAKOTA					
Bismarck Tribune	1	flat	1	1	0
Forum (Fargo)	1	flat	1	1	1

State	FT Staffers in 1998	Trend from Early 1990s	FT Staffers in 1999	FT Staffers in 2000	FT Staffers in 2002
Grand Forks Herald	0	down	0	0	0
Minot Daily News	0	flat	0	0	0

OHIO

Columbus Dispatch	6	up	6	6	4
Plain Dealer (Cleveland)	6	down	6	6	5
Cincinnati Enquirer	2	up	2	2	2
Akron Beacon Journal	3	flat	3	2	1
Cincinnati Post	1	flat	1	1	1
Dayton Daily News	2	flat	2	3	2
Dix Newspapers	1	up	1	1	1
Gannett Newspapers	1	up	1	3	2
Thomson Newspapers	3	up	3	NA	NA
Blade (Toledo)	2	flat	2	2	2
Morning Journal (Lorain)	0	down	NA	NA	NA
Brown Publishing Company	NA	NA	1	1	0
Copley Newspapers	NA	NA	NA	NA	1

OKLAHOMA

Daily Oklahoman	3	flat	3	3	3
Tulsa World	3	flat	3	3	3
CNHI Newspapers	NA	NA	1	1	1
Journal Record (Oklahoma City)					2

OREGON

Oregonian (Portland)	1	down	1	2	3
Register-Guard (Eugene)	1	flat	1	1	1
Mail Tribune (Medford)	0	flat	0	0	0
Statesman Journal (Salem)	3	flat	3	3	2
Wall Street Journal	NA	NA	1	1	0
East Oregonian (Pendleton)	NA	NA	1	1	0
Bulletin (Bend)	NA	NA	1	1	1

PENNSYLVANIA

Philadelphia Inquirer	4	flat	4	3	3
Philadelphia Daily News	1	flat	1	1	0
Pittsburgh Post-Gazette	2	flat	2	1	1
Patriot-News (Harrisburg)	4	up	4	4	3

State	FT Staffers in 1998	Trend from Early 1990s	FT Staffers in 1999	FT Staffers in 2000	FT Staffers in 2002
Lancaster New Era	0	flat	0	1	1
Allentown Morning Call	2	up	2	2	2
York Daily Record	0	down	1	1	1
Ottaway News Service	1	flat	1	1	1
Erie Daily Times	1	up	1	1	0
Calkins Newspapers	1	flat	1	1	1
MediaNews Newspapers	1	flat	1	1	1
Tribune-Review Newspapers	2	up	2	2	1
Gannett Newspapers	1	flat	1	1	0
Delaware County Daily Times (Primos)	0	down	0	NA	NA
Times Leader (Wilkes-Barre)					1

RHODE ISLAND

State	FT Staffers in 1998	Trend from Early 1990s	FT Staffers in 1999	FT Staffers in 2000	FT Staffers in 2002
Providence Journal-Bulletin	4	up	3	3	2
Newport Daily News	1	up	0	0	0

SOUTH CAROLINA

State	FT Staffers in 1998	Trend from Early 1990s	FT Staffers in 1999	FT Staffers in 2000	FT Staffers in 2002
State (Columbia)	3	flat	2	2	4
Post and Courier (Charleston)	2	flat	2	2	1
Greenville News	2	down	2	1	1
Sun News (Myrtle Beach)	0	flat	0	0	0
Herald-Journal (Spartanburg)	0	down	1	1	0
McClatchy					1

SOUTH DAKOTA

State	FT Staffers in 1998	Trend from Early 1990s	FT Staffers in 1999	FT Staffers in 2000	FT Staffers in 2002
Argus Leader (Sioux Falls)	0	flat	1	1	1
Rapid City Journal	1	flat	1	1	1
Aberdeen American News	0	flat	0	0	0
Capital Journal (Pierre)	0	up	0	0	0

TENNESSEE

State	FT Staffers in 1998	Trend from Early 1990s	FT Staffers in 1999	FT Staffers in 2000	FT Staffers in 2002
Commercial Appeal (Memphis)	2	down	2	2	2
Tennessean (Nashville)	2	down	2	2	2
Knoxville News-Sentinel	2	flat	2	2	2
Chattanooga Times	0	flat	1	1	1
Chattanooga Free Press	0	flat	NA	NA	NA
Jackson Sun	0	flat	0	0	0

State	FT Staffers in 1998	Trend from Early 1990s	FT Staffers in 1999	FT Staffers in 2000	FT Staffers in 2002
TEXAS					
Dallas Morning News	8	up	8	8	6
Houston Chronicle	5	flat	5	5	5
Fort Worth Star-Telegram	3	flat	3	3	3
Austin American-Statesman	7	flat	7	9	5
El Paso Times	1	up	1	1	1
Scripps Howard Newspapers	3	flat	1	2	2
Lubbock Avalanche-Journal	1	flat	NA	NA	NA
San Antonio Express-News	2	up	2	2	3
Freedom Newspapers	1	flat	1	1	1
Beaumont Enterprise	0	down	1	0	0
Amarillo Daily News/Globe Times	1	up	NA	NA	NA
Wall Street Journal	1	up	1	1	0
Morris Newspapers	NA	NA	1	1	1
UTAH					
Salt Lake Tribune	2	flat	2	2	2
Deseret News (Salt Lake City)	6	flat	2	2	2
Ogden Standard-Examiner	1	flat	2	2	1
Daily Herald (Provo)	0	down	0	0	0
Herald Journal (Logan)	0	flat	0	NA	NA
VERMONT					
Burlington Free Press	3	up	3	1	2
Vermont Press Bureau	3	flat	3	3	3
Valley News (Lebanon, NH)	0	flat	1	1	0
VIRGINIA					
Richmond Times-Dispatch	5	flat	4	4	4
Virginian-Pilot (Norfolk)	4	flat	3	3	1
Washington (DC) Post	2	flat	3	2	2
Roanoke Times	1	up	1	1	1
Washington (DC) Times	1	flat	1	1	1
Daily Press (Newport News)	1	flat	1	1	1
Fairfax Journal	0	flat	0	0	0
Free Lance-Star (Fredericksburg)	0	flat	1	1	1
News & Advance (Lynchburg)				1	1

State	FT Staffers in 1998	Trend from Early 1990s	FT Staffers in 1999	FT Staffers in 2000	FT Staffers in 2002
WASHINGTON					
Seattle Times	2	flat	3	3	3
Seattle Post-Intelligencer	0	down	1	2	2
Olympian (Olympia)	2	flat	2	2	2
News Tribune (Tacoma)	1	flat	1	1	1
Spokesman Review (Spokane)	1	flat	1	0	1
Columbian (Vancouver)	0	flat	1	1	1
Wall Street Journal	NA	NA	1	1	0
WEST VIRGINIA					
Charleston Daily Mail	3	flat	3	2	2
Charleston Gazette	2	flat	2	2	2
Herald-Dispatch (Huntington)	1	up	1	0	0
WISCONSIN					
Milwaukee Journal Sentinel	3	down	3	3	3
Capital Times (Madison)	2	flat	2	2	2
Wisconsin State Journal (Madison)	1	down	2	2	2
Post-Crescent (Appleton)	1	flat	1	1	1
Green Bay Press-Gazette	1	flat	1	1	1
Janesville Gazette	0	down	0	0	0
Lee Enterprises					1
WYOMING					
Star-Tribune (Casper)	2	flat	2	2	2
Wyoming Tribune-Eagle (Cheyenne)	2	flat	1	1	1
TOTALS	513	—	532	543	510

2 | The New Washington Merry-Go-Round

By *John Herbers and James McCartney*
ORIGINALLY PUBLISHED IN APRIL 1999

IN 1995, INTERIOR SECRETARY Bruce Babbitt was trying to let the world know what dire things would be in store for the national-park system if hundreds of millions of dollars in proposed budget cuts were actually adopted, but he seemed to be getting nowhere with Congress—or, frankly, with the Washington press corps. So Babbitt took to the road.

He went bass fishing on Chickamauga Lake in southeastern Tennessee. He canoed along the Little Miami River in Ohio. He spoke before St. Louis's shimmering Gateway Arch. At every stop, Babbitt found local media receptive to his story, one wherein he cast Republican congressmen as villains for wanting, in effect, to shutter some of the country's hundreds of National Park Service sites. "We had twenty-eight stories in New Jersey papers alone," recalls Stephanie Hanna, a department press assistant. The blitz worked. After this regional drumbeat, the national media began paying genuine attention to Babbitt's admonitions, and the budgetary threat to the parks died.

Now, you can read Babbitt's tour as a savvy exercise in public relations, which it surely was. But you can also read it as a commentary on the shifting, uneasy state of Washington press coverage today. The Department of Interior controls the use of 500 million acres of public land, including a national park system that attracts 275 million visitors a year. It oversees the U.S. Geological Service, the U.S. Fish and Wildlife Service, the Bureau of Land Management, and the Bureau of Indian Affairs. Day in and day out, Babbitt's department is involved in such lightning-rod issues as mining, logging, water rights, and the protection of endangered species. And there are no newspaper reporters assigned full-time to cover Interior. None.

This is a marked departure from the past, when the *Denver Post* and at least a handful of other Western papers thought it important to have someone more or less stationed in Washington to keep an eye on the region's biggest landholder. Now they largely endeavor to cover Interior from their hometowns. In any event, the department has learned its lesson. Today when it seeks to generate news, Interior bypasses Washington altogether. If Babbitt wants to talk about efforts to save the condor, for instance, he'll do it in California. Or he'll fly to Florida to discuss preservation of the Everglades—this despite the fact that both stories have much more than regional significance. The secretary's assistant, Michael Gauldin, says department officials have realized that if enough regional outlets pay attention to a given story, the national press just may follow. "We'd rather appear in the *Washington Post* through AP, coming from the outside," he says.

So far the strategy seems to be working—for Interior, anyway. Whether it works for the public is a far more dubious proposition, considering that under this system the "news" is basically whatever the department decides it is, and there are no reporters left to tell us otherwise.

THE WASHINGTON PRESS CORPS has always been as susceptible to fad and fancy as the politicians they cover. The practices of daily journalism inside the Beltway evolve with the times and with changing media mores, and we're clearly in such a transition now. In today's confused, hypercompetitive environment, Washington's newspaper bureaus are struggling to define their basic mission, and in the process they have fundamentally altered what their reporters are covering and how they are deployed. So it is that some federal departments, such as Interior, have witnessed a steep slide in beat coverage. At the same time, the number of Washington journalists covering business and finance has exploded. (See chapter 6.) Tracking economic trends now far overshadows the once strong commitment of the capital press to social concerns such as poverty and equal opportunity under the law.

To help assess this evolution, the Project on the State of the American Newspaper recently surveyed newspaper and wire-service beats at nineteen federal departments and agencies, most of which have some direct influence on everyday life. How has the newspaper industry's commitment to covering these entities—as measured by full-time, or nearly full-time, beats—changed in the 1990s? We found that in eight cases (the departments of Interior, State, Agriculture, Labor, and Veterans Affairs; the Supreme Court; the Federal Aviation Administration; and the Nuclear Regulatory Commission) commitment is clearly down, sometimes to the point of nonexistence. In seven other cases—most having to do with business and finance, but also the technology, health, and science fields—

coverage has increased. And in four cases, the commitment appears to be roughly the same as it was a decade ago. (See chart, page 61.)

Peek behind the numbers and you find other notable, and sometimes worrisome, trends. For one, it can scarcely be reassuring how much the newspaper industry has come to rely on just four key outlets—the *New York Times, Washington Post, Los Angeles Times,* and Associated Press—to monitor vast portions of the federal government. (And that's just the major agencies we're talking about, much less the more arcane and virtually ignored specialty bureaucracies like the Federal Maritime Commission or the National Institute of Standards and Technology.) Conversely, many chains that reach huge segments of the reading public—Gannett, MediaNews, Cox, and Scripps Howard alone sell some 20 percent of America's daily papers—constitute a proportionately tiny fraction of the capital press corps.

The irony here is that more reporters are prowling Washington than ever. But that's not because the mainstream media have laid on thousands of extra people. To some extent it's due to a proliferation of newsletters, trade magazines, and specialty publications running the gamut from *Army Times* to *Women's Wear Daily.* Mostly, though, the capital boom is attributable to an appetite for business news that in the 1990s has become seemingly insatiable. Reuters, for instance, employs nearly 150 reporters and editors in its Washington office alone. Bloomberg News Service, which didn't even exist a decade ago, has nearly 60—or roughly three times that of such newspaper bureaus as Cox or McClatchy. Bridge News, formerly Knight Ridder Financial, stays abreast of federal activities moving the commodities and capital markets with 30 Washington journalists.

More people means more heat, and more pressure on the newspaper bureaus to somehow keep up. That pressure is the driving force behind the two most dramatic changes in Washington journalism, both of which involve the way reporters are being used. First, there has been a distinct move away from "covering buildings," jargon for the traditional practice of tying a specific beat to a specific agency. More and more beats today are built around broad themes—national security, law, science, economics—in which the reporters have the latitude to flit from agency to agency in pursuit of stories. So one day may find a national security correspondent at the State Department, the next day at CIA headquarters, and the day after that at the Pentagon.

The second major shift involves a concentrated push to get reporters in Washington to write stories with strong angles for the reader back home. "Local, local, local," says Clark Hoyt, vice president for news for

Knight Ridder and former chief of its Washington bureau. "Local news is the heart of the franchise. . . . If you look at reader research, the thing that readers are most intensively interested in is, first, local—my area, my neighborhood."

The fact is, Washington, with its multitude of public and private research agencies, increasingly is seen as a center for information rather than a center of government—and the new Washington journalism reflects this thinking. Virtually all the increase in coverage of business and economic affairs, for example, is based on a search for statistics and other information with little regard for what is happening within the agencies that produce it. But this evolution comes with some risk. If no one is covering Washington's "buildings," who will cultivate the kind of deep sources it takes to really know what's going on inside them? If everyone is looking for stories with "local angles," how many serious national stories will go unreported? If in trying to differentiate themselves from their electronic brethren Washington's print reporters become fixated with personalities or political process or today's spin, who will monitor actual governance on behalf of the public?

To UNDERSTAND THE EXTENT of these changes it is useful to look back to a time, before Monica Lewinsky was born, when presidents often were treated with a respect due kings, when reporters fought for the chance to travel with the secretary of state, when government actions weren't widely discussed until they had been read on the front page of the day's paper or heard on the nightly news. News from Washington was often high drama. It was about life-and-death issues of moment, not cynical gamesmanship. It seemed to matter.

Citizens were best connected to Washington by their local newspapers through the news dispatches, analyses, and columns of their paper's staff in the capital, with numerous regional papers competing with their larger and more influential counterparts for leaks and exclusive information. In the process, they were able to follow and judge, at least to some extent, the policies and actions of the national government. Not anymore. Except for papers in the biggest markets, most dailies have drastically reduced the amount of foreign and national news they publish. Washington has scarcely been immune. "We are no longer there waiting for the call from the red phone," says Charles Lewis, Hearst's Washington bureau chief. "The Cold War for fifty years defined Washington coverage . . . but when it ended, it changed the relevance of Washington."

In terms of journalistic coverage, this truth is perhaps most evident at the State Department, where standing press representation is way down from its Vietnam-era peak. In the past decade, however, a kindred erosion has occurred throughout official Washington. With relative peace abroad and unprecedented prosperity at home, the Washington bureaus of many major papers, such as those of the *Detroit News, Chicago Sun-Times,* and *Denver Post,* have virtually abandoned efforts to personally report national news stories. Even papers in such labor-conscious communities as Detroit, Milwaukee, and St. Louis no longer maintain a regular presence at the Labor Department.

All these newspapers see their current mission as much more difficult than in the past because of the pressures to do more analysis of news events and to go behind the issues involved—and to do it all instantly, since they now compete with a daunting array of electronic media. "News is very different in the CNN era than in the pre-CNN era," says Carl Leubsdorf, Washington bureau chief of the *Dallas Morning News.* Andrew Glass, senior correspondent for Cox and its former bureau chief, elaborates: "In the old days, on the first day we would report what happened. On the second day, we would tell what the reaction was. On the third day, we would analyze what it means. Now CNN tells you what happened and five minutes later some professor from Fordham University is telling you what it means. That's the problem. We have to find a way to package it all the first day or we're out of business.

"If we tried today to do traditional coverage in the traditional way, it would be ignored," Glass continues. "The papers wouldn't run it."

Therefore an increasing number of chains and newspapers—Cox, Hearst, Newhouse, the *Los Angeles Times,* the *Boston Globe,* Cleveland's *Plain Dealer,* Copley, and Scripps Howard, to name just a few—don't do it the traditional way. They have revamped their Washington bureaus to cover trends and issues that might take a reporter to a full gamut of government agencies and out into the country. Under these circumstances, they are more than willing to leave much of the "basic" Washington coverage—what the White House said, or the Supreme Court decreed, yesterday—to the wires and news services of the largest papers.

AP's veteran State Department correspondent Barry Schweid finds the new culture deeply distressing. "The papers are trying hard to get away from hard news," he says. Even those reporters still assigned to State are less and less visible. They come around occasionally to pick up transcripts of old briefings and follow up anything of interest they might find, Schweid says, but he believes important news is being lost in the process.

One reason why is that bureaucratic Washington, taking its cue from the White House and Congress, is decidedly more sophisticated about managing the flow of news. When officials want something publicized, everything is scripted. And when they don't, they are much more adroit at keeping unpleasantness under wraps. The State Department "has three times more flacks than they used to," says Schweid. "They don't tell you anything unless you ask about it." As an example he cites the March murder of eight tourists, including two Americans, in Uganda. State was aware of the atrocity but did not share the information with the press until a reporter heard about it elsewhere and solicited comment. For Schweid, it reinforced the notion that there is simply no substitute for being there. "You need to go to State daily," he says, "and elicit information."

Lyle Denniston, the longtime *Baltimore Sun* reporter and dean of the Supreme Court press corps, concurs. He regrets the severe hemorrhaging in the press gallery, which he blames in part on a court that takes on only about half the cases, and less controversial ones, than it did a decade ago. But another factor, Denniston says, "is that in the eyes of news editors the court is not a highly respected beat. They are not really keen on it." Today's court reporters try to stay on top of developments with occasional visits and by reading decisions electronically from miles away, but Denniston says you can't really do an adequate job that way. "The court is a small, tight-knit community. You run into justices in the hall or on the elevator. Being there is vital to knowing the human dimensions of the court."

NOW, EVEN IN THOSE gauzy days when Washington's influential newspaper bureaus had the capital essentially to themselves, not every chain felt the obligation—or wanted the considerable expense—of fielding widespread beat coverage of the federal government. One that has shouldered the obligation through the years is Knight Ridder, which has maintained one of Washington's largest and more prestigious bureaus.

But even here the combined pressures of budget and competition increasingly are being brought to bear. The Knight Ridder bureau in 1998 embarked on its second reorganization in seven years. The 1992 restructuring was traumatic enough, leading to a number of notable departures of seasoned journalists, a sharp redefinition of its essential mission, and a change of beats and coverage areas. Some feared the latest changes amounted to another step away from the bureau's hard-news tradition, but the company maintained that taking a new approach didn't mean diminishing its commitment to aggressive reporting in the capital.

The latest move was prompted when the chain surveyed its top editors about Washington's performance. For the most part they felt the bureau's coverage was too duplicative of major wires, that the operation was too costly, and that perhaps it should be shrunk. In response, only a handful of the fourteen national reporters were kept on conventional beats, two at the White House, two covering Congress. National politics, national security, and foreign affairs were assigned one reporter each. Longtime Supreme Court reporter Aaron Epstein retired, and his job became a "legal-affairs" beat looking not only at the high court but also at action in other federal courtrooms. Other areas of concentration included the environment, health, national economics, and consumer economics, as well as "federal cops," focusing on Justice, the FBI, the Drug Enforcement Agency, Customs, and the Immigration and Naturalization Service.

The number of regional reporters working out of the Knight Ridder bureau shrank from twenty-three to nineteen when the company stopped subsidizing the salaries of four reporters who covered Washington on behalf of the chain's ten smallest papers.

Similar changes are taking place in smaller bureaus that formerly took pride in their daily coverage of "the big picture" in Washington. The *Plain Dealer,* with five reporters and a writing bureau chief, has made dramatic shifts in both function and approach. "It's hard to cover anything news-worthy as news anymore because of television and the Internet, which give ordinary people great access to information," says Tom Brazaitis, who was bureau chief for years before becoming senior editor. "We still have a full-time Senate and House correspondent, but we no longer consider the regular daily events at the White House. In the [past] I would be at the White House most days. That's over. I tend to do more work on projects based on issues that can be talked about from a Cleveland perspective.... We have turned more to softening, to explain what is behind events rather than relating the events."

The notion of covering Washington through a local prism is every-where as embattled papers focus on what they perceive to be their biggest competitive edge. Another case in point: the *Detroit News*. After the Persian Gulf War in 1991, says former Washington bureau chief James Gannon, editors in Detroit seemed to lose interest in covering govern-ment, politics, or diplomacy. "The appetite in Detroit for that kind of news was minimal.... If it didn't have a local angle, they didn't want it."

Needless to say, Washington offers up local angles everywhere you turn. It is common practice for a bureau to staff the Supreme Court only when it is considering an appeal from a case of regional interest, or to report on new legislation only when a local member of Congress is its author. To some extent news from Washington with a local connection has always been prized copy back home. A host of small and medium-sized newspapers have long had reporters in the capital primarily to follow the home state's congressional delegation. In the 1960s a story circulated in the House and Senate press galleries about a regional wire-service reporter assigned to cover only Texas developments. One day a member of the House fell dead in the underground corridor leading to his office. The reporter, one of the first to happen along, saw the dead man's face and promptly went on his way. Asked why he didn't call his desk, he replied, "Well, he wasn't from Texas."

That yarn sounds less outrageous today, as what once was considered provincialism has become an established way of doing business. In recent years, a number of energetic new bureau chiefs have arrived on the scene armed with reader surveys and directives from their home offices determined to alter the way Washington is reported. Much of their criticism of past practices was well-founded: too many reporters standing around waiting for handouts, too much cozying up to high officials, too much redundancy in reporting among papers and agencies with little originality in news dispatches, too much allowing government officials to set the news agenda, too much pack journalism.

Deborah Howell, Washington chief for Newhouse, was one of the pioneers in structuring a bureau designed to avoid traditional beats and to focus on issues believed to be of greater reader interest. But she makes no claim that her forty-person bureau is covering Washington. Newhouse editors believed they received adequate hard-news coverage from Washington from many other sources; they made clear to her that "they did not want another version of the story of the day. They wanted something different."

To say the least, many of her beats are not traditional. Among them are money and jobs; race and ethnicity; family and children; violence; cyberspace; the American scene; and "doing good." Howell believes the bureau's primary function should be focused on enterprise stories that nobody else has, and claims considerable success. "I want to have important trend stories," she says.

Stephen Hess, a senior fellow at the Brookings Institution who has been studying Washington journalism for a quarter of a century, takes the side of the new generation of bureau chiefs in their efforts to reduce redundancy, which he sees as large numbers of reporters all writing virtually the same story while other news goes unreported.

Still, the new approaches to Washington coverage do have real draw-backs. They have helped fuel a record amount of turnover at the Washington bureaus. Despite the competence and commitment of the large news organizations that serve multiple papers, competition is reduced and some important stories invariably go ignored. The term "parachute journalism" used to suggest intrepid writers dropping into unknown terrain overseas, but with the downplaying of conventional beats we now have reporters in our own capital parachuting into the State Department or the Supreme Court. And while more coverage of health, crime, immigration, technology, economic trends and the environment is a laudable thing, in Washington it usually occurs without regard to the state of governance by the federal institutions involved.

And make no mistake: Washington is still very much in business. For all the efforts to shrink the vast bureaucracy, despite the return of so much power to the states, official Washington continues to exert a huge impact on people's lives. "The demise of big government has been greatly exaggerated," says Doyle McManus, who runs the Washington bureau of the *L.A. Times*. "I'm actually surprised at how obsolete we aren't."

O F COURSE, THE INHERENT problem in assessing the impact of the new Washington coverage is what we don't see—stories reporters never find, or ones they do but cannot get printed. Morton Mintz keeps a fat file of occurrences he considers important but were never printed, or were buried on back pages of the major newspapers he reads. Mintz had a distinguished career as an investigative reporter for the *Washington Post* (among other big stories, he alerted consumers to the dangers of thalidomide in the early 1960s), and today he is a kind of conscience-scold who directs his ire in long memos and op-ed pieces. Last fall, writing in the *Nation*, he observed: "In the four months ending in mid-September, for example, news of deliberate, even criminal, corporate misconduct with dire consequences for people and the environment—news that could be plucked from the wires like plums from a tree—too often drew either scant attention or none at all. Some great newspapers shrink-wrapped these stories into brief, one-shot items, causing them to sink without a trace. No follow-up, no commentary, no editorials."

One of several examples Mintz cited occurred last summer, when the St. *Paul Pioneer Press* "drew on Minnesota tobacco-industry documents to expose 13 well-credentialed scientists who took more than $156,000 from the industry for writing letters—or signing letters written or edited by tobacco law firms—discrediting links between secondhand smoke and lung cancer." The *Washington Post* ran an AP summary, he said, while the *New York Times, Wall Street Journal,* and *Los Angeles Times* carried nothing at all.

Mintz and others believe that the new order of journalism in Washington stems in part from how today's editors define news. The trend is away from hard news about how the government is functioning and evolving to softer stories and analysis about events and personalities. Some see in it a conscious, albeit futile, effort to mimic television's more entertainment-oriented approach to news, where, even in light of the cable TV boom and the twenty-four-hour news cycle, genuine depth and context remain rare. (Indeed, the network news divisions have led the march away from fixed Washington beats.)

Certainly there's no shortage of longtime reporters who feel their hard news copy is being downgraded. When he left an editing slot at the *Washington Post* to return to reporting, Bill McAllister asked to cover the Department of Veterans Affairs. Not exactly the sexiest beat in town— which was the point. "I had always thought of the VA as a great gray whale that sits almost unnoticed in Washington, second only to the Pentagon in the number of people it employs," McAllister says. He figured there must be a lot of good stories in a department that has 255,000 employees nationwide, spends $38 billion a year, administers benefits for 25 million veterans, guarantees 15 million home loans, and operates one of the world's largest insurance programs.

He was right. One story from last fall offered a case in point. For years government auditors have been calling on the VA to shutter many of its 173 hospitals, calling them obsolete and complaining that they contain too many empty beds. Just as regularly, Congress, under pressure from the powerful veterans organizations, blocked such reform efforts. No veterans hospital had been closed since Lyndon Johnson was president. But McAllister detected a new wind blowing through the dusty corridors where such decisions incubate. For the first time, he reported, there seemed a willingness at both the VA and in Congress to take on this once taboo subject. And they weren't just talking about closing tiny hospitals in obscure areas, but big ones like one of the four facilities in Chicago.

The story was initially slated for page one, McAllister says. Yet day after day it was held over, losing out not only to the drumbeat of the Lewinsky scandal but to a variety of local, business, and international stories (the *Post* being one of the few American papers that still maintains a large foreign staff). Finally it ran on A15—the "Federal Page," which appeals largely to government employees in what is, admittedly, a company town. Still, the great gray whale remained out of sight for most readers.

"It is hard to get good play on veterans' stories," says McAllister. "They are thought of as appealing just to the old-farts crowd." Of course, the story that never made page one was less about veterans than reforming a dysfunctional area of government whose profligacy has cost billions of dollars and affects the entire nation.

All of this raises perplexing questions about the long-term impact of the new order in Washington journalism. After all, democracy is not a matter of entertainment, it's a matter of engagement. The Constitution requires close citizen attention if the grand experiment is to continue to work. Paul West, bureau chief of the *Baltimore Sun,* is one of those in Washington who worry about the ramifications if the press veers too far from hard news. "More people are writing off the news, not digging up the news, and I think there is a danger there," he says. "If your job is to provide basic information about the function of the government, then the system of government that we have is not well-served."

The changes also tend to lend Washington journalism an increasingly transitory feel, and with it a disturbing myopia. Late last year, for example, the Senate debated a long-pending and controversial bill to allow banks, insurance companies, and securities firms to merge under common ownership. Rarely mentioned in news coverage of the debate was the fact that some eight hundred community-based organizations around the country strongly opposed the bill on grounds that it would concentrate too much power into the hands of relatively few institutions.

In years past these organizations, now treated as of little importance, were important players in gaining legislation for consumer protection and rebuilding central cities. But in keeping with today's fascination with Wall Street, most of the reporters working the bank story wrote only from the perspective of the high-profile financial interests then lobbying Congress. The situation caused consumer advocate Ralph Nader to charge that "surely legislation which is reshaping the entire financial landscape and which affects the economic well-being of the entire population deserves more than repeated articles which reiterate the spins of industry lobbyists."

As Stephen Hess warns in a recent book, *Media Power, Professionals and Policies:* "In a moment of general prosperity, such as the United States is presently experiencing, it is easy for news organizations to ignore most of what Washington does and is expected to do, dismissing the grunt work of government as only of interest to unblooded academics. When the rate of inflation and unemployment rise again, perhaps the media's attention will snap back to the purposes of governance."

Or as James M. Naughton, president of the Poynter Institute for Media Studies and a longtime newspaper editor, puts it, what is needed from Washington is coverage of the government, with intelligence and depth. "We only have one national capital," he says. "The main obligation [of a Washington bureau] is to cover the way the federal government and the people taking part in it are serving the public."

The Project on the State of the American Newspaper's first survey of which newspapers and wire services regularly cover nineteen federal departments and agencies first appeared in April 1999. Revisiting the same departments and agencies two years later, reporter Lucinda Fleeson found that the trend away from full-time beat coverage had deepened somewhat. Not only had coverage declined at the Nuclear Regulatory Commission, the Department of Veterans Affairs, and the Internal Revenue Service, but there were also defections from traditionally obligatory beats such as the State Department and the Department of Defense. In all, coverage had dropped at eight beats and increased at five.

The update did show increased vigilance at some agencies now in the news. In 1999, there was not one full-time reporter devoted to the Department of Interior. Since then, the Washington Post and Denver Post reactivated those beats to focus on the Bush administration's controversial environmental policies. Likewise the Wall Street Journal and New York Times added coverage at the Federal Communications Commission, which is undergoing a policy revolution. Some increases came as a result of newcomers to the field who assigned reporters to Washington beats because of regional interests. The Hartford Courant, for instance, added a reporter at the Environmental Protection Agency, as well as at the Defense Department.

In 1999, financial beats—anything to do with the stock market—were more numerous than ever before; two years later the Chicago Tribune, Scripps Howard, and the Washington Times had shuttered those full-time beats. In other areas papers shifted coverage. The Los Angeles Times, for instance, dropped its IRS reporter, but added a Social Security Administration beat; the St. Petersburg Times closed its full-time Washington watch on Veterans Affairs but added a Food and Drug Administration reporter.

Where Are the Watchdogs?

The following tables reflect the reporting levels at nineteen key federal departments and agencies. The column on the right is from the first survey, in 1999, which found that during the decade of the 1990s coverage of many of these beats had fallen off considerably. An update in 2001 showed that the slide in coverage was continuing.

Agency	Annual Budget	Bureaus Covering as of May 2001	Coverage Changes since 1999
Veterans Affairs	$46 billion	None	Dropped: Washington Post, St. Petersburg Times
Agriculture	$73 billion	Reuters, Associated Press, Des Moines Register	Dropped: Wall Street Journal
Interior	$10 billion	Washington Post, Denver Post	Added: Washington Post, Denver Post
Nuclear Regulatory Commission	$482 million	None	Dropped: New York Times
Treasury/SEC/FTC	$14 billion	New York Times, Boston Globe, Newsday, Associated Press, Dallas Morning News, Reuters, Knight Ridder, United Press International, USA Today, Washington Post, Wall Street Journal, Los Angeles Times	Added: Knight Ridder, United Press International; Dropped: Chicago Tribune, Scripps Howard, Washington Times
Supreme Court	$38 million	Washington Post, New York Times, Los Angeles Times, Baltimore Sun, Wall Street Journal, Houston Chronicle, USA Today, Associated Press, Newsday, Washington Times, Reuters	Added: Reuters; Dropped: Dallas Morning News

Agency	Annual Budget	Bureaus Covering as of May 2001	Coverage Changes since 1999
Federal Aviation Administration	$10 billion	Washington Post, USA Today, Reuters, Associated Press, Los Angeles Times, Wall Street Journal, Dallas Morning News	Added: Los Angeles Times, Wall Street Journal, Dallas Morning News; Dropped: New York Times
Internal Revenue Service	$9 billion	Wall Street Journal, New York Times, Washington Post, Associated Press	Added: New York Times; Dropped: USA Today, Los Angeles Times, Scripps Howard
Defense	$291 billion	Washington Post, New York Times, Los Angeles Times, Baltimore Sun, Wall Street Journal, Hartford Courant, USA Today, Associated Press, Newsday, Washington Times, Reuters, Knight Ridder, Copley, United Press International	Added: Hartford Courant, Copley; Dropped: Christian Science Monitor, Scripps Howard, Chicago Tribune
Federal Communications Commission	$237 million	Washington Post, USA Today, Los Angeles Times, Associated Press, Reuters, Wall Street Journal, New York Times	Added: Wall Street Journal, New York Times; Dropped: Chicago Tribune
State	$7 billion	New York Times, Washington Post, Los Angeles Times, USA Today, Washington Times, Baltimore Sun, Wall Street Journal, Boston Globe, Newsday, Associated Press, Knight Ridder, Reuters, United Press International	Dropped: Christian Science Monitor, Chicago Tribune

Agency	Annual Budget	Bureaus Covering as of May 2001	Coverage Changes since 1999
Justice	$25 billion	New York Times, Washington Post, Los Angeles Times, USA Today, Chicago Tribune, Wall Street Journal, Washington Times, Newsday, Associated Press, Reuters, Knight Ridder	Added: Knight Ridder; Dropped: United Press International
Food and Drug Administration	$1 billion	New York Times, Washington Post, Wall Street Journal, Los Angeles Times, Associated Press, Reuters, St. Petersburg Times	Added: St. Petersburg Times
Environmental Protection Agency	$8 billion	Associated Press, USA Today, Hartford Courant	Added: USA Today, Hartford Courant; Dropped: New York Times, Des Moines Register
Labor	$39 billion	Washington Post, Associated Press, Wall Street Journal, Reuters	Added: Reuters
Social Security Administration	$7 billion	New York Times, Associated Press, Los Angeles Times	Added: Los Angeles Times; Dropped: Cox, Scripps Howard

3 | Goodbye, World

By Peter Arnett
ORIGINALLY PUBLISHED IN NOVEMBER 1998

C ITY STREETS RADIATE from Monument Circle in Indianapolis like the spokes in the wheel of an old race car. Designed as the hub of an imposing series of veterans' memorials and plazas, the circle was downtown's main landmark until the Circle Centre shopping and entertainment complex opened in 1995. With its flashy eight-story glass rotunda and nearby museums, the center revivified downtown and put the lie to the old slur that the only thing that ever happened here was the Indy 500.

But for longtime residents, Monument Circle remains the reference point for the heart of the city, and for none more so than the 185 reporters and editors who work for the morning *Indianapolis Star* and the evening *Indianapolis News,* whose parent, Central Newspapers Inc., is the seventeenth-largest newspaper company in the United States.

That their preference is for news close to the circle was evident in the May 12, 1998, edition of the *News* I bought after arriving at Indianapolis International Airport. There were front-page stories on a tobacco-industry suit, a business merger, and, of course, the upcoming Indianapolis 500—but no mention of India's explosion of a hydrogen bomb the previous day. In fact, in the thirty pages of that day's *News,* I found only a few international briefs. Nine paragraphs, total.

Indianapolis was one of more than a half-dozen stops I was making to determine why most American newspapers, like the *News* and the *Star,* have come to focus so overwhelmingly on news from home. I had my reasons for picking Indianapolis, as I did with a couple of Manhattans (New York and Kansas). The other cities, among them Kalamazoo and Atlanta, I chose more serendipitously—no scientific sampling, but enough exposure to America's newsrooms to obtain at least an anecdotal explanation as to why so many papers have given up on the world.

What drew me to Indiana's capital was the memory of a time—the late 1960s—when international news dominated the agenda of America's media. The story was Vietnam. The Indianapolis papers were run by the cantankerous Eugene C. Pulliam, the most powerful publisher in two states, Arizona and Indiana. Despite initial reservations about U.S. involvement in

Southeast Asia, Pulliam had switched his full support to President Lyndon Johnson. The Pulliam papers in Indianapolis and Phoenix carried pro-war editorials, and the old man lambasted anti-war protesters at any forum he could.

Pulliam also served on the board of the Associated Press, a prestigious seat because the wire service was such a dominant force in the news business. I happened to meet him in early 1966 at AP's New York headquarters at 50 Rockefeller Plaza. An AP correspondent, I had just returned from Vietnam to receive that year's Pulitzer Prize for international reporting. Wes Gallagher, the legendary AP chief who could out-growl any newspaper titan, invited me to lunch. Pulliam would be a guest.

"He's louder in his support of the war than LBJ is," Gallagher warned me, then smiled. "Don't worry, I'll protect you."

But during the meal Gene Pulliam asked nothing but sensible questions about my experiences covering the war. As we dined in Rockefeller Center's Rainbow Room, the seventy-seven-year-old Pulliam reminisced of his travels to Europe and the Middle East in the 1950s. His grasp of developments overseas was confident and informed. Later I treasured any stories of mine that ended up on the front page of a Pulliam paper.

So now, thirty years later, I was traveling to Indianapolis. Pulliam's son, "Young Gene" Pulliam, in his eighties and his health declining, still ran the papers. I was armed with a rough survey I'd taken of the *Star*'s use of international news the previous November. The big story had been Saddam Hussein's defiance of the United Nations weapons-inspection teams. American members had been expelled precipitously from Iraq. The U.S. military buildup seemed to presage another round in the Persian Gulf War, with American lives at risk once more.

Yet the *Star* had little coverage beyond the obvious headlines. Only a tiny percentage of the newshole was international, even though this was once world-traveler Gene Pulliam's proud flagship, the main provider of news to central Indiana. What had happened?

I'LL PUT IT SIMPLY: International news coverage in most of America's mainstream papers has almost reached the vanishing point. Today, a foreign story that doesn't involve bombs, natural disasters, or financial calamity has little chance of entering the American consciousness. This at a time when the United States has become the world's lone superpower and "news" has so many venues—papers, magazines, broadcast and cable TV, radio, newsletters, the Internet—that it seems inescapable. So how is it that Americans have never been less informed about what's going on in the rest of the world? Because we, the media, have stopped telling them.

Sadly, that includes the vast majority of our newspapers. "The top fifty papers in the country do a good enough job—the other 1,550 dailies don't do anything," says Edward Seaton, owner-editor of the little *Manhattan Mercury* (circulation 13,000) in heartland Kansas. The worldly Seaton is the current president of the American Society of Newspaper Editors (ASNE) and is so concerned about the disappearance of foreign news that he made reversing the trend his top priority at ASNE. "For the average citizen of the United States," he says, "there is no international news available anywhere unless there is a major crisis."

Newspapers have been among the last holdouts. A few of the big boys —the *New York Times, Washington Post, Los Angeles Times, Wall Street Journal*—have stubbornly maintained substantial foreign-reporting staffs and produce sterling reports. Many major metros still do a serviceable, if spotty, job. Coverage of global finance and such hot-button regional issues as immigration and trade is on the upswing. But that said, the rest of the newspaper industry has capitulated to the ominous trend that began in the wake of Vietnam and accelerated with the end of the Cold War.

Broadcast television has essentially left the field. (Ironically, the rise of my own employer, Cable News Network, exacerbated this situation.) Magazines followed suit; foreign covers, we've been told, are the newsstand kiss of death.

At newspapers, when the money crunches of the early 1990s forced editors to pare budgets and newsholes, foreign reports were a major casualty. With the fall of communism, Washington bureaus for such chains as Cox, Gannett, Hearst, and Scripps Howard eliminated or greatly pared their coverage of the State Department.

Individual papers that once rightly bragged on their own foreign-affairs coverage—*Cleveland's Plain Dealer,* the *Detroit News,* and the *St. Louis Post-Dispatch,* to name a few—virtually gave it up. As paper after paper wrestled with priorities, what resources there were stayed home. Local ruled.

Consider Indianapolis. In the thirty days of November 1997, by simple yardstick measurement, foreign news accounted for just under 3,900 column inches. That equals one full page of news a day. Not great for those big Thanksgiving-season issues; not bad, either. But if you consider the same month in 1977, the *Star* totaled 5,100 inches (adjusted for today's wider measure) of international report. So there was a 23 percent drop over two decades.

Of course, that's only a snapshot and should be taken as such. Frankly, there's precious little data on this subject. But in the late 1980s, in one of the few consequential attempts to get a handle on the trend, a California State University professor of journalism, Michael Emery, measured the space that ten major American papers devoted to foreign news. Emery found that it constituted only 2.6 percent of non-advertising space. That figure, Emery discovered, was down precipitously from similar (albeit less rigorous) surveys during the early 1970s. And the papers he examined were standard-bearers—like the *New York Times, Washington Post, Christian Science Monitor, Chicago Tribune,* and *St. Louis Post-Dispatch.* One can only wonder how minuscule the percentages would be at the smaller papers most Americans read.

Beyond quantity, the trend also involves an overall reduction in the prominence of foreign news. Even at metro papers that still offer a reasonable diet of stories from abroad, a subscriber can go for days at a time without seeing one crack the front page. And the sheer number of foreign stories is clearly down. If you want to find out what actually happened the day before in a far-off place, the news is apt to be in those now-ubiquitous "World Roundups." On many days, in the smaller papers, those roundups are all you get.

My travels turned up no indications that this decline will be reversed. We would do well to fear the consequences of such a benighted state of affairs. In a new introduction to his 1996 book, *International News and Foreign Correspondents,* scholar and media critic Stephen Hess points out that "the United States is increasingly one nation and two media societies. Particularly as this gap relates to knowledge of the rest of the world, Americans who have the time, interest and money will be awash in information, while those with limited resources, who probably rely on an evening network television program and a local paper for news, will not get the information that reflects the importance of the world for their lives."

So many editors embrace the canard that readers don't want foreign news. Yet surveys just don't bear this out. In a 1996 poll, for instance, the Pew Research Center for the People and the Press asked readers what kinds of news stories they regularly follow. Fifteen percent said international affairs—just one point below Washington politics, and slightly ahead of consumer news (14 percent) and the celebrity stuff (13 percent) that gets cranked out these days by the boatload. American newspaper readers instinctively realize that with today's interconnectedness, what happens halfway around the world directly affects them. A one-day, five-hundred-point swan dive on Wall Street is laid to the collapsing Asian and Russian economies. Recessions abroad threaten American jobs. Terrorists blow up U.S. embassies. We launch cruise missiles in response. Iraq continues to flout U.N. resolutions and the American will. India and Pakistan engage in nuclear one-upmanship. There's the Mideast. Korea. Kosovo.

The world presses in on us, even in Indianapolis.

MY TAXI DRIVER, Earl Gibson, told me the *Indianapolis News* was his paper. He talked enthusiastically about its coverage of the Indiana Pacers basketball team. I asked if he cared for international news. "Hell," he responded with a laugh, "all those years they were talking about the SALT talks with the Russians? I thought they were talking about salt like in shakers, not nuclear bombs!" Earl dropped me off at the turn-of-the-century brick building at the corner of Pennsylvania and New York that houses the *Star* and the *News*. He pointed to the large black-checkered flags tied to power poles and to the rows of benches temporarily erected along sidewalks: "We got an Indy 500 parade comin' up!"

An old AP pal, Chip Maury, now director of photography for the two Indianapolis papers, met me upstairs in the second-floor newsroom. He started right in: "Proximity, proximity, proximity—that's what it's all about, that's what they're saying at the J-schools." Maury is gray-bearded, fifty-nine, and near retirement. By "proximity," he meant the ascendancy of local news. At the four o'clock meeting to determine page one of the next day's paper, I saw exactly what he meant.

Bob di Nicola, the acting wire editor, dealt his budgets round the table. He had culled several pages of national and international story suggestions from hours of scanning wires from the Associated Press, the *New York Times,* the *Washington Post,* the *Los Angeles Times,* the Knight Ridder–Tribune service, and others, a blue-ribbon news motherlode that costs the Indianapolis papers nearly a million dollars a year.

Di Nicola, a fifty-eight-year-old news veteran, was pinch-hitting for Jennifer Morlan, an assistant news editor. His picks for page one: President Clinton on a stepped-up campaign against organized crime; Secretary of State Madeleine Albright in Israel squabbling with Prime Minister Benjamin Netanyahu; and a follow-up story to India's nuclear blast.

Executive editor Frank Caperton took his seat at the head of the table. "Where's local?" someone asked impatiently. Moments later "local" arrived in the person of Thomas Leyden, the brassy master of the city desk's sixty-five editors and reporters. He bustled to his chair and shoved around his lists. A police reporter in Chicago before joining the *Star,* Leyden has been a fixture here for eighteen years. The meeting began.

Editors talked mostly about local stories. An Indiana man with cancer was arrested after admitting on television that he grew marijuana as medicine. A murder exposed the dark side of a high school romance. The governor threatened to sue his auditor. Each of these made it to page one, along with the Clinton press conference on crime. After some debate that evening, an *L.A. Times* analysis on India's nuclear tests cracked the front. The U.S. demand that Israel give up an additional 13 percent of the West Bank went inside.

Leyden seemed to dominate the meeting, and he did nothing to alter that impression when we talked by telephone a few weeks later. "Hey, in terms of play in the most precious part of the paper—the A section—it's the survival of the fittest," Leyden told me, with an almost gleeful laugh. "I am a partisan of local news. I want the local story to be played. I fight with everyone if I have to."

Until the early 1980s, the *Star* set aside ten or more A-section columns —nearly two open pages—for national and international news. But over the past decade, local news has gradually consumed more and more of that space and the front page as well. "A great day for me is an all-local front page," Leyden proclaimed, doubtless speaking for city editors everywhere. Indeed, a few days earlier severe tornadoes had strafed Indiana and blown all other news off page one.

The tornado stories belonged there, without doubt. But the point is, in Indianapolis "there is a temptation to be local to a fault," conceded Ted Daniels, managing editor for news. International stories have to meet a higher threshold just to get into the paper, much less be awarded prominence. Fifteen years ago Daniels himself was wire editor. At the end of the day, he said, he felt fully informed but was frustrated at being able to pass along to readers only 1 or 2 percent of what he'd read. Important regional papers like the *Star* and *News*—combined circulation 275,000—ought to avoid the temptation to go all-local, Daniels said.

I also followed up with Jennifer Morlan. It's her job to stay on top of both foreign and domestic news. She told me about her first news meeting. It was late July 1990. The wires were reporting ominous troop movements in southern Iraq. Neighboring Arab countries were concerned. Morlan pushed the story at the page-one meeting. But perhaps her newness at the job or her youth—she was twenty-three—went against her. "Someone muttered, 'Sounds like a helluva long way from the Circle,'" she recalled.

The story didn't make page one. It didn't even make the paper. The next day Saddam Hussein invaded Kuwait.

Morlan had better luck a year later. As political instability roiled the Soviet Union, she argued vociferously to move the story onto the front page. This time she had a formidable ally. Myrta Pulliam, the granddaughter of old man Pulliam and the paper's director of electronic media, had just returned from the Soviet Union. She said Morlan was right. The day after the story hit page one in the *Star,* there was an attempted coup against Mikhail Gorbachev. "I live for moments like that," Morlan said.

Most days, though, she must bow to the inevitable. "If there are three great international stories and three great local stories and I'm page-one editor that day," she said, "I'll pick the local stories. That's the way it is here. Sometimes you want to share wonderful stories and events with readers, but you cannot."

Executive editor Caperton, who came to the *Star* fifteen years ago, was blunt. "We print the best stories of the day, and that's it," he told me. "No favorites, no biases. I have to worry about readers enjoying our paper enough to renew their subscriptions. You ask about international news? We just cannot shove things with interesting datelines in the paper and serve it like breakfast cereal. We are in more than 55 percent of Indianapolis homes. We want to stay there."

But I reminded him: When Gene Pulliam ran the papers with an iron hand, one of his objectives was to "let everyone's view be known." Pulliam's heightened awareness of the uniqueness of America's free press caused him to change the motto of his papers to read, "Where the spirit of the Lord is, there is liberty," words that remain on the masthead today. Caperton shot back: "At that time, no matter how bad the paper, 90 percent of the population would read it—read it as entertainment. You were assured readership then. Today, people are much more discriminating. We must be more discriminating."

Discriminating, as in more local news. Of the newspapers in all the communities I visited, the *Indianapolis Star* ran the least international news.

My journey made one thing obvious: The very culture of today's newsroom puts wire editors at a disadvantage. They work in solitude, watching the news roll across their screens. Meanwhile, the army of local reporters and editors fills the newsroom with buzz. These days, there aren't even bells from the old clattering teletypes—the once-familiar signal that something happened in the world.

Of course, there are reporters and editors in Indianapolis who remember —as I do—those bells, the wire-room staffers running in with takes, straight to the copy desk. But that's what it is now, memory. The victors write the history . . . and the local editor, Tom Leyden, made it a short history: "That was another era—long gone."

I WATCHED INTERNATIONAL NEWS fade from America's newspapers in the 1970s. International news was my life's work, so I worried as my stories for the AP appeared in fewer and fewer papers. I was stunned by the editorial indifference. I had lived through the Vietnam War, the last great era of the wire services. AP's Saigon staff battled fiercely with United Press International, and a two-minute beat on a big story was still worthy of celebration, and headlines, from Maine to Montana.

But after the war ended, international news fell dramatically out of favor with editors. They were armed with surveys that suggested readers wanted more local news and service-oriented features (though not necessarily in place of world and national news), and they were scarcely immune to the country's inclination to turn inward after the decade-long nightmare of Vietnam. There was less room for crisis stories, much less longer series with exotic datelines.

AP foreign veteran Mort Rosenblum, now senior international correspondent, was so concerned that in 1981 he wrote *Coups & Earthquakes*, the first book to identify the diminishing interest of news executives in international coverage. Rosenblum quoted Harris and Yankelovich surveys showing that nearly half or even more readers were interested in international news. Yet a Harris poll revealed that news executives believed only 5 percent of readers cared. "Many of them allowed themselves to be guided by their own instincts—and prejudices—[rather] than by the polls," Rosenblum concluded.

Which may explain why there has never been a full-scale debate over this peculiar idea that there's room to publish an adequate local report, or room to publish an adequate foreign report, but not both. To me, it's a case of journalists making an ideological issue out of what is, in fact, a cost issue—and not a very big cost issue. Building in one additional page a day to beef up a paper's existing international coverage would cost a fraction of 1 percent of its operating expenses, yet would do much to ensure a foreign report that at least touches all the bases. Most newspapers of any size guarantee a certain amount of space for, say, the sports report, but except for the *New York Times* and maybe a handful of other top papers, how many set aside minimums for international news?

At the AP, whose showcase foreign report has won a fistful of Pulitzers over the years, editors struggled to cope with the growing apathy. The wire service has always hewn closely to the inclinations of member newspapers, so it responded to suggestions that foreign news be better related to the audience, that detail be traded sometimes for explanation, that "people reporting" become an important element in explicating complex international crises.

I did my own lobbying with America's editors at the annual AP Managing Editors conferences and on assignment around the country. One editor assured me, "Peter, when your byline's on a story on the wire, I can tell you our editors are eager to read it. Whether they use it in the paper is another matter." What came through to me in these conversations was that the editors believed my stories had already been told—on network TV. Walter Cronkite's avuncular "and that's the way it is" seemed to bring down the curtain on that day's news. For many newspapers, it meant curtains for foreign news. We'd been scooped.

The technological advances of TV news coverage in the 1970s were a wonder to behold but a horror for print hacks like me. I remember scribbling in my notebook at Clark Air Force Base in the Philippines early in 1973 as American POWs returned home from Hanoi. They came off the planes into the lenses of cameras beaming their emotional reunions around the world. Bernie Kalb and Liz Trotta had already told the story to network audiences before I could even get to my typewriter to bang out a bulletin.

The cost of those live broadcasts was enormous, but the networks operated their news divisions under relatively altruistic management. Bernard Kalb's brother Marvin, another CBS News star of those years, recalls meeting with network founder William Paley, who encouraged his staff to get the POW story on the air at any cost. "I have the *Jack Benny Show* to pay for it," Paley told him.

I, too, marveled at the immediacy of TV news, the powerful synergy of picture, sound, and voice. But all the while I knew: Print reporters were dispensing far more substantial information. Cronkite himself, a former wire-service man, had no illusions about this. At the height of his considerable fame, Cronkite encouraged viewers to turn to their newspapers each morning to get the stories behind the networks' thirty-minute nightly summaries. But as more and more people told pollsters they relied primarily on

TV for national and international news, mainstream newspapers opted increasingly for what networks could not cover—local news and sports. The hometown paper could get an outright clamp on local coverage. Meanwhile, I got tired of wheedling my own AP stories into the nation's newspapers. I couldn't beat the enemy, so I joined it. In 1981 I signed up with Ted Turner's infant Cable News Network.

Doom-criers predicted that an all-news channel could never be profitable. CNN quickly proved them wrong. It provided viewers with an exhilarating immediacy and rode the cable boom. Then, unexpectedly, the major networks began to stumble. In the mid-1980s, corporate owners sliced budgets and trimmed staffs. Foreign-news coverage plummeted. A 1987 *New Yorker* cartoon noted the retreat: "Owing to cutbacks in our news department, here is Rod Ingram to guess at what happened today in a number of places around the globe." The decline was detailed poignantly in the 1991 autobiography of former NBC News president Reuven Frank, *Out of Thin Air.* He wrote, "Like all American companies and later than most, broadcasting had moved from supplying customers to maximizing stock prices and their managers' bonuses. . . . The old role, our way, had served a long time. Never had Americans known so much about the world in those years. It would be enough to be remembered by."

In the heyday of Walter Cronkite, John Chancellor, and Frank Reynolds, at least 40 percent of television news was international. These days the figure is at best 12 percent and dropping to as low as 7 percent. Americans who'd developed the habit of getting at least a fix on international affairs from network news were now getting virtually nothing. That CNN had introduced a new era in dramatic, real-time TV news coverage was salutary but beside the point; the audience was too small.

In the print world, a harbinger of the decline of foreign news was the meltdown of UPI in the 1980s. From a peak of two hundred bureaus in the United States and around the world, with more than 1,200 employees and several thousand clients, UPI tottered into bankruptcy twice after Scripps Howard unloaded it in 1982. AP, a cooperative owned by America's newspapers, had effectively knocked UPI out of business. After Vietnam and with the emergence of Watergate, the energy crisis, and other domestic concerns, the industry wanted less international news—and fewer papers could afford to subscribe to both comprehensive services. Today UPI is owned by Middle East Broadcasting, a Saudi company, and is down to a dozen bureaus in the United States and abroad. Said one former staffer, "UPI's only real assets are its name—and Helen Thomas," referring to the legendary doyenne of the White House press corps.

Ironically, the demise of UPI encouraged the supplemental wire services, such as Knight Ridder–Tribune, Cox, and the *Los Angeles Times–Washington Post* syndicate, to fill the breach. There was renewed commitment on the part of some major papers, in the early and mid-1980s, to an overseas presence. For instance, Knight Ridder, starting from scratch in 1979, had eighteen foreign correspondents by 1986. Its news service went from serving mainly its own papers in the early 1970s to upwards of 350 clients in recent years. Other premiere and emerging papers, such as *Newsday,* the *Boston Globe,* the *Christian Science Monitor,* and the *Dallas Morning News,* moved to keep pace.

But the supplemental services were not immune to the recession of the early 1990s and the waning appetite for foreign news. Knight Ridder's foreign correspondents have always belonged to its major subsidiary papers, but in the past year the company began consolidating the foreign operation in Washington. More than a few editors—inside and outside the company—fear that Knight Ridder will now essentially duplicate AP's work and deprive the chain's metros of the chance to tailor a foreign report to their own audiences. But the company said the centralization came about in part from frustration: Knight Ridder's own papers were using too little of their foreign report.

Media specialist Hess, a fellow at the Brookings Institution, made the same point in his book: Foreign coverage is there, but not the commitment to publish it. "The newspaper industry almost requires us to move to certain large cities if we wish to be well-informed about the state of the world," he wrote. To prove his argument, he examined the two thousand news stories used in twenty mainstream papers (ranging in size from the *Arizona Republic* to the *Grand Rapids Press*) that appeared on one day— September 28, 1994, a date chosen because no major global events occurred to skew things. Hess found the papers used an average of only 4.5 international stories a day, other than briefs. He also found that the AP still set the agenda for international news in the United States, and that in addition to its trademark breaking news, it produced interesting enterprise pieces. "But few get published," Hess asserted, "and what is even more troubling is my finding of how few first-rate overview articles coming from the supplemental services . . . are chosen by newspaper wire editors."

Hess was right. There are still talented reporters out there producing terrific stories. They're just not getting used. As part of this examination of foreign coverage, the Project on the State of the American Newspaper canvassed papers around the country to find out how many staffers they have working full-time (or on exclusive contract) in foreign postings. Not

including the *Wall Street Journal*, whose overseas reporters focus predomi-
nantly on financial matters, our count is 186—not a lot, considering there
are nearly 1,500 daily newspapers.

If you include the *Journal*, the total is a more respectable 286. In fact,
the overall number of newspaper reporters abroad may actually be up in
recent years, a development almost certainly attributable to the exploding
interest in business and finance. Today thousands of business journalists
(and quasi-journalists) around the world are doing largely specialized
work for specialized consumers who can and will pay for the information.
Not much of this work, however, trickles down to everyday consumers.

That is the discouraging reality the AP must face. It puts out a superb
international news report, paid for by all of America's newspapers, that's
hardly being touched.

I WALKED THROUGH the AP portals at 50 Rockefeller Plaza, New York,
for the first time in October 1962, a year after signing up as a young correspondent in Southeast Asia. I had worked in cramped, often fetid, one-
room bureaus overseas, but the fourth-floor newsroom in New York
stretched across a vast landscape of clacking teletype machines, clattering
typewriters, and editors bent low over copy. In the distant southwest corner
was the foreign desk, presided over by the formidable Ben Bassett in his
green eyeshade, the last in the building, I'm sure. His steadiness and urgency
had piloted the AP through the Korean War, the uneasy years of the Cold
War, and into Vietnam. His dictum was expressed in frequent messages to
his far-flung staff in times of crisis: "It's time for cool heads . . ."

Bassett was already a legend, but only later would I realize that this was
the golden age of AP. Giants walked the halls. There was Relman "Pat"
Morin (two Pulitzers—the Korean War and school desegregation); Don
Whitehead (a Pulitzer for his Washington reporting); Dan Deluce and Hal
Boyle (both Pulitzer winners from World War II). At night they swapped
tales at the crowded bar of the Overseas Press Club on 42nd Street, one of
the most coveted memberships in town. The valorous Wes Gallagher, veteran of World War II reporting, was just taking the helm at AP. The Cuban
missile crisis was at its peak. New York's major newspapers—there were
seven—headlined the threat of nuclear war. Within two decades, the
nation had been through two wars and was embarking on a third. What a
time to be a foreign correspondent!

Today, more than thirty years later, AP remains at 50 Rock. The newsroom still covers the fourth floor. But the noise is gone. Editors stare,

unblinking, into computer terminals. There are no green eyeshades; wrist pads guard against carpal tunnel. Once you caught everyone's eye as you walked through the place. Now they're closeted in cubicles; what you catch is their backs. The old foreign desk, now the "international desk," has moved to the southeast corner, where its boss, Tom Kent, a forty-eight-year-old former AP Moscow bureau chief, struggles with uncertainties that never once plagued Ben Bassett.

Kent spent all of his working life in international news before moving to become AP's deputy managing editor for projects and administration in May 1999. He oversaw ninety-three international bureaus—a third more than during the height of the Cold War, when there was limited coverage behind the Iron Curtain—and he was under the gun to reverse the trend of diminishing international news in America's newspapers.

Traditionally, AP has taken the high road. It gathers and disseminates the stories. Newspapers can do what they will with them. But Tom Kent was willing to bear a greater burden. He told a seminar organized in 1998 by the Freedom Forum that he believed some papers were willing to publish quality projects, such as major takeouts on regions in crisis. "I am a very harsh judge of us, and I think if we do it right, it will be used," Kent told the gathering. "If they don't, it's our fault. I can't blame the American educational system or the fact that people don't read anymore or that everybody's watching *Seinfeld*. I just blame us.

"We are trying to provide more explanatory copy," he said. "We are trying to gauge the moment at which a story suddenly is likely to attract attention and to give people a point of entry to that story at that time. For example, we've been writing forever about the euro [currency], but recently they actually had a summit on the euro and made a decision. I can imagine a lot of people saying, 'Oh, yeah, what is this euro thing that I've sort of. . . . It's been vaguely on the edge of my consciousness, but now it's in the news.' So we did a Q&A on 'What is the euro?' that probably five or ten years ago we wouldn't have done—would just assume, 'Well, you should have been listening.' Now we're realizing that points of entry to stories, the key time, are important."

After newspapers complained that AP didn't provide enough advisory information, that it left wire editors awash in wordage as deadlines approached, the service started making recommendations for page one. Still, for some that just wasn't enough. John Simpson, a senior executive of *USA Today,* weighed in at the Freedom Forum session, too. "I look at [the AP page-one list] sometimes and I say to myself, 'Well, you guys are crazy.' But I also look at it and say, 'Well, if this is what most of the papers who are relying on the AP are going to have for their front pages tomorrow, this is important to me.'"

John Maxwell Hamilton, dean of journalism at Louisiana State University, told the seminar, "The [wire] advisories should tell you why a story is relevant, why you should use a story—in a sense, almost an instruction manual for stories, giving people ideas for what they can build on at the local level."

But Kent worried that AP editors are already hard-pressed for time, trying to stay ahead of the news curve, too busy to warn editors about crises in advance. AP gives some advance word with interpretive stories, Kent said, but "frankly, there are many places around the world where we are told things can explode. Sometimes they do, sometimes they don't. Often, newspapers don't find the room for the interpretive."

Many media observers blame the gatekeepers. David Anable, president of the International Center for Journalists in Washington, told the Freedom Forum group, "Virtually every paper has a mass of international news available—the AP, the *New York Times,* and other syndicates. Using more of it is cost-free. But most senior editors are reluctant to buck their publishers and money managers who are fixated on the public-opinion surveys. And some gatekeepers are like some of their readers: They don't know what matters, what's relevant, what appeals or how to make it so."

At the AP, the man who must somehow juggle all these competing concerns is the cooperative's president, Louis D. Boccardi. An assistant managing editor at the old *New York World Journal Tribune* before joining the AP in 1967, Boccardi took over the wire service in 1985. He and his top editors have worked hard to overcome AP's longtime image of a bulletin-board service. Boccardi once told an AP annual meeting, "We want to make it impossible for anybody to disparage anything we do with the old insult that it's just 'wire-service journalism.'"

Yet today Boccardi has a worse worry. Diminishing use of international news might cause newspapers to invest less in it, therefore restricting the AP's own ability to cover the world—and shutting off from the American public the best source of accurate, balanced news that it could ever get.

AZLAN IBRAHIM IS a lone figure tucked away in a corner of a busy newsroom. He is wire editor of Michigan's *Kalamazoo Gazette,* arriving at four in the morning to begin poring over the AP, Newhouse, and *New York Times* wires. ("I will name four or five stories that just have to run and pray that some of the others make it," he told me.) He keeps his eye on the CNN monitor across the room for tips on breaking news. But since the TV is closer to the sports department, the channel is often mysteriously switched to ESPN.

Ibrahim is one of those gatekeepers Lou Boccardi and others are counting on to advance foreign-news play. To be sure, Ibrahim wants to help. But he's up against it.

The *Gazette,* an afternoon paper with 63,000 daily subscribers, is local and proud of it. "Local news is our franchise," explained editor James Mosby. "We're original, and we want to stand out from the other papers around here." He conceded that in "the eternal pull and tug of daily news decisions, non-local news might not make it as much as it should." But he pointed to the paper's letters to the editor to buttress his views that local matters most. There, Kalamazoo readers teed off on such social issues as crime, abortion, and hometown politics. I also noticed some vociferous diatribes, a few laced with bigotry or extreme ideology. This southwestern part of the state, the *Gazette*'s circulation area, gave rise to the notorious Michigan Militia.

On the other hand, there is a flourishing cultural life here, due in large part to the presence of Western Michigan University and Kalamazoo College. The city, once best known for Glenn Miller's 1940s hit "(I Got a Gal in) Kalamazoo," has its own symphony orchestra, a new museum, a renovated civic theater and public library, and an arts center that recently doubled in size. In the 1950s Kalamazoo conceived the nation's first outdoor pedestrian mall, but now the mall is considered an obstacle to progress. The trees will be cut down, and traffic once again will flow along Burdick Street after a four-decade hiatus.

The *Gazette* is a Booth paper, owned by Newhouse. Mosby, editor here ten years, contends he is publishing a sufficiently nutritious product. "My readers can live with the *Gazette* alone," he told me. "I don't think they could with five-minute radio [news] or the thirty-minute TV news." Not all his readers agree. The content of the *Gazette* plays "to the lowest common denominator," complained Gail Griffin, an English professor at Kalamazoo College. "The *Gazette* is more parochial than it needs to be, and what's not local is often celebrity stuff. We talk about it—that it's more and more like *People* magazine."

At the hub of these conflicting passions is Azlan Ibrahim.

But he has found an ally in *Gazette* veteran Mary Tift. She has been at the paper since 1962 and has run the editorial page since 1987. A quietly commanding figure with a vigorous intellect, Tift writes two editorials a day, often six days a week. One of every five deals with international affairs.

"I have a personal belief that Joe Sixpack desperately needs to know what is happening in the world," she said. "He has an abysmal understanding of how international events affect his everyday life. The newspaper is the last stronghold of informational reality today. Many people around here rely on talk radio for what they think about the world. Or they visit militia-group sites on the Internet. What we have in our community are people ranging from the well educated to the determinedly ignorant."

Ibrahim contends there's more interest in the world-beyond-Kala-mazoo than management believes. Sometimes in the supermarket, he said, people stop him, want to know where he's from, then chat fondly about old college roommates from Africa or Asia. He said his neighbor, a blue-collar worker, listens to National Public Radio. A car that recently pulled up alongside him at a traffic light had the BBC news report blaring from its speakers.

In August, months after my visit, I checked back in with Ibrahim. He told me how the bombing of the two embassies in Africa and the American retaliation had warranted "power headlines" in Kalamazoo. "This is what we are in business for, the big story played in a big way," he said.

As for Mary Tift, she had painstakingly researched the collapse of the Russian economy, carefully wording her editorials to bring the disparate readership of the *Gazette* into the global picture. "I try to tell them, 'These events happen far from you, but they affect your lives,'" she said. Then she laughed, "I can't wait to get the mail."

Editor Mosby seemed grateful for their input. "We don't want to lose that," he told me. But he added, "Don't forget, happenstance dictated play. International events took over for a while. Our franchise is still local news."

MORE THAN A DECADE ago when I lived in Atlanta, I sometimes ate at the Varsity burger and hot dog joint on North Avenue. The place was capacious, outfitted in chrome. The waiters dressed like bellhops and scuttled across the floor bearing plates piled high with tasty Vidalia onion rings. Atlantans liked the Varsity because it was a throwback to the 1950s. At the Varsity time stood still. The rest of Atlanta was changing. Fast.

As I drove to work each day I passed beneath an electronic billboard that stretched across a main thoroughfare, blinking the daily increase in the metro population—over a million, and still counting. On Atlanta's out-skirts, greeting arrivals from the airport, was another billboard, boasting, "The World's Next Great City." Boosters mused about bidding for the Olympic Games. The city's industries and institutions tried to mold them-

selves to the new prosperity and sophistication. None did this more reso-
lutely than Cox Newspapers' morning *Constitution* and afternoon *Journal.*

In late 1986 the Atlanta papers recruited Bill Kovach, then Washington
editor of the *New York Times,* as their new editor. Kovach championed an
East Coast aggressive style of journalism. He aimed to win prizes and to
cover the world. But he struggled from the outset with a kind of culture
clash. He was trying to bring a *Times* worldview to papers whose most
popular writer was down-home humorist Lewis Grizzard (who once
allowed that "the *Constitution* and *Journal* sure as hell should worry more
about Cobb County than Botswana").

After two years Kovach was gone, and Cox brought in Ron Martin, a
USA Today veteran. Four years later, in 1992, the Atlanta papers finally
vanquished their suburban rival, the *Gwinnett Daily News,* whose doors
were shut by an embarrassed New York Times Company. Cox moved to
consolidate its position—and its costs. The morning and afternoon papers
were merged. And Atlanta continued to boom. Today more than 3 million
people live in the greater metropolitan area, and the *Journal-Constitution*
woos them with a blend of local news, short stories, features—and upbeat
style.

I visited the paper's international editor, Keith Graham, on the same
day he met with representatives of the Japanese consulate. They noted that
some three hundred Japanese enterprises had established themselves in the
Atlanta area. The businesses had a combined workforce of nearly twenty
thousand. Aggressive marketing by state officials had made Georgia second
only to California in Japanese investments in the United States. Yet the
Japanese had noticed that Cox Newspapers had closed its Tokyo bureau.
News from China was getting better play.

They left with Graham's sympathy and understanding. He'd been
appointed international editor only the previous year but was making a
determined bid to strengthen international coverage. He'd already given
top management a moving memo, which he showed me:

"Thirty years ago when I moved to Atlanta from Phoenix there was one
Mexican restaurant. There were maybe three or four Chinese places and a
single pseudo-English pub. You had to go out of your way to discover an
international presence. A few minutes ago I had lunch down the street at a
brewhouse where people were watching soccer broadcasts from both
England and South America. The woman who cuts my hair is from
Uzbekistan. I shop at the Korean grocery. The plumber who came to my
house the other day is from Israel. People from Germany and Pakistan and
Canada and Switzerland have moved into my neighborhood. The world

has come to us and it will come in a bigger way in the future. Our readers need to know about key events that could affect their lives—wars, ecological disasters, trade disputes, and, sometimes, they just need to know enough about other cultures to be able to talk to their neighbors."

Was anyone listening? I asked.

Graham grinned. He knew the odds. Yet he has posted a few victories. Management gave him two staffers to cover international events in Atlanta, including activities at the Carter Center and stories around the South, with a foreign-affairs slant. Graham even resurrected an idea from Kovach's days, suggesting in his memo: "For our market, we need to push more strongly for an African position or at least Africa stringers." No dice. But in August he did send reporter Don Melvin to Nairobi after the U.S. embassy bombing and later to Khartoum to inspect missile damage after America's retaliatory strike.

Graham's team also produced a weekly "International Atlanta" page. The page happened to be on the schedule for the day I visited. The lineup included two stories from Atlanta's sister city, Tblisi, Georgia—one about baseball fever in the former communist country, the other about a nurse from Atlanta's Grady Memorial Hospital who was helping develop a nurse-training program there. There was also an interview with Carter Center officials en route to China with computers for remote villages. The page floats from section to section. It runs wherever there's room.

But that afternoon, a bulletin interrupted the news meeting. Paula Jones's lawsuit against President Clinton had been thrown out. The next morning's *Constitution* had to undergo major reshuffling. Graham sighed. "Well," he said. "We won't make it today."

That evening he phoned me with an update: "We lost 'International Atlanta' at 4:30—but we got it back an hour later. It's in tomorrow's paper." A small victory, but worth cherishing.

O N BUSY INTERSTATE 70 just beyond Lawrence, Kansas, road markers point the way to the Oregon Trail. Locals say if you search long enough you can still find the wagon wheel ruts in the hard clay gulches of the Flint Hills. Farther west you reach Abilene, a rip-roaring frontier town long after the pioneers moved on. Some 170 miles southwest is the Dodge City of Wild West legend. Add to those tales the struggle of abolitionists who help escaped slaves travel north ahead of the approaching Civil War, and the unrest that followed, and you have a nineteenth-century Kansas where local news was far more interesting to frontier editors than anything else in the world.

Fast-forward 130 years or so and not much seems to have changed—at least with the editors. I stopped off to buy a copy of the *Topeka Capital Daily*, reputedly one of the best papers in the region, and it carried not one international story and virtually no national news. Local stories on politics and crime prevailed.

Yet it is here, in Kansas, that a campaign is beginning to put international news back into America's newspapers. The trailblazer is a mild-mannered hometown editor, Edward Seaton, whose family owns the *Manhattan Mercury*. Manhattan is almost literally middle America, 120 miles east of the geographic center of the contiguous forty-eight states. Seaton's campaign aims to rehabilitate foreign coverage in the small and medium-sized daily papers that most Americans read.

That such a journalistic initiative comes from an out-of-the-way place like Manhattan is less surprising than it first seems. With 44,000 people, it is one of the bigger communities in the state. Kansas State University is located here, and a former president was Milton Eisenhower, brother of Dwight. Manhattan was settled by abolitionists from Boston in the mid–nineteenth century, and a landmark building outside town is the clapboard Beecher Bible and Rifle Church, so named because in the wars against pro-slavery forces, Henry Ward Beecher's abolitionists shipped guns here in boxes marked for Bibles.

Manhattan also has close links to the wars of the twentieth century. When I drove into town on my visit late one evening, distant storm clouds seemed to be discharging bolts of lightning that reminded me of artillery explosions. It turned out they were real. My motel desk clerk later informed me that a brigade of the First Infantry Division from neighboring Fort Riley was on maneuvers in the rolling hills.

Ed Seaton's campaign will be an uphill fight, even at home. *Mercury* executive editor Bill Felber and Seaton's son, Ned, the news editor, are sympathetic but not entirely supportive.

"I don't pretend that we on the *Mercury* are doing much better than anyone else. We are learning, too," Seaton said as he gave me a tour of his paper's modern downtown plant. As editor in chief, Seaton prefers the persuasive approach with his staff, and says of Ned, "He never gave a rat's ass about international news until India and Pakistan exploded the bomb this year, and then he told me, 'Wow, now that's a story.'"

Felber is an outspoken adherent of local news first. With the circulation of the *Mercury* down a bit in the past year, Felber's voice is a commanding one in the newsroom—and with the accountants. "You have to understand Kansas editors," he told me. "They operate from a concentric circle, with the most important news coming from their hometown, with diminishing interest as those circles widen. It's a zero-sum game. You put one story in and that means another is kept out. The local makes it, the others don't."

But Ed Seaton is the boss, and so Felber said in acknowledgement of that reality, "Should Americans know what's happening in the world? Yes, but we can only communicate a few things in our paper. But if we don't tell them, where will they get it?"

Seaton's passion for international news doesn't surprise anyone who knows him. Seaton grew up on a farm in Coffeyville, Kansas. His dad was publisher of the *Coffeyville Journal,* his grandfather was publisher of the *Mercury,* and his great-uncle's brother was Ned Beck, the longtime editor of the *Chicago Tribune.* Seaton went to Harvard, where he majored in government and was a varsity swimmer. He wrote a senior honors thesis about the regime of Francisco Franco of Spain. A Fulbright scholarship took him to Quito, Ecuador. After a stint as general-assignment reporter for Louisville's *Courier-Journal,* he became editor in chief of the *Mercury.* He was twenty-six.

He has been in Kansas ever since, but his love of Latin America has had a powerful influence on his life. He has been heavily involved in the Inter American Press Association for more than twenty-five years, and in 1977, on one of his many humanitarian trips south of the border, Seaton helped secure the release of jailed Argentine editor Jacobo Timerman.

It was no surprise, then, that when Edward Seaton became president of ASNE he quickly went on record about his chief goal: make international news more interesting, more relevant, more enjoyable, and more available to newspaper readers across America. He named his campaign Project ASNE for International News.

Seaton rejects the often-heard view that slipping circulations warrant less foreign news. "That just won't wash," he said evenly. "Newspapers should be the vehicle for giving Americans a better view of the world because we have more space than the other media, and that space is expandable." He also sees a unique opportunity for the print press. "International news has been pretty much abandoned by network television and weekly magazines. What a chance for us to be back into the game again."

Seaton's ASNE initiative will specifically target editors, giving them the knowledge and the techniques to explore how international forces affect their own communities. "All this talk about 'local, local, local,'" Seaton said. "I figured, why not make a local story of international news? The average reader has to be guided into understanding how international news affects them. Just one example—look at the clothes they wear. I'll bet they weren't made in the USA."

Driving me around Manhattan, he showed me what he meant. We passed the McCall Pattern Company factory that exports its products to the far corners of the earth. I remembered in New Zealand in the 1940s, when material was scarce, my mother carefully traced McCall's patterns on yards of cotton for the school clothes she hand-sewed for me. Near McCall's was an auto plant that modified vehicles for alternative fuels for markets in Asia. And the sprawling Kansas State University campus is an assignment editor's dream. The Grain Marketing and Production Research Center has close connections with grain-producing countries in Europe and Asia. The American Institute of Baking, also on campus, attracts cooking specialists from home and abroad. Wichita, 130 miles to the south, is home to three major aircraft manufacturers—Beech, Cessna, and Lear—and Boeing remains the state's largest private employer.

"All this and Fort Riley, too," Seaton said. "Most American communities have similar linkages if editors take the trouble to look for them. That is the principle of our project. By [our] writing more about how our communities have become internationalized, and about the international connections to their lives . . . the reader will make the connection to the international country. If these stories are written, then people will become more interested in the policy stories that drive them."

Seaton has devised a practical way to advance these ideas. With assistance from the Freedom Forum, ASNE is taking a look at how mainstream daily newspapers can improve foreign coverage. "Then we will produce a handbook for every U.S. editor on covering the world, and then hold workshops around the United States," Seaton said. "We even plan to offer, as part of the annual ASNE writing awards contest, a prize for the best writing about the impact of international forces on the writer's local community."

Similar efforts percolate elsewhere. The Pew Charitable Trusts (which underwrites the State of the American Newspaper series) is establishing a four-month-long biannual program to send seven journalists to Washington and overseas to study such issues as population, the environment, immigration, refugees, and human rights. The Associated Press Managing Editors (APME) will send four staffers from small newspapers abroad each year to interact with AP bureaus. Editors are being advised to take advantage of the U.N. Development Program's annual trips overseas for journalists; they are inexpensive and have flexible schedules. Several newspapers are introducing "sister" programs with overseas papers to give their staffs foreign reporting experience.

The editors and media experts who give their support to Ed Seaton and his Project ASNE for International News have no illusions that the effort will be easy. They agree it's a matter of getting the news editors, the reporters and everybody else in the newsroom to appreciate what's at stake and to rethink how they approach the news every day.

Louisiana State University's John Maxwell Hamilton says that in his endeavors around the United States to promote the use of international stories, he learned that the top editor was the first who needed convincing. "If we found an editor who wanted to do it, we were always successful. If a reporter alone in the newsroom wants to do it, it's a constant fight."

Ed Seaton is one of those editors who want to do it. As we drove about his hometown, he pulled over to a lookout on the crest of one of the rolling Flint Hills that stretch from Nebraska in the north to Oklahoma in the south. Seaton talked of his heartland legacy. "Our congressional district abuts the districts that Harry Truman, Ike and Bob Dole came from," he said, pointing east and then west over grassy fields and green hills. "Those three Plains-states political figures had a hell of a lot to do with shaping American foreign policy in the last half of the twentieth century, [with] giving us the great advantages we enjoy at home and abroad today."

Then he added, "Our obligation, surely, as editors of the nations' newspapers who labor in their shadows, is to provide the public all they need to know about the world."

The terrorist attacks of September 11, 2001, changed many editors' attitudes toward foreign news. A follow-up survey by the Project on the State of the American Newspaper in 2002 found many newspapers putting more energy and resources into their foreign reports. Papers found more space for stories with international datelines, and page-one editors no longer grimaced when wire editors promoted foreign stories for the front page. Keith Graham, world editor of the Atlanta Journal and Constitution, *spoke for many of his peers when he said that, after September 11, top editors were "more aware that foreign news is important, and that people need to be exposed to it."*

In an effort to quantify the difference this awareness might have made, writer Steve Seplow reviewed the coverage of three midsize regional papers —the Journal and Constitution, *the* St. Louis Post-Dispatch, *and the* Indianapolis Star—*both before and after the attacks of September 11. Before the terrorist attacks he found only four to six columns a day in each of these papers devoted to international news. Their reports consisted mainly of eight- to twelve-inch stories that laid out the facts but offered little background, little flavor, and little analysis.*

"And to some extent," Seplow wrote after the terrorist attacks, "that hasn't changed. There's still not much foreign copy beyond the big stories, and there is little to illuminate the values and cultures of different countries—the very kind of stories that might explain the anger seething in the Muslim world." He did find slightly more space devoted to foreign news, but most of it was taken up by the two major stories, Afghanistan and the Middle East.

According to a survey of 218 editors conducted for the Pew International Journalist Program, 95 percent said reader interest in foreign news had increased since September 11, and 78 percent said their newshole for foreign news had increased as well. But 64 percent said they expected their readers to gradually lose interest, and 58 percent said they expected their foreign newshole eventually to shrink back to previous levels.

It also remained true that very few newspapers were willing to invest in foreign bureaus.

Even before September 11, the dynamics between foreign and domestic events had been changing. Not long after Arnett's article was published, protesters in Seattle and Washington, D.C., organized spirited mass demonstrations at meetings of the World Trade Organization, the World Bank, and the International Monetary Fund to protest the fiscal, labor, and environmental policies of those organizations. Other foreign stories intruded on the American consciousness. OPEC cut oil production, and oil prices in the United States tripled. The United States went to war in Kosovo. A young Cuban exile, Elian Gonzalez, dominated headlines for months. New waves of immigrants, especially from Latin America and Asia, had a considerable impact on American culture. And global trade took on increased importance.

"The line between foreign and domestic issues has blurred," said John Maxwell Hamilton, dean of the Manship School of Mass Communication at Louisiana State University. "It's a mistake to see them as being separate categories."

With this idea in mind, the American Society of Newspaper Editors and the Freedom Forum launched a campaign to encourage newspapers to increase their coverage of foreign news. The result was a series of workshops around the country and an eighty-three-page how-to booklet for editors called "Bringing the World Home: Showing Readers Their Global Connections."

Still, the heightened interest did not translate into more column inches devoted to news from abroad.

4 | Then and Now

By Carl Sessions Stepp
ORIGINALLY PUBLISHED IN SEPTEMBER 1999

O N THURSDAY, JANUARY 9, 1964, readers of the *St. Louis Post-Dispatch* awoke to a five-degree day. Their paper cost seven cents. Its front page featured fourteen stories and three photos. Four bumping heads tombstoned their way across the top. A four-column lead reported that President Johnson, trying to budge a nation still numbed by the assassination of John F. Kennedy, was pushing his legislative agenda on Congress.

The paper was a happy mishmash of serious news and oddities. From the three local, nine national, and two world stories on page one, readers learned about a proposed merger involving seven local towns, infighting among county Democrats, a reform plan that South Vietnam's premier hoped would help win a war there—and a sixteen-year-old girl caught running a moonshine still.

At the bottom of the page they discovered that the local YWCA was launching an anti-girdle campaign. "A girdle is a girl's worst enemy," the unbylined, six-inch story began, accompanied by art of local women throwing away the offending undergarments.

That issue of the *Post-Dispatch* was crammed with no fewer than 137 local items—about news, sports, business, and society matters. On page three, an excruciating local photograph showed five sad-faced children left motherless after a shooting in which their father was charged. A four-page editorial section included three long analytical articles, but otherwise few stories throughout the paper exceeded six column inches. Only two A-section stories topped twenty inches.

Thirty-five years later, on Thursday, January 14, 1999, St. Louis arose to another brisk day (twenty-four degrees) but a different-looking newspaper. The *Post-Dispatch* now cost fifty cents. Its modular front page, with no bumping heads, carried four stories (three local, one national, all jumping) and five photos, the most prominent a four-column color shot of an ice storm that had paralyzed the region the day before. A digest-index ran four inches deep across the bottom.

A banner headline previewed the noon opening of President Clinton's impeachment trial. The front page also covered the ice storm (story, two photos, fact box), a local nurses' unionization vote, and local nuns' efforts to prepare by hand 130,000 communion hosts for the impending visit of Pope John Paul II.

Overall, the broadsheet paper featured fewer but longer stories (sixty-nine local items, about half the 1964 total), far fewer oddities, and far more graphics and reader-service material. There were fewer national and international pieces and local personal items. A thirty-six-page entertainment tab, unmatched by anything in the 1964 edition, contained five local bylines plus hundreds of listings, from "jaunty jalopies" at an area auto show to local casino-gambling events.

Times had changed, and so had the *Post-Dispatch*, one of ten papers reviewed in an extensive State of the American Newspaper survey of how newspaper content has evolved over a generation.

The survey sought to answer a simple question: Amid all the turbulence in society and in newsrooms, with all the talk of the need to innovate, has the newspaper itself, the bundle that ends up in the reader's hands every day, really changed all that much?

The short answer is yes. But if many of the changes are self-evident, some are surprising and others even alarming.

Today's newspapers are strikingly different, in looks, content, and tone, from their 1960s counterparts. Whether you call it the paper (1960s) or the product (1990s), whether you find it on the doorstep (1960s) or somewhere in the yard (1990s), the actual fruit of all the journalistic tumult and sweat has indeed been transformed.

Today's papers have bigger newsholes, longer stories, lengthier leads, and more jumps than those of a generation ago. They pay dramatically more attention to business and sports. They give more front-page coverage to local stories and less to world news. They are more diverse (but not as much as you might think), use anonymous sources less often (but barely), and still like their pun headlines on occasion. They also publish enough calendars in a day to choke a Palm Pilot.

The most visible change is in appearance. Older papers look homely and drab compared to their artful, color-splashed modern cousins. With content, the most noticeable difference also starts with something visible: Older papers were jam-packed with short items, overflowing with local names, places, and activities. In tone, today's papers are far better written. Writing in older papers carried a traditional, just-the-facts style, even as the pages brimmed with more peculiarities and sensationalistic crime stories than we may remember.

In most ways, today's papers are more featurized than the older ones, and features have changed. Gone for the most part are "women's" pages, social and personal items, and full-page daily photo spreads. Supplanting them are themed sections (on fitness, gardening, relationships) and what former editor James Squires has called "marketing-driven editorial content" —ad-rich sections on real estate, automobiles, travel, dining out, and the like. Some serious topics, notably religion, have gained attention, as have all sorts of lifestyle subjects (like the *Fresno Bee*'s "Petishes," a page of "advice for and about your pets").

Papers have also experienced an agate revolution. They publish exponentially more business, sports, and TV agate, along with lists of everything from participatory sports to local support groups.

Today's papers offer more interaction, more reader-service content, growing attention to high tech and money management, and a clear effort to appeal to younger readers through such vehicles as teen pages and entertainment sections. Still, considerable hard news remains, and, to my eye at least, it appears that government coverage—the subject of so much dismissive criticism among many editors—remains high at the federal and local levels but lower at the state and regional levels.

The bottom line is that modern newspapers read different. They are, by almost any measure, far superior to their 1960s counterparts: better written, better looking, better organized, more responsible, less sensational, less sexist and racist, and more informative and public-spirited than they are often given credit for.

Yet something significant, perhaps vital, seems to be in decline. When you carefully read scores of papers from both eras, as I did, it is hard not to conclude that modern papers are less flavorful, less surprising, and— distressingly—less imbued with a distinctive sense of place.

If yesteryear's papers strutted with the happy-go-lucky vanity of impregnable monopolies, today's hum with professionalism but lack some of their predecessors' wayward charm and unabashed embrace of community.

There was much to criticize and reform in the 1960s newspaper world. But revisiting it now brings a wallop of nostalgia. For all their faults, those newspapers exuded a guileless and infectious charm, a goofy amiability that can make today's technically superior editions seem stiff and remote.

If nothing else, newspapers have mirrored their world in one profound way over the past thirty-five years: Like society at large, they have gained sophistication and glitz but at a conspicuous cost to their innocence and gusto.

FOR THIS STUDY, we sought mainstream papers, deliberately avoiding the very best, worst, largest, and smallest. We kept in mind diversity of ownership and locale. We chose papers known for influencing their states or regions, mid-range papers in both circulation and status. Our aim was not so much to achieve a statistically pure sample of all American papers as to get a reasonable look at evolving heartland journalism. Thus, our ten: the *Fresno Bee, Houston Chronicle, Las Vegas Review-Journal, Macon Telegraph, Richmond Times-Dispatch, St. Louis Post-Dispatch, Topeka Capital-Journal, Wilmington News Journal,* Cleveland's *Plain Dealer,* and Memphis's *Commercial Appeal.*

Using a ninety-nine-question form, we analyzed the papers for one week each in May 1963, September 1963, and January 1964, and then for those same weeks in 1998 and 1999. To help understand how various trends phased in over time, we also conducted a similar analysis for comparable periods in 1985 and 1986; we hoped that by examining this intermediate period, we could learn which changes were already well in place by the 1980s and which were relatively recent.

This analysis constitutes one of the most comprehensive examinations ever into newspaper content. Even so, the data should be read not as absolutes but as indicators of trends. Our papers represent an important slice of newspapering, but not all newspapers: Eight of these ten rank in the top one hundred in circulation, and all ten rank in the top 16 percent. (Put another way, the smallest of our picks, the sixty-thousand-circulation *Topeka Capital-Journal,* is still larger than 1,300 of the nation's dailies, most of which are small-town enterprises.) This report also includes personal impressions from an informed reading of many of the survey papers. Taken together, the observations and data are meant to provide some baseline evidence to enlarge our understanding—and challenge some myths—about how newspapers are changing.

Some of our chief findings:

- Today's newshole is double that of 1963–64. Among these ten papers, total newshole rose an average of 101 percent, from 59 percent at Cleveland's *Plain Dealer* to 161 percent at the *Macon Telegraph.* Newshole grew at all ten papers between 1963–64 and 1985–86, and at nine of the ten it grew additionally between 1985–86 and 1998–99.

While total news space clearly has risen, three factors somewhat offset the gains. First, eight of these ten cities have lost at least one daily newspaper since the 1960s, reducing the overall newshole within the market. Second, in the intervening years the papers have shrunk their page size by an average of 10 percent (the tables on page 114 reflect the specific shrinkage at each paper). Third, most have increased the size of their body type. Even so, the rise in news-hole looks significant at every paper we studied.

- Hard news now gets relatively lower priority for space. Bear in mind that a doubled newshole means that today's papers print more of almost every kind of news. But as a percentage of total newshole, business coverage has doubled (7 percent to 15 percent), and sports (16 percent to 21 percent) and features (23 percent to 26 percent) have risen notably. Hard-news categories have fallen: local from 19 percent to 14 percent, national from 11 percent to 7 percent, and foreign from 5 percent to 3 percent. One telltale indicator of today's priorities: business agate has jumped from an average of four columns a day to fifteen. All these trends were well under way by the 1985–86 period, with one key exception: The percentage of space devoted to foreign news stayed constant into the 1980s and then dipped between 1985–86 and 1998–99.

- Front pages are much more local. Local stories, as a proportion of page-one copy, are up from 41 percent to 55 percent; foreign stories are down sharply, from 20 percent to 5 percent. National news stayed about the same (39 percent to 41 percent). Among the topics getting more front-page coverage: business, court, science, and sports news. (Scandal news also soared, but the study was doubtless skewed on this point since the final week of our sample coincided with the Clinton impeachment trial.) Among the topics getting reduced front-page play: world and celebrity news. Interestingly, front-page attention to two key topics stayed almost constant: crime and government/politics. Again, many of these changes were under way by the 1980s intermediate period, with the one obvious exception of international news, which still accounted for 19 percent of front-page stories during the 1985–86 period.

- Front pages are more featurized. Today's front pages average fewer stories (twelve in 1963–64 to five now), more features (up from 10 percent to 20 percent), more soft leads (up from 9 percent to 29 percent), more jumps (up from 37 percent to 88 percent), and more length (up from an average of nine inches to twenty). They have 25 percent more art and, of course, color. Modern pages have fewer bumping headlines, banner headlines, or leads in the traditional top-right position. Pun headlines rose a tad; the average 1998–99 paper ran three in the twenty front pages we studied, compared to two in 1963–64. These trends could be clearly seen by the 1980s intermediate period.

- Diversity has increased. Bylines that were apparently female quadrupled, from 7 percent to 29 percent. In photographs, the papers averaged thirty-eight male faces and twelve females (our count reflects page one images for all three weeks) over the 1960s period, forty-four male and sixteen female in the 1990s. They averaged forty white faces and five nonwhite faces in the 1960s period, forty-two white and sixteen nonwhite in 1998–99. These directions can be seen in the 1985–86 papers as well.

- Stories are longer. In their main news sections, the older papers averaged thirty-six items a day under six inches, compared to thirteen for the modern papers. Older papers averaged just one item a day over twenty inches inside the A section, compared to three today. Letters to the editor jumped from three a day to seven. The 1980s papers show these changes in progress.

In a snapshot look at sources (we recorded the first source mentioned in front-page stories), we found that anonymous sources were down (18 percent to 14 percent), "regular people" sources up (10 percent to 15 percent), and government sources about the same (39 percent to 38 percent). For reasons that are unclear, the 1980s papers showed the lowest percentage of anonymous sources (8 percent) and the highest percentage of government sources (46 percent).

Behind the figures are a host of personality changes. If newspapers were relatives, and sometimes they do seem part of the family, then the 1963–64 papers seem like dotty Aunt Zelda and Uncle Ernie—unkempt, eccentric, and footloose, yes, but full of high spirits, tall tales, and a get-a-load-of-this exuberance. Today's papers come across as more the Cousin Edwina or Grandfather Benjamin type—proper, polished, and professional, but also starched, sanitized, and short on spontaneity.

Consider the *Houston Chronicle* of September 26, 1963. The paper's lead story kicks off with this grabber: "The Texas Department of Public Safety knows the identity of all Communist Party members in Texas."

Three other stories line the top of page one, headlines bumping:

- A local police chief accuses the "P-TA" of being "aligned with gambling interests."

- "Stool pigeon Joseph Valachi" is reported "'singing' freely to Senate investigators about operations of the sinister 'cosa Nostra' [sic] gangland syndicate."
- And, chillingly: "President Kennedy is planning to visit Texas late in November on a political foray. . . . Sources said there was likelihood he would visit Dallas."

To read 1963 newspapers is to reenter a pre-Watergate, pre-Vietnam, pre–Dealey Plaza world. It is to roll back a gigantic cultural loss of idealism.

Papers of the 1960s seem naively trusting of government, shamelessly boosterish, unembarrassedly hokey, and obliging. There was apparently no bottom to the threshold for local news and photos. Writing was matter of fact, and stories were surprisingly often not attributed at all, simply passing along an unquestioned, quasi-official sense of things. The worldview seemed white, male, middle-aged, and middle-class, a comfortable and confident Optimist Club bonhomie. With it came a noblesse oblige sense of purpose. A paper was inextricably woven into its community, a self-anointed major player almost preening with pride and duty.

The 1960s papers appeared to take some forms of news—particularly state and foreign coverage—more seriously than today's do. Their sweeping accumulation of short and sundry items, the nonstop parade of local names and faces, the plentiful local photos recording quotidian community themes, together built a powerful shared appreciation of local life. But the communities they reflected tended to be narrow and noninclusive.

Overall appearance is the first change you notice. The type-heavy front pages of the older papers—all in black and white, of course—cram fifteen or more stories into eight gray columns, relieved by only a few small photos and almost no relaxing white space. Clashing headlines, jigsaw-puzzle design, and vertical makeup intensify the harsh effect.

Inside pages seem disorganized and lackluster. Stories wrap out from under their headlines and frequently end in midsentence (a common problem in those hot-type days). News, features, fillers, and art are combined into indifferent hodgepodges. For instance, a single page in the May 3, 1963, Las Vegas Review-Journal contained a news story from Yugoslavia, a report on local building permits, and a "Tips for Teen" feature column with a perky drawing.

Older papers are sprinkled with idiosyncratic shorts and "did you know?" fillers ("Prizes awarded to winners in the ancient Greek Isthmian games consisted of a wreath of wild celery"). They also scatter local photos throughout all sections, breaking up type on national and world pages and providing a stream of local flavor. Today's computer-formulated pages fit more neatly and rely on wire photos and computer graphics outside the local section. The gain in attractiveness and orderliness is clear, but it is off-set, at least partly, by a loss in localness and personality.

Granted, many of the 1960s photos were best-forgotten bathing-beauty and grip-and-grin shots. Macon featured eight "pretty milk-maids" on page one. A Las Vegas cutline referred to "chorus cuties." But local events and faces showed up in many other ways:

- A full photo page of local people and their pets (Macon)
- A local couple waving from the airplane stairway as they embarked on a "coast-to-coast" trip won in a sales contest (Las Vegas)
- A cast shot of ten schoolgirls who will be "doing the boogie woogie" at an upcoming recital (Las Vegas)
- A thirteen-year-old eighth-grader sent home from school because her skirt was too short (Cleveland)
- The state printer holding up the new budget as it rolls off the press (Topeka)
- A local rabbi launching a series of book lectures, the mayor donning a ten-gallon hat to open the livestock show, and a picture page of "one day's social activities" (Houston)

In terms of content, the older papers seem a little like old-fashioned hardware stores, with items stashed into every nook.

The May 2, 1963, *St. Louis Post-Dispatch* contained, by my count, 145 local news, business, sports, and social items—from a health-department study of radioactivity in milk to items about a hometown girl winning a speed-typing contest and a man who shot himself in the finger.

One Saturday in 1964 the *Topeka Daily Capital* carried box scores for a staggering 101 high school basketball games. A single page in the January 8, 1964, *Commercial Appeal* contained twenty local stories, nineteen of them under one-column headlines.

Virtually everything qualified as news: minor crimes, kids' birthday parties, speeches to civic clubs. When Miss Georgia sang for the Rotary Club, Macon reported it. When Nevada's U.S. senator came down with flu, the *Las Vegas Review-Journal* took notice. When a junior-college student council presented a "panel discussion of mutual problems," the *Topeka Capital* advanced it with a story.

This item, reprinted in its entirety, earned front-page play in the *Houston Chronicle:*

A blonde with a patch over her nose fatally shot a waitress, Juanita Daniels, 32, at Grimm's Cafe, 1610 Cullen, today. A waitress said the blonde pulled a pistol and threatened "to shoot everyone." Police arrested the blonde.

These days, social and personal items have almost vanished from the paper. But news of bridge parties, visiting grandchildren, out-of-town vacations, and debutante balls filled 1960s feature sections. It was news in Houston, for instance, when Cecile (Mrs. Carl) Stuebing treated her friends to a post-holiday party to "rest up from parties" (on the same day that Dan Rather, the southern bureau chief for CBS News, was named "outstanding young man of 1963" by the Jaycees). St. Louis alerted readers that "Mr. and Mrs. John R. Kirk Jr. . . . have returned home from a 10-day trip east." Club news abounded; if the Toastmasters, the Geranium Society, or the VFW Auxiliary met, they made the paper. Boy Scouts and Camp Fire Girls drew regular coverage, often through weekly columns.

The 1960s approach to public service seemed assuredly community-centered, almost didactic.

A January 1964 *Plain Dealer* story devoted almost twenty inches to a Kiwanis Club speech by the paper's editor and publisher, Thomas Vail, headlined, "Vail Calls for Dynamic Leadership to Put Cleveland Ahead of Rivals."

That same month, Macon reported "Sermons Set on Problems of Youth." The story began, "A series of 'frank and straight to the point' sermons especially directed to the problems and interests of youth will begin Sunday at Mulberry Street Methodist Church."

On another day, the *Richmond Times-Dispatch* published a front-page essay by former President Truman, detailing his advice on world issues, and a local anti-drug feature, headed "Dope Addict Needs $30 a Day."

The older papers seemed duty-bound to chronicle news of record. They produced regular lists of marriages, divorces, and births—as do most of today's papers—but also often listed court dockets, grand-jury actions, hospital patients, newly naturalized citizens, ships in port, driver's-license suspensions, and burial permits. Some listed every fire call. Others even covered elementary school sports results.

Overall, government coverage was ample and prominent in the 1960s, focusing largely on basic executive- and legislative-branch stories about presidents, governors, mayors, Congress, statehouses, and city councils. Speeches and local ordinances were often printed verbatim. Preview stories, rare today, frequently appeared before even routine meetings ("City Council may ease up on regulations requiring cabbies to wear hats").

As for tone, reading the older papers challenges at least two common criticisms of today's papers—that modern journalism veers more toward sensationalism and shows less respect for privacy than the media once did.

The 1960s pages brim with "brites" and peculiarities ("Crazed Elephant Terrorizes City"). Cleveland put a mate-swapping case on page one ("Two couples who traded spouses finally settled their differences out of court here yesterday as to who will rear whose children"). Richmond did the same when a British doctor announced there was no cure for hangovers. "Bites Off Ex-Wife's Ear," a page-two story in St. Louis blared.

Crime coverage was extensive and often wallowed in personal details. Houston, for example, delivered a painful play-by-play on the suicide of a local dentist who had learned he was going blind. It described how the man and his wife, both named, fought over a packet of sedatives until he wrested them away and swallowed a fatal dose.

Much of the 1960s-era coverage now seems wildly dated, of course. One paper reported on a mother jailed for not cleaning her house. Photos and stories regularly patronized women ("trusted grandmother accused of forgery," "sextress Brigitte Bardot is seeing Brazil with boyfriend"). A Sunday-magazine story was headed, "Women Will Buy Anything!" A photo showed a local employee dipping her feet in a fountain, and the cutline concluded, "The photographer caught her just before she peeled off her stocking."

For a story about a local woman moderating a panel of federal officials, the *Plain Dealer* led with, "No one in Cleveland underestimates the power of a woman when that woman is Mildred Barry." It ended: "And it can be said without fear of contradiction that [she] will be the most attractive person on the stage at Hotel Statler Hilton."

Black people were barely visible, except in photos of civil-rights demonstrations. Macon provided a zoned page labeled "Social and Personal News of Our Colored Community"—a department, the paper reported, "edited and managed exclusively by colored people." (Macon also ran a hard-hitting 1963 editorial favoring church integration: "A church that professes, Sunday after Sunday, to be engaged in a great crusade to bring all men into the fellowship of Christ should not be shocked when someone of another color presents himself to partake of that fellowship.")

Some references to race were shocking, even allowing for the segregationist times. A Las Vegas photo of freedom marchers in Georgia carried an all-caps overline that screamed, "'GIMMIE THAT SIGN, BOY.'" And Houston juxtaposed photos of civil-rights protesters being beset by dogs and fire hoses beside a cheery feature story headlined, "Dogs Valuable Law Enforcers."

S TATISTICALLY, ONE DAY'S comparison means little. Still, zooming in on a single day's coverage—the Thursday in our January sample for 1964, 1986, and 1999—helps illustrate many changes we found.

The January 9, 1964, *St. Louis Post-Dispatch* came in seven sections (more than most papers of its time): main news, sports, combined food and business, classifieds, a four-page "editorial section," the "Everyday Magazine" feature section and a zoned community-news section.

The *Loretta Young Show* and *Queen for a Day* highlighted the day's TV offerings, with *Rawhide, Dr. Kildare,* and *Perry Mason* coming up that night. For 50¢, you could see *Days of Wine and Roses* at the Tivoli; for $7.77 you could get snow tires at Western Auto. Classifieds were divided into "help wanted—men, boys" ("time study and methods man" needed) and "help wanted—women" ("claims girl" sought).

The paper was a news-features soup. One of the two twenty-inch-plus A-section stories had Defense Secretary Robert McNamara assailing Sen. Barry Goldwater, who had criticized U.S. missile readiness. The front page also reported on a man who recorded his neighbors' yapping dog and played back the tape, aimed at the neighbors' home, at three A.M.

The four-page editorial section included seven local editorials, three longer analytical articles, five "letters from the people," two editorials reprinted from other papers, two op-ed columns, one book review, and an editorial cartoon.

Besides the local photo of the orphaned children, there were shots showing new county medical-society officers, six delegates heading for a Junior League conference in Winnipeg, a lesser kudu born at the local zoo, and the visiting National March of Dimes Poster Girl.

In the news, the governor was appealing for tougher traffic laws. Cab drivers had elected union officers. East St. Louis was about to vote on requiring taverns to close earlier. The Catholic archdiocese was deploring attacks on the home of a black family that had moved into a "white neighborhood." The school-lunch menu featured Texas hash.

In separate stories, two apparent suicides were reported, with names. Dorothy Jane Atwood's "By, For and About Women" column led with debutante Ann von Weise's visit to college friends and then covered nine other social items.

In the community section, readers found a twenty-six-inch story with five-column art on a local annexation proposal, a photo of a prize-winning baton twirler, and a report that Constable Thomas McNiff was "seriously considering running for mayor of Kirkwood." Local ninth-grader Mary

Ann Kosin had just completed a scale model of England's Globe Theater, a project that took her a month and a half.

By January 9, 1986, the *Post-Dispatch* was far more pleasing visually, with a larger newshole and doubled sports and business coverage. In many ways the sixty-eight-page, twenty-five-cent paper had clearly moved into the modern journalistic era; its modular, six-column front page had fewer stories, two graphics above the fold, and the makings of an index-digest box across the bottom. Gone were most of the eccentricities of the 1960s, the local tidbits and quirky photos. But the paper was sticking with tradition in other ways; all nine front-page stories (compared to fourteen in 1964) were hard news with traditional leads, and the top three carried Washington datelines. Two A-section pages slugged "Missouri Capitol" carried nine state-government items, including legislative committee deliberations on medical malpractice costs and the naming of a new warden for the state penitentiary.

So-called local-local news, spread through the 1960s newspapers, was by 1986 cubbyholed into four-page zoned sections ("North Area Post"), where prep sports, school lunches, and local library news could be found. The paper looked and felt more polished and professional than it had in the 1960s, but carried itself with a clear, ongoing commitment to serious news coverage.

By January 14, 1999, the *Post-Dispatch* was even more distinct from its 1960s predecessor, dramatically different in design (four stories on the front page, a six-column digest-index across the bottom, color everywhere). The paper's overall newshole had grown another 9 percent from the 1980s, and space devoted to sports, business, and features was still rising. Reader-service material, almost unknown in the 1960s and just taking hold in the 1980s, was now plentiful. The paper offered a full-column list of numbers to call about school schedules affected by the previous day's ice storm; two-thirds of a page devoted to an impeachment guide in graphic format (with timetable, Q&A, television-coverage plans, and mugs of the central characters); and a "help yourself" column in which readers submitted questions or sought help with small projects and received answers in future columns.

The sports section devoted six columns to prep sports, with an eleven-item "honor roll" of kids' achievements in basketball, wrestling, and hockey. The entertainment tab listed a march honoring Dr. Martin Luther King Jr., fishing seminars, wine classes, pet first-aid clinics, and dozens of other activities covering music, bands, fine arts, and galleries.

In the news, the mayor was leaving on a business-development trip to Greece. The Girl Scout cookie sale was opening. Local letter carrier Steve Wolters had saved a woman from a fire. An alderman's committee wanted to expand the number of vendors allowed on city streets. The eight-page community-news section described how local utilities were handling the Y2K problem, the library was revamping its Web site, and aldermen were reconsidering snow-removal policies.

Local display photos concentrated on the ice storm and the heroic letter carrier. The community-news front included two color shots of local Wal-Mart employees collecting toy bears for children involved in accidents.

The editorial and commentary space—down to a conventional two pages from the four in the 1960s—contained three editorials, eight letters, a local editorial cartoon, six reprinted cartoons, and three op-ed columns.

Here's how the days' coverage compared statistically:

Newshole
1999:   264 columns, 16 percent to local news, 14 percent to business, 17 percent to sports, 36 percent to features
1986:   191 columns, 17 percent to local news, 14 percent to business, 15 percent to sports, 28 percent to features
1964:   138 columns, 14 percent to local news, 10 percent to business, 11 percent to sports, 32 percent to features

Item length
1999:   twenty-one items under six inches, six over twenty inches in eighteen-page A section
1986:   thirty items under six inches, zero over twenty inches in twenty-page A section
1964:   fifty-eight items under six inches, two over twenty inches in sixteen-page A section

Changing newspapers mean changing newsrooms, of course. To appreciate that point, drop in on any daily news meeting, such as one unfolding on a rainy spring day in Georgia.

A faraway war in a little-known land is sucking the United States in an international maelstrom. Bombs have begun to fall, and editors at the *Macon Telegraph* are brainstorming their coverage.

It is 1999, but it could be—almost—the 1960s. Certainly at first glance things don't seem that much different from news meetings of a generation ago. Sixteen people gather around a cluttered conference table, plugging their stories and jockeying for scarce news space. The tone is a typical newsroom blend of big-story gravity and mordant humor. "Any casualties so far?" an editor wonders. "Well, I'm not feeling so good," another cracks. The state editor bets a colleague five dollars that she can go all day without using the F-word. She loses.

Even the daily budget seems to carry over from distant times. There's that war, an eerie echo of Vietnam ("Kosovo—why now?" reads the slug for one sidebar). The state budget leads with news of the legislature, as it has on many days over many decades. The sports staff is, as always, blanketing Georgia college hoops and the opening of trout season. And Macon's Cherry Blossom Festival poses its annual test of editors' twisted ingenuity; today's installment has a reporter and photographer riding along on a tour bus. "Should be a good piece with color from the blue hairs," the budget entry deadpans.

But it soon becomes obvious that a 1960s editor time-traveling into this meeting would feel like an alien encountering a foreign language and landscape. The person standing in front of the room, for instance, is the *presentation editor.* The two people questioning him from the conference table are *paginators,* and they are discussing what data to give to the *Web editor* for *posting.* Talk flows about *timelines* and *centerpieces,* 1A *promos* and *swapouts* for the *zoned sections.* There's a move to take the paper up two pages, but it creates a problem with the *color positions.*

Through the glass windows of the conference room, wall-mounted monitors are tuned to play-by-play war coverage on CNN. The carpeted(!) newsroom is quiet and clean, with reporters peeking out from behind the dividers between their cubicles and computer stands. Smokers have been exiled. To get into the building, staff members and visitors must pass a security console and trip an access panel to enter the locked newsroom.

Once inside, you find a remodeled version of the same downtown building in use in the 1960s. It still breathes Deep South hospitality. A secretary is busy ordering drinks for an upcoming function ("That's fourteen sweet teas and eight unsweetened, honey"). Editor Cecil Bentley, fifty-one, an easygoing Macon native, answers his own phone and keeps a grits advertisement above his desk. His love for the paper goes back to the days when it covered the kids' league baseball games he played in. He still has the clippings.

But he too has CNN playing in his office and up-to-the-second online news on his computer. Later that day Knight Ridder brass from the chain's California headquarters will drop by for a visit. Long gone are the days when local owner-publisher Peyton Anderson had negligible competition and a stranglehold on Macon's information franchise.

Bentley now presides over a 176-year-old newspaper that, in 1964, came as two editions: the morning *Telegraph* (circulation 48,000 daily, 66,000 Sunday) and evening *News* (24,000), both owned by Anderson. In 1969, the Knight chain bought the papers, and in 1983 the morning and evening papers merged. Today the *Telegraph*'s circulation is 71,000 daily and 97,000 Sundays.

Bentley has been editor here since 1996. After attending the University of Georgia, he went on to edit several smaller papers before coming home to run the *Telegraph*. The editor has a marketing degree; on the other hand, Bentley offers with a grin, the *Telegraph*'s publisher and marketing director both have journalism degrees. And the fact is, he sometimes considers himself "as much of a change agent as a journalist." In the past three years, he says, Macon has redesigned the paper, restructured the newsroom, and replaced the computer system—steps few editors dreamed of in the 1960s.

Yet Bentley doesn't mean to radicalize the place. For example, the *Telegraph,* like many papers, tried dividing its newsroom into topic-based teams, but finding it unwieldy soon returned to a more traditional organization. Instead, Bentley aims to move the *Telegraph* back to the future—to regenerate the paper's essential but elusive status as the town's trusted supplier of indispensable local news.

He is a walking carrier of the let's-shake-things-up gene. "To be around Cecil Bentley is to learn to live with change," one of his section editors says dryly. But Bentley says he spurns change for change's sake. "You hope all the change is leading to better content in the paper," he declares. "If it doesn't do that, then don't do it."

In the 1960s, newspapers owned the town—or thought they did. Television was nowhere near the competitor it would become. The "web" was something spiders made in the curbside metal boxes where people's daily papers were stuffed. Suburban papers, aggressive weeklies, and alternative city tabloids weren't yet fearsome rivals. Daily newspapers competed among themselves, but as an institution the daily press reigned supreme.

Cecil Bentley knows those heady days are history.

Today's editors live, instead, in an oddly paradoxical age. Newspaper profits are rocketing, but circulation—and confidence—continue to slip. In the most pessimistic circles, something approaching a death watch is on, and even the optimists can be caught looking over their shoulders, or, worse, gazing at the backsides of competitors that already seem to have surged past them. In a sober-up-or-else comment at this year's American Society of Newspaper Editors convention, Intel chairman Andrew Grove warned that newspapers could be three years away from meltdown. "Nothing sharpens the awareness of a situation like the sight of the gallows," he said.

Most editors disagreed, but everyone listened anxiously. They know the figures. In 1964, average weekday adult readership of newspapers was 81 percent; by 1997, according to the latest Newspaper Association of America data, it had fallen to 59 percent. In 1964, there were .5 newspapers sold per adult; by 1997, the figure was .3.

That helps explain why Bentley considers himself a change agent, welcomes focus groups and readership research, and tries to marry the five Ws of journalism with "the four Ps of marketing: price, promotion, product, and place." Like many other editors, he believes newspapers can survive and thrive, but must transform themselves to do so.

"A lot of what we are doing is going back to the basics," Bentley says. "We have quit defining government as such—because that makes people's eyes glaze over. But you think of it as taxes and services and the stuff that makes a difference in your community. Instead of public journalism and civic journalism, we're just talking about good journalism. The public is going to buy us more than ever if we can tell them what's going on, how it affects them, and why it matters."

Bentley's paper backs up his talk. A May 1998 edition, for example, front-pages a thoughtful examination of how a local county is coping with booming growth. The article brims with quotes, facts, and insights from regular people as well as government officials, taking a broad look at an issue concerning both government and citizens.

The numbers, too, underline the *Telegraph*'s preoccupation with local matters. From 1963–64 to 1998–99, according to our survey, local news doubled, from 224 total columns to 454.

And the attractive, well-arranged, modern *Telegraph* all but wags with reader-friendliness. Page two starts with a "Day by Day Event Planner," a compendium of local happenings. The editor's phone number is listed, as are the e-mail addresses of a half-dozen executives and, naturally, the *Telegraph*'s Web address.

Local listings are everywhere. If anything, the *Telegraph* runs calendar-wild: "Doers and Watchers," dozens of sports events from baton twirling to paintball tourneys; "People's Agenda," on local government; "Support Groups," six columns of contacts on topics from amputees to grief; "Healthy Dates," listing flu shots and weight workshops; "Datebook," a business-section list of meetings and conventions; "Praise Dates," a religion calendar; "Dates to Dig," for gardeners; "Senior Calendar"; "Parents'

Notebook." There are lists of family reunions and wedding anniversaries, "News 2 You" (for kids) and "Next Level" (for teens), a "Happy First Birth-day" column, and the "75-and-Over Happy Birthday Club."

The zoned-news section features "Local Shots," photos submitted by readers; school, sports, and military items; lists of volunteer opportunities. One day's club calendar carried fifty-nine separate listings. A "Neighbors" tab ran twenty-four pictures of local people, mostly kids, at parades, elementary schools, and church festivals.

Yet despite such impressive tallies, you still encounter the wistful feeling that the newspaper, as a place and as a product, just isn't what is used to be.

John Krueger has worked at the *Telegraph* since 1963. Now the editorial-page copy editor, he has been a reporter, assistant sports editor, wire editor, news editor, and Sunday editor, among other jobs. He enjoys his work and feels today's paper has more depth and variety—but he finds the newsroom less sociable and collegial. He misses local owner Peyton Anderson, who "knew everybody." "He would have picnics at his house," Krueger remembers. "Now it's more impersonal and the [corporate] head-quarters is out in California. There is more emphasis on making the bottom line. There was more of a family-type atmosphere back then."

Longtime reader Hyman Weiss, who moved to Macon in 1958, finds the contemporary paper more willing to stand up to local politicians and businesses, but he too misses something. "Local color," he calls it. "They just don't have it." And, he echoes, "Today everything is dollars and cents."

Juanita Jordan worked for Anderson in the *Telegraph* newsroom of the 1960s. Now she runs the Peyton Anderson Foundation—his legacy to Macon—from a building elsewhere in town. Here is her perspective:

"The paper back in the 1960s was very, very much local news, more about citizens doing things that were not necessarily earth-shattering. Today, you either have to be crowned king or shot almost to have a story written about you. I really think that's a loss."

But, I ask her, what about the zoned-news and neighbors sections and multitude of local listings and nuggets?

She pauses. "Usually the pictures are small, and the items are small, and it's not easy reading. So I usually pass it by."

NOSTALGIA CAN BE a trap, and not just for newspapers. Modern medicine saves more lives than ever, yet we still grouse about HMOs and yearn for the days of house calls. Schools teach students more today than their parents ever learned, yet we carp about failing education.

Jon Margolis titled his recent book about 1964 *The Last Innocent Year,* and clearly the tidal forces of those times proved pivotal for newspapers as well as society. But as former *Miami Herald* publisher David Lawrence pointed out in a recent speech, "Journalists ought not to be suckered into feeling that they somehow missed some 'golden era.' The day of the idealist in newspapers is not gone. Good journalism will always be able to make its mark on our world."

And so it does. During one of our sample weeks in September 1998, the *Wilmington News Journal* published an eight-page special section, "A State of Tolerance," exploring race relations in Delaware. Beautifully designed and crammed with local names, faces, and thoughts, the section drew on polls, interviews, specialists' insights, and reader contributions. While it offered hope and encouragement, the package rendered a tough conclusion: "Outside of the workplace or schoolroom, most of us still choose to stay apart. . . . Overt racism is behind us but a subtle new form now challenges us. The expectations of the Rev. Martin Luther King Jr.—of black children and white children holding hands—for the most part remain a dream."

Indeed, our sample papers are reflexively trying to humanize and deepen their approach to covering public issues and the community at large. To check the results of a new federal law revamping public housing, the *Commercial Appeal* interviewed local officials but built its story around one resident's experience. The *Las Vegas Review-Journal,* filled in the 1960s with promotional photos and puff pieces for local showplaces, fronted a January 1999 piece entitled, "Gaming Executives: What's A CEO Worth?" The *Review-Journal*'s Sunday "In Depth" section dealt with the aftermath of a deadly explosion at a local rocket-fuel plant.

Our survey shows that today far more space is given over to such issues as welfare, transportation, food safety, justice, and the environment, and in more parts of the paper.

The *Topeka Capital-Journal*'s sports section devoted more than seven columns to an illustrated essay on canoeing the Kansas River—part typical adventure tale, part plea for environmental reform: "It's all too easy to view the [river] as simply a political issue and forget that it is in fact a river, a river that is the lifeblood of this entire region."

Likewise, trend stories and bright writing abound. Fresno's page-one profile of a high school principal's high-wire life began, "Cynthia Quintana left McLane High School three years ago as a self-professed 'bitch-witch.' She had worked as vice principal: the enforcer of discipline, the one who waded into fights to pull apart the swinging arms, the woman with a quick mouth and a huge heart who oozed with authority. She left because she felt her energy and enthusiasm draining away. But then McLane beckoned, again. And Quintana flung herself back." Memphis launched a piece on the fate of regional-literature studies with the lead, "A course in Southern literature may be gone with the wind from Rhodes College."

Call these examples of a "high-end" expansion of many contemporary newspapers—offering readers more big-ticket items like news features, issues packages, analyses, and an elevated design esthetic.

But they have been equally busy on the "low end." Newspapers are running voluminously more tiny type, such as mutual-fund listings, sports results, calendars, entertainment guides, full-page TV grids. And the small-news trend has its dutiful side. Among many examples: Wilmington's "Your Help Is Needed" column, seeking blood donors and drivers for the elderly and tutors; Cleveland's "Grapevine," featuring local people's accomplishments; Fresno's "Almanac," listing daily events, births, obituaries, and police reports; and Houston's "At City Hall" roundup of local civic happenings.

Especially heartening is that so many papers are interactive, and becoming more so by the second. Our study found not just more letters to the editor today, but more reader-comment columns, more reader-participation offers, more telephone and electronic outreach to readers, and far, far more published phone numbers and e-mail addresses for reporters and editors.

Consider one day's *Fresno Bee.* Page one refers readers to its Web site. Page four lists phone numbers for nine executives, ten editors, and two bureaus, plus numbers for news tips, news faxes, and faxed letters to the editor. The religion page contains a "how to reach us" box. The back page lists five different phone numbers for calling in corrections. The local section has a call-in poll and directs readers to a twenty-four-hour newsline. The op-ed page contains three columns by local writers and a box on how to submit yours. And the weather page lists still another set of phone lines for current and extended forecasts.

For all these advances, contemporary newspapers have their flaws. They seem less attentive to state and foreign news, trends that seem to have accelerated mainly in the past decade or so. Their featurey feel, in topic choice, writing style, and front-page display, appears to signal a relative shift toward entertainment at the expense of news. One disappointment that showed up in all periods of our survey: a surprising dearth of original investigative reporting.

Beyond the hard data, a close reading of these ten papers and others like them yields signs of the newsroom anxieties that have been documented elsewhere in the State of the American Newspaper series, and that I have seen firsthand in a decade's worth of editorial consultations. These include increased mistakes in copy (tied to such factors as reduced quality control and overstretched copy desks), demoralization over rising productivity demands in an age of downsizing and cost cutting, and a clash between marketing and public-service mindsets. Forces like these have plunged the industry into a crisis of confidence at a time when many papers are, arguably, at a peak in terms of quality.

Yet one wonders, at heart, if it isn't another intangible that should be an even greater worry: the question of personality and connection—that essential, ephemeral quality that can make the difference between readers speaking fondly of "our paper" or simply "the paper."

One day in Macon, I stood in the newsroom lobby waiting for Cecil Bentley. The phone rang, and a clerk answered. From what I heard, the caller wanted to inform the paper about an upcoming religious revival. The clerk courteously took the information and promised to list the event. But the caller evidently wanted more. Finally, the clerk explained with a sigh, "We have a form that we follow, ma'am."

Thirty-five years ago, the paper probably would have run a three- or four-graf item on the revival, listing a couple of local names and a sermon topic or two, maybe with a photo of workers erecting the revival tent. Today it follows the form. The item gets in, in small type, making room for many more such items. There is more coverage, but it sometimes feels like less.

It is a bedeviling quandary. Newspapers today undeniably run far more news than their 1960s cousins. But a strong perception lingers that some essential local ingredient—be it a fixed sense of region, state, or even state of mind—has been lost.

That shifting perception may be the most worrisome change of all.

ABOUT THIS SURVEY

The purpose of this study was to get a strong sense of how American newspapers have changed by analyzing ten mainstream dailies—the papers they publish now compared to what they were printing a generation ago, before the transformational Vietnam and Watergate eras.

To do that, we picked three weeks from then and now—one each from May and September of 1963 and 1998, and the third from January of 1964 and 1999. In addition, we also analyzed papers from the comparable weeks in 1985–1986, as a check on how various trends phased in over time. In all, we analyzed more than six hundred issues of our ten sample papers, which are listed below. In each case, researchers applied a ninety-nine-item questionnaire that dealt with everything from story length to types of leads to picture use to attribution.

Major stories during the 1963–64 samples were civil-rights demonstrations in the South, the anticipated John F. Kennedy–Barry Goldwater presidential race, riots over the U.S.–controlled Panama Canal, the aftermath of Kennedy's assassination, and President Johnson's declaration of a war on poverty. Top news during the 1998–99 periods included the Monica Lewinsky scandal and the opening of President Clinton's impeachment trial.

Charts accompanying this chapter show the results. Newshole figures were adjusted to account for two important changes: the conversion of all the papers from eight-column to six-column formats, and the shrinkage of their front pages (which came down an average of 10 percent). We did not adjust for such factors as increased body-type size or changing formulas for leading and white space, but those have probably reduced actual content by another 10 percent or so.

One other key factor: Since the early 1960s, seven of the ten cities in our survey have gone from having two newspapers to one, and Houston has gone from three papers to one. So even though the surviving papers are much larger than their 1960s forebears, the closings and consolidations offset some of the gains.

Here are the papers we surveyed, with their daily circulations then and now:

	1964	1999
Plain Dealer (Cleveland)	328,000	395,000
Fresno Bee	107,000	160,000
Houston Chronicle	227,000	542,000
Las Vegas Review-Journal	37,000	159,000
Macon Telegraph	48,000	71,000
Commercial Appeal (Memphis)	217,000	168,000
Richmond Times-Dispatch	143,000	206,000
St. Louis Post-Dispatch	345,000	312,000
Topeka Capital-Journal	68,000	60,000
Wilmington News Journal	81,000	126,000

Principal researchers were Carl Sessions Stepp, Rachel Powers, and Steve Frankel. Also contributing were A. C. Benson, Todd Burroughs, and Meg Cederoth. The 1985–86 papers were analyzed by a team headed by Penny Bender Fuchs and including Rachel Powers, Laurent Thomet, and Howard Unger. Jeff Stepp provided technical assistance.

The Changing Face of Newspapers
The Evolution of the Front Page

	CLEVELAND			FRESNO			HOUSTON			LAS VEGAS			MACON		
	1964	1984	1999	1964	1984	1999	1964	1984	1999	1964	1984	1999	1964	1984	1999
Average number of stories on 1A	11	6	5	9	6	5	12	5	5	12	5	5	11	6	4
Percentage of 1A stories that are news	90	83	80	91	89	81	89	72	86	92	83	85	95	80	66
Percentage of 1A stories that are features	6	17	19	9	27	19	9	25	13	8	11	13	4	20	33
Percentage of 1A stories with hard leads	91	71	70	94	92	73	88	57	78	93	89	78	94	74	60
Percentage of 1A stories that jump	55	89	96	34	97	96	63	95	99	37	64	99	3	88	90
Percentage of 1A stories that are local news	50	59	54	43	43	59	40	46	52	46	37	31	42	35	64
Percentage of 1A stories that are national news	33	27	48	41	31	37	35	37	37	41	40	60	38	45	36
Percentage of 1A stories that are international news	17	13	8	16	20	4	25	11	11	13	23	9	20	20	1
Average length of leads on 1A (in words)	26	30	32	20	34	31	24	28	31	27	31	33	28	31	27
Average length of 1A stories (in inches)	11	19	19	7	19	22	9	20	24	7	13	23	7	17	15
Percentage of 1A bylines apparently female	7	28	31	0	38	35	10	40	30	8	26	26	6	15	30

Topics of 1A Stories

World news involving U.S.	5%	11%	1%	3%	2%	0%	7%	6%	5%	5%	13%	4%	7%	12%	1%
World news not involving U.S.	12%	7%	8%	13%	9%	4%	15%	4%	7%	7%	8%	6%	13%	10%	0%
Business	9%	15%	15%	5%	7%	11%	4%	14%	13%	8%	12%	10%	5%	6%	8%
Celebrity	4%	2%	1%	2%	3%	1%	3%	0%	2%	4%	0%	1%	1%	1%	3%

MEMPHIS			RICHMOND			ST. LOUIS			TOPEKA			WILMINGTON			AVERAGE PER PAPER		
1964	1984	1999	1964	1984	1999	1964	1984	1999	1964	1984	1999	1964	1984	1999	1964	1984	1999
12	6	5	11	7	5	14	8	4	16	6	5	9	5	5	12	6	5
79	77	86	91	94	80	87	88	79	84	82	80	88	84	65	89	83	79
20	21	8	7	4	17	12	14	21	14	18	20	12	15	35	10	17	20
79	76	81	94	88	70	93	88	61	95	85	76	85	56	65	91	78	71
18	69	96	50	81	85	45	92	88	30	73	61	36	58	65	37	81	88
43	43	54	38	31	51	28	49	58	37	61	68	41	57	67	41	46	55
34	29	43	39	38	40	52	32	42	44	23	31	37	31	31	39	33	41
23	25	7	24	29	9	20	21	1	19	15	1	22	13	2	20	19	5
28	28	34	27	32	30	28	30	27	28	30	30	24	31	29	26	31	30
8	16	24	12	18	17	11	15	21	8	14	16	10	14	18	9	16	20
12	20	34	8	19	22	0	29	23	15	20	15	0	35	43	7	27	29
8%	18%	0%	9%	19%	4%	6%	11%	0%	5%	10%	0%	4%	11%	0%	6%	11%	2%
16%	9%	2%	16%	9%	5%	12%	10%	0%	13%	5%	1%	18%	2%	2%	14%	6%	4%
8%	6%	7%	2%	5%	15%	10%	14%	16%	6%	9%	6%	9%	5%	15%	7%	8%	11%
9%	3%	2%	0%	0%	0%	7%	0%	0%	7%	0%	1%	2%	1%	0%	4%	1%	1%

The Evolution of the Front Page, continued

	CLEVELAND			FRESNO			HOUSTON			LAS VEGAS			MACON		
	1964	1984	1999	1964	1984	1999	1964	1984	1999	1964	1984	1999	1964	1984	1999
Crime	14%	9%	10%	19%	6%	19%	13%	6%	7%	13%	11%	10%	11%	19%	10%
Court	8%	11%	9%	4%	5%	18%	6%	5%	10%	5%	6%	11%	4%	2%	3%
Education	2%	4%	1%	1%	1%	2%	2%	10%	3%	2%	2%	0%	3%	2%	7%
Human Interest	2%	3%	5%	2%	3%	3%	4%	10%	1%	5%	9%	1%	2%	9%	5%
Government	23%	23%	17%	22%	24%	12%	18%	10%	34%	23%	17%	24%	30%	16%	35%
Obituaries	1%	0%	1%	1%	0%	1%	1%	0%	1%	1%	0%	3%	1%	0%	0%
Politics	5%	7%	11%	5%	2%	3%	6%	5%	2%	10%	3%	6%	5%	1%	2%
Protests	5%	0%	0%	3%	1%	1%	3%	0%	0%	4%	2%	0%	8%	0%	0%
Religion	0%	0%	0%	0%	0%	0%	1%	4%	0%	1%	0%	0%	1%	0%	0%
Science	2%	4%	8%	3%	3%	6%	8%	4%	5%	6%	3%	6%	2%	12%	1%
Sports	2%	0%	9%	0%	0%	4%	2%	2%	10%	0%	2%	9%	2%	1%	9%
Weather	3%	3%	7%	6%	0%	8%	4%	5%	4%	4%	1%	5%	8%	2%	9%
Other news	1%	0%	0%	0%	4%	5%	2%	0%	0%	3%	0%	0%	1%	0%	2%
Other features	3%	0%	2%	6%	1%	5%	2%	0%	0%	1%	1%	1%	0%	2%	0%

Front-Page Traits

	CLEVELAND			FRESNO			HOUSTON			LAS VEGAS			MACON		
Number of pieces of art	51	39	50	41	53	73	63	52	63	36	39	80	46	57	65
Number of male faces	37	20	30	31	34	48	49	29	34	27	24	55	31	41	40
Number of female faces	15	9	9	9	19	19	21	16	17	7	13	16	8	14	10
Number of white faces	35	18	25	32	31	39	63	30	36	31	26	51	35	41	40
Number of nonwhite faces	8	8	15	4	11	27	4	11	13	0	4	14	1	7	9
Number with top-right lead	14	8	19	14	10	15	20	16	13	19	14	13	20	8	11
Number with bumping heads	20	2	4	14	5	13	18	1	1	20	0	3	17	4	8
Number with banner heads	7	15	1	0	13	8	14	7	4	20	5	3	0	15	3
Number of pun heads	2	0	1	0	2	2	1	0	5	0	0	3	2	2	5

Sources

	CLEVELAND			FRESNO			HOUSTON			LAS VEGAS			MACON		
Anonymous or none	20%	8%	14%	9%	9%	13%	32%	1%	19%	22%	6%	14%	22%	11%	9%
Government	33%	53%	30%	47%	42%	33%	45%	49%	43%	48%	59%	45%	43%	34%	41%
Laypersons	17%	13%	22%	13%	12%	20%	8%	16%	6%	6%	13%	10%	5%	25%	24%

	MEMPHIS			RICHMOND			ST. LOUIS			TOPEKA			WILMINGTON			AVERAGE PER PAPER		
	1964	1984	1999	1964	1984	1999	1964	1984	1999	1964	1984	1999	1964	1984	1999	1964	1984	1999
	9%	14%	14%	16%	11%	6%	10%	10%	14%	14%	9%	18%	11%	14%	19%	13%	11%	12%
	2%	3%	13%	2%	1%	4%	3%	8%	11%	4%	1%	12%	8%	11%	3%	5%	5%	10%
	1%	3%	4%	4%	4%	5%	2%	5%	6%	4%	5%	1%	0%	3%	5%	2%	4%	3%
	9%	9%	5%	4%	1%	4%	5%	5%	2%	2%	9%	6%	3%	7%	2%	4%	7%	4%
	20%	15%	18%	20%	12%	27%	15%	16%	20%	19%	29%	18%	18%	16%	22%	21%	17%	23%
	1%	0%	1%	1%	0%	1%	1%	1%	1%	2%	1%	0%	1%	0%	3%	1%	0%	1%
	6%	0%	15%	6%	11%	9%	6%	2%	1%	5%	1%	14%	3%	0%	2%	6%	3%	7%
	2%	0%	0%	5%	1%	0%	6%	0%	0%	4%	3%	1%	2%	1%	2%	4%	1%	1%
	1%	0%	1%	1%	0%	2%	1%	0%	4%	1%	0%	0%	1%	0%	0%	1%	0%	1%
	2%	6%	2%	2%	10%	11%	3%	7%	4%	1%	4%	0%	1%	4%	9%	3%	6%	5%
	2%	5%	3%	1%	1%	3%	1%	3%	14%	1%	0%	3%	0%	2%	3%	1%	2%	7%
	4%	2%	5%	3%	5%	4%	6%	1%	6%	8%	1%	3%	8%	7%	3%	5%	3%	6%
	1%	2%	1%	2%	1%	0%	2%	0%	2%	1%	2%	4%	5%	0%	2%	2%	1%	2%
	1%	3%	0%	2%	1%	0%	2%	1%	1%	1%	1%	5%	8%	0%	5%	3%	1%	2%

Front-Page Traits

	MEMPHIS			RICHMOND			ST. LOUIS			TOPEKA			WILMINGTON			AVERAGE PER PAPER		
	51	51	54	81	49	106	76	66	76	82	55	56	40	43	86	57	50	71
	30	30	35	51	25	54	39	32	41	62	31	39	22	24	60	38	27	44
	8	9	17	11	6	21	10	12	16	16	19	17	10	6	20	12	12	16
	29	31	41	52	21	48	29	27	36	65	40	41	24	25	58	40	29	42
	3	7	8	6	6	25	17	10	21	3	9	7	6	3	16	5	8	16
	20	12	3	20	16	14	19	14	15	20	9	9	17	12	15	18	12	13
	20	2	5	8	8	1	20	8	12	18	6	12	17	0	6	17	4	7
	0	6	4	1	1	10	0	5	1	3	3	5	10	7	3	6	8	4
	8	4	5	2	0	5	7	5	0	0	2	0	1	10	3	2	3	3

Sources

	MEMPHIS			RICHMOND			ST. LOUIS			TOPEKA			WILMINGTON			AVERAGE PER PAPER		
	8%	14%	6%	13%	6%	9%	9%	9%	13%	11%	12%	15%	36%	7%	26%	18%	8%	14%
	33%	34%	38%	30%	56%	51%	44%	41%	33%	40%	58%	38%	26%	38%	26%	39%	46%	38%
	12%	17%	15%	12%	5%	8%	10%	14%	17%	6%	1%	14%	14%	14%	18%	10%	13%	15%

The Changing Face of Newspapers
Dividing Up the Newshole

	CLEVELAND			FRESNO			HOUSTON			LAS VEGAS			MACON		
	1964	1985	1999	1964	1985	1999	1964	1985	1999	1964	1985	1999	1964	1985	1999
Change in newshole 1964 to 1999	Up 59%			Up 92%			Up 145%			Up 98%			Up 161%		
Percentage of newshole devoted to general local news*	14	14	13	25	21	16	18	9	10	20	10	12	23	13	17
Percentage of newshole devoted to national news	7	5	6	12	8	7	9	8	6	15	14	9	10	10	9
Percentage of newshole devoted to international news	3	3	3	5	6	4	5	4	4	6	6	4	3	5	2
Percentage of newshole devoted to business news	11	17	16	6	10	13	10	18	13	3	15	15	4	14	12
Percentage of newshole devoted to sports	15	19	22	17	16	20	14	18	23	14	18	21	18	18	19
Percentage of newshole devoted to features	35	19	29	22	20	24	25	25	30	24	25	27	16	20	26
Percentage of newshole devoted to weather	1	2	1	1	2	3	1	1	1	1	1	1	2	1	2
Percentage of newshole devoted to comics	6	8	3	5	5	3	5	7	6	5	6	3	11	8	4
Percentage of newshole devoted to editorials/opinion	7	10	5	6	6	7	10	8	4	11	6	6	11	7	5
Percentage of newshole devoted to obituaries	2	1	2	2	2	2	2	0	3	1	1	1	3	3	4
A-section items under six inches	588	357	274	582	392	405	840	487	276	818	152	274	689	131	123
A-section items over twenty inches	25	58	30	18	42	63	16	9	74	5	13	78	1	33	30
Number of letters to the editor	87	169	105	85	131	187	80	264	148	9	97	115	19	127	73
Columns devoted to business agate	153	372	375	38	154	208	143	356	373	40	205	269	33	171	213
Columns devoted to sports agate	92	348	358	38	115	161	64	190	584	43	203	264	30	122	169

(Papers surveyed were from the same three weeks in 1963–1964, 1984–1985, and 1998–1999.)

* Includes local stories from main and local news sections

MEMPHIS			RICHMOND			ST. LOUIS			TOPEKA			WILMINGTON			AVERAGE PER PAPER		
1964	1985	1999	1964	1985	1999	1964	1985	1999	1964	1985	1999	1964	1985	1999	1964	1985	1999
Up 68%			Up 145%			Up 77%			Up 90%			Up 76%			Up 101%		
17	15	11	20	18	12	13	15	12	20	20	17	22	15	19	19	15	14
7	6	6	11	8	6	16	7	7	13	7	9	13	7	7	11	8	7
5	4	2	7	5	4	6	6	4	7	3	2	5	4	3	5	5	3
12	13	15	9	12	18	9	14	17	6	10	13	4	9	16	7	13	15
14	18	21	18	19	18	14	18	22	17	22	25	14	21	21	16	19	21
28	21	29	16	21	33	25	23	24	20	16	19	22	24	19	23	21	26
1	2	2	1	1	1	1	1	1	1	2	2	1	2	2	1	2	2
6	7	5	6	6	3	7	6	4	5	5	4	5	9	3	6	7	4
7	8	7	10	7	5	8	6	5	10	6	6	9	9	7	9	7	6
3	3	2	2	1	1	1	1	1	1	3	4	3	3	3	2	2	2
															AVERAGE PER DAY		
601	229	130	436	419	295	787	394	398	1090	241	177	794	291	266	36	15	13
45	30	53	25	34	48	28	50	30	35	53	84	29	9	84	1	2	3
26	44	152	95	73	147	81	131	190	14	27	79	58	95	130	3	6	7
128	187	246	133	194	502	144	322	425	44	142	158	18	58	234	4	11	15
41	95	173	41	103	249	67	162	217	36	122	139	33	146	157	2	6	12

5 | What Do Readers Really Want?

By Charles Layton

ORIGINALLY PUBLISHED IN MARCH 1999

BOB OLINTO'S OFFICE, on the fifth floor of the *Orange County Register* building in Santa Ana, California, is a sunny little domain that looks out across a broad, dry suburban landscape split by a river of cars on the No. 5 freeway. It's a fine vantage point from which to ponder the fitful moods of the newspaper-reading public, which is what Olinto does as the *Register*'s market-research director. An ebullient man with snow-white hair and a matching, neatly trimmed beard, Olinto is eager to show off the readership surveys he has commissioned in his fourteen years here. He lives with the numbers in these surveys, knows them intimately, and can, within seconds, put his finger on any reference.

The only trouble is, as we look them over, some of the numbers don't seem to make sense.

In a survey in 1990, people in the *Register*'s circulation area were asked whether they would read the paper more often if fewer of the stories jumped.

Sixty-three percent said yes, they would.

Olinto explains that *Register* management had wished to start minimizing jumps anyway, but there were objections in the editorial ranks. "The reporters, they want to write," he says. "They just want to all win Pulitzers." But with such dramatic survey results, "we were able to cut down the resistance from the newsroom."

This morning's *Register* has five stories on page one, two of which do not jump. The Metro front has six stories, three of which do not jump. The average length of all those stories (jumpers and nonjumpers alike) is not quite thirteen column inches.

"That is a direct result of the research," Olinto says.

Now he shows me an item in his 1997 survey, the most recent one. Again, people were asked whether they'd be more likely to read the paper if fewer stories jumped. And 59 percent said yes.

So let's get this straight. In 1990, 63 percent say they'd read the paper more often if it had fewer jumps. The *Register* gives them fewer jumps. And now, 59 percent answer the same question the same way, as if nothing happened.

Here's another problem: These people are fickle. After the paper gave them fewer jumps, they did not read it more, like they said they would; they read it less. From 1990 to 1997, the percentage of adults who read the daily Register at least once a week slid from 75 to 71 percent. The percentage of its most *loyal* readers, those who tend to read the paper every day, has dropped even further—from 55 to 50 percent.

Olinto shows me another figure. The number of people wanting shorter stories is 39 percent. But again, they're already getting short stories. How should the newspaper respond to this? Cut stories even more? And jump them even less?

"No, it just means they have a vote," Olinto explains. "They're basically saying they like shorter stories, they like fewer jumps. It further reinforces streamlining the paper even more."

Yet consider this: In the latest survey, 44 percent said they'd be more likely to read the paper if it had "more in-depth stories." In other words, the vote for more depth is as strong as the vote for less length.

And what of this question about "more explanation of complex issues"—what percentage say they'd be more likely to read the *Register* if it had that?

Olinto looks it up. The answer: 59 percent.

MORE COMPLEXITY in less space? Greater depth with fewer jumps? Measuring the likes and dislikes of newspaper readers was not supposed to be this tricky. In a 1993 essay, Andy McMills, then executive editor of the *News-Leader* in Springfield, Missouri, summarized the newspapering philosophy of his employer, Gannett, by saying: "First, go out and ask your readers what they want in their daily newspaper. Then give it to them. It's that simple."

Well, it isn't.

After moderating a series of focus groups for the American Society of Newspaper Editors (ASNE) in 1989, researcher Kris McGrath made no bones about the "consistently contradictory" results she was turning up. They were not unlike the contradictions in the Orange County surveys (which, by the way, her company conducted). "People want complete news coverage, but they don't want to have to spend too much time with the paper," she wrote in her report. "They want in-depth stories, but they want jumps to be avoided at all costs. They want the important news, but it has to be personally relevant. They want substantial newspapers, but they don't want bulky newspapers that pile up unread."

These contradictions arose as McGrath asked focus groups to compare traditional newspaper layouts with prototypes containing the splashy graphics and quick-read features that came into vogue in the 1980s. As she looked at who was saying what, it seemed to be the occasional readers—those not very interested in newspapers to start with—who liked the skim-the-surface prototypes. Loyal, regular readers tended to find them offensive. "The comic book is not my idea of news," one said. Another said, "People who would read this would be people who don't want anything in depth."

From a research and marketing point of view, a newspaper turns out to be a maddeningly complicated consumer product. When Knight Ridder asked one thousand people their reasons for buying a newspaper, it got 188 distinct answers—far more than you'd get for running shoes or breakfast cereals or even an automobile. The moral of the story, according to Jenny Fielder, the company's vice president for research, was this: "Simplistic answers to content and strategy will almost always be wrong."

Intelligent people with opposing policies can, and often do, cite the same research. Consider the perennial problem of the time-starved reader. On surveys, the most common reason people give for canceling a subscription is, "No time to read." To Burl Osborne, publisher of the *Dallas Morning News*, this challenges the industry to make newspapers more compelling, so people will commit more time to them. "If you create more value—that is, if readers spend more time with your newspaper—the advertising works better," he says. "You can charge more for it. And that's where you get the resources. . . . You can stairstep your way into continual improvement if you keep adding value to readers. Because that will translate into value for advertisers, and that will translate into increased revenue."

But Bob Olinto has a different take on the "no time to read" problem. He says, "If we interview people and they say, 'I'm only going to give you twenty minutes to read the paper,' then we want to give them a satisfying read. And if they get into a [long] article that they want to read and it wipes out the whole twenty minutes, they're frustrated, because they've got a lot of stuff they have to do and they've only gone through the first part of the paper."

Ed Batson used to do consumer research for Taco Bell. Now that he's director of marketing research at the *Los Angeles Times,* the world looks different. "A newspaper . . . is not just another consumer product," he says. "At Taco Bell, if we found out people didn't like the green sauce, they like the brown sauce better, well I mean to tell you the green sauce was history tomorrow morning. Who's got ego involvement with the green sauce?"

The news, unlike a taco, is an unknown quantity. It changes daily, hourly. Consumers of news expect to be surprised—by something new! So asking people what kind of news they want is like asking them to plan their own surprise party.

If market research has trouble predicting which automobile design will be a hit in the showroom, or what new trend in fashion will dominate the market a year from today, imagine trying to predict people's appetite for news. We can say with confidence that people want the paper delivered on time and that they want the ink not to rub off. We can say they want accurate, fair reporting and that good writing and compelling headlines are a plus. And we can make some other broad generalizations, most of them rather obvious. Beyond that, the results of market research, as applied to news, are disappointing.

Although skepticism is a job requirement in journalism, newspaper people have not been skeptical enough about the claims made for readership research. They have not much questioned the accuracy of the surveys that land on their desks or the pitfalls of the methodologies researchers use. Most have not even questioned research's single most obvious failing —that it has not arrested the decline in readership, as its advocates have claimed it could. Over the past twenty years, at their annual conventions and in their trade magazines and in-house publications, news executives have spoken more and more of the need for journalists to think like marketers. As if it were easy, or possible, to know in advance what people want to read. As if the average citizen, in a brief telephone survey conducted by a part-time, poorly paid, not-very-well-trained surveyor, could articulate that. And as if compelling content somehow originated with readers and not in the individual mind of a journalist with interesting things to say.

For years now, editors and reporters have been told that their journalistic instincts were out of sync with readers, and that the cure for this occupational malady was research. In 1989, James Batten, then CEO of Knight Ridder, declared in a widely noted speech that newspapers had to become "more reader-driven, customer-driven, looking much more outward and less complacently inward." That same year, Batten is reported to have told a meeting of the company's editorial-page editors, "The balance of power has shifted from editors to readers."

A decade on, however, it is apparent that newspaper research yields as much uncertainty and confusion as clarity. Much of it is subjective, unscientific, and amenable to manipulation. Its heavy reliance on focus groups constitutes a serious weakness. Its results always depend on the questions asked. And questions of interest to serious journalists (for instance, what's the impact of challenging a community's cherished assumptions?) are almost never explored.

If, as Batten suggested, the balance of power is with the readers, and if what readers say is malleable and unclear, then in fact the real power resides with whoever gets to interpret their responses. This may be the researcher herself, but more likely it's a paper's marketing and advertising directors, its publisher, and perhaps its corporate executives. Maybe even the editor . . . or maybe not. I haven't found a single case where a newspaper's research department reports unilaterally to the editorial side.

Given the lack of consensus and the vagaries of interpretation, it's been easy for some newspaper companies to talk about "reader-driven journalism" even as they followed policies that readers could not possibly endorse. Publishers and CEOs have sometimes used research as a cover for downsizing news staffs and trivializing news content. When surveys have found that readers want more substantive coverage, papers have often responded by cutting the space for news. When people said they couldn't trust newspapers because they were rife with errors, papers reduced the number of copy editors, then saddled the ones who remained with pagination and other tasks that make it nearly impossible to give each story a critical, thoughtful read.

While researchers have not raised their voices as a community against such cynical practices, one does find, in individual conversations, the occasional frustration that publishers don't spend enough money to improve their papers. Just before his death in 1998, I interviewed Tom Holbein, chairman of Belden Associates, the pioneering newspaper-research firm. I asked him about the conflict between what readers want and what Wall Street wants. "The implied message of a lot of our research," he said, "is that to improve readership, to reverse the trend, you need better products and better promotion of those products. Both of them cost money."

I broached the same subject one afternoon with Greg Martire, of the research firm Clark, Martire and Bartolomeo, at his office in Englewood Cliffs, New Jersey. Martire stretched his legs out in front of him, tilted his head up toward the ceiling, and said, almost with a sigh, "How many more surveys do we have to do in which people say they want more local news before we give it to them?" When I asked whether he saw even the tiniest groundswell of support for spending more money to give readers more value, he paused a moment and then said, "No. What you more often get is like the *L.A. Times* saying, 'We're going to give you more local news and we're going to get rid of two hundred people who cover it.' I don't know how they're going to do that."

W HILE NEWSPAPER RESEARCH has been around for decades, its recent growth—and its clout within the industry—are notable. In 1977, researchers founded their own trade organization, the Newspaper Research Council, with a membership of 75. Today, that group's successor organization, the Research Federation of the Newspaper Association of America, has more than 450 members, mostly newspaper staff researchers. Ten years ago, hardly any paper under 100,000 circulation had an in-house research specialist or commissioned serious market surveys. Today, Belden says one of its newest clients is an independently owned paper with a circulation of only 15,000. A readership study these days can cost anywhere from $10,000 to $500,000 or more, depending on its sophistication and the size and complexity of the market. A few of the country's largest papers now spend between $1 million and $2 million a year on market research— not much by the standards of some industries, but a big increase for newspapers.

When researchers gather at conferences and conventions, a recurring question is, "How can we get the newsroom to buy into what we're doing?" Researchers work hard to gain the respect of all the major departments of a newspaper, because these are their "internal clients." But editorial departments often present a special problem. After all, a researcher's conclusions may validate a paper's traditional editorial judgment and values, or challenge and undermine them.

This challenge became apparent to journalists about twenty years ago. This was a time of fear in the newspaper industry. Some major papers— especially afternoon papers—were failing, and daily readership had been in decline since the mid-1960s. At a 1981 convention of newspaper publishers, Ted Turner, whose Cable News Network was then celebrating its first birthday, predicted that "newspapers as we know them today will be gone within the next 10 years, or certainly . . . serving a very reduced role. . . . You're becoming very rapidly technologically obsolete." Words like "dinosaur" and "survival" were beginning to enter our common parlance.

In 1979, Ruth Clark of the Daniel Yankelovich research firm had published a report so influential that two decades later it is still being cited. It was called "Changing Needs of Changing Readers," and in it Clark wrote, "Is there a communications gap between editors and readers? The overriding conclusion of this research is that there is indeed a gap—and a serious one at that." She thought the problem was, at least in part, due to "the mind-set in the newsroom" and the feeling among readers "that newspapers are slow to change." Her solution was to find out through focus groups and other means what readers really do want. She thought they wanted newspapers to be better organized, easier to read, and more useful to people in their daily lives.

Many of her ideas were put to use by Al Neuharth, then chairman of Gannett, when in 1982 he launched *USA Today,* a striking editorial departure said to have been based on the most thorough market research ever performed on behalf of a newspaper.

Neuharth was blunt in his assessments of what readers wanted. And to many journalists, this didn't seem to include serious news. In a speech to ASNE, he declared that when it came to national and world affairs, "Coffeyville, Kansas; Muskogee, Oklahoma, they don't give a damn; the less they hear about Washington and New York the better they feel about it." He heaped contempt on more traditional competitors; in his autobiography, *Confessions of an S.O.B.,* he wrote of "the blue-blood owners of the *New York Times* and the *Washington Post*" and said he "really didn't expect 'Punch' Sulzburger [*sic*] or Kay Graham to do anything very bold or risky" because they lacked "guts." This being the same Arthur Sulzberger who printed the Pentagon Papers, the same Katharine Graham who ran such risks publishing Woodward and Bernstein's Watergate stories.

The more Neuharth belittled reporters and editors—declaring that newspaper writers "saw their jobs more as essayists than as reporters" and that "we never designed *USA Today* for journalists. We were after readers" —the more it felt like an assault on the basic values of the trade. But because Neuharth and Gannett had poured millions into readership research, and because *USA Today* was gaining readers as other papers lost them, many journalists heeded Neuharth's pronouncements.

In doing so, they overlooked the fact that in most cities, the papers that survived or dominated tended to be those most invested in serious news— papers like the *Washington Post, Philadelphia Inquirer, Boston Globe,* and *Los Angeles Times.* Also underemphasized was the consistent research finding that the most read portion of a newspaper is the most serious one, the A section.

In fact, many of Neuharth's claims about the wants and desires of readers were patently at odds with what research has always shown. In just about every major survey ever conducted, for instance, national and world news are among people's top concerns. In a highly regarded national survey done in 1997 by Clark, Martire and Bartolomeo, 71 percent of those polled said they were either extremely interested or very interested in world and national news. The only news interests that ranked higher were local news, investigations of important issues, and news about the weather.

Or take the young *USA Today*'s ironclad adherence to short, easy-to-read stories—"facts rather than endless prose," as Neuharth once expressed it. Here was an innovation that infiltrated countless mainstream dailies, but research shows it to be a dubious one. (In fact, as *USA Today* became a more responsible paper in recent years, it backed off of its original policy on story length.)

Deanne Termini is president of Belden Associates, which conducts about sixty newspaper studies a year and is the longest-established newspaper research firm in the country. She says that in Belden's experience about 10 percent of those questioned have always said stories were too long, about 10 percent have said they were too short, and about 80 percent have said it wasn't much of an issue.

Greg Martire has come to believe there's no way to generalize about story length, so he never puts a question about it in a survey unless the client twists his arm. "How long should a story be? Well, it should stop when it gets boring," he says, "and that depends on the story and how well-written it is."

Fifteen years ago, Christine Urban of Urban & Associates, a leading research and consulting firm, wrote a short essay for the *ASNE Bulletin*. It was called "10 Myths about Readers," and one of the myths was this: "Stories must be short and easy to read." In fact, Urban wrote, all of her company's experience had shown that "important news stories should be long, less important ones should be short."

"This seems a blinding glimpse of the obvious," she wrote, "and it is. Readers pay for and expect good editing in their newspaper, and a part of their definition of a good editor is one who knows what the news priorities should be. . . . Simplistic 'rules' about maximum story inches or minimum story count violate reader expectations."

I called Urban, read a bit of her old article back to her, and asked if her point still stood. "For twenty-four years we've been finding this," she said, "and I can't imagine why it isn't obvious."

But, I persisted, if the research is so obvious, why would there be these "myths" about readers? And why would Gannett and Belden draw such different conclusions about story length?

"Well," she said, "you've stumbled on a metaphysical question that you're trying to answer on deadline."

Here's another ambiguous issue—the matter of jumps. Deanne Termini says that, while people have complained for years about not being able to find jumps, this may not mean they oppose jumps per se. "We're not really sure that jumps—if they're easier to find—discourage readers," she says.

The *Dallas Morning News* was a pioneer in avoiding jumps. According to Burl Osborne, "We at one point here, in the '70s I guess, had a no-jump rule off page one. You couldn't jump off page one. The fact is, it made page one very dull. And very inactive. And the system always circumvents that, so we created these fake jumps. You would end the story on page one and you'd have a 'refer' to another story on page eight, and on page eight you'd have basically a one-paragraph pickup into the jump. And so—no jump, well maybe—but it was clear that was an artifice to get around the rule." Around 1980 the *News* scrapped its no-jump policy.

Today, virtually every paper that does limit jumps compromises the policy in the way Osborne describes. Gannett has published detailed editorial guidelines for its newspapers, and on the subject of jumps they say, "Severely limit or eliminate jumps because readers don't follow them." But the rules go on to say, "Use billboard stories and other similar techniques instead of jumps to give readers the essential news and impact of a story on page one, and then direct them to in-depth coverage inside the newspaper that expands on the page one report."

It's unclear whether readers follow simple jumps more or less willingly than they follow jumps disguised as refers.

Butch Ward, managing editor of the *Philadelphia Inquirer,* says, "Like everybody else, we've talked to people about jumps, and we've heard people say they don't like jumps. But we've heard significant numbers of people say things like, 'I like jumps. Jumps always take me to a story I wouldn't have read otherwise.' Or they say, 'That's the way I go back through the paper. I see jumps, I read them.'

"So are jumps good or are jumps bad? Jumps are jumps."

IN THE SEMI-DARKNESS of a small viewing room, Jennifer Files and three of her newsroom colleagues sit facing a large glass wall—actually a one-way mirror that lets them see out but prevents those on the other side from seeing in. Files and her friends are peering through this magic window at a group of nine men and women, gathered at a table, discussing the pros and cons of the *Dallas Morning News*. Only, mainly, it's the cons. These nine people have been invited here because (a) they said they were interested in local news, and (b) they said they weren't satisfied with how the *News* covers it. Now that they're being prodded and probed by a moderator, and being paid fifty dollars a person for their opinions, they aren't bashful about giving them.

Files has never seen a focus group before. She is a young business reporter, well groomed and smartly dressed the way business reporters tend to be, especially in a fashion-conscious place like Dallas, and she's clearly proud of the acclaim the *News'* business section has received in journalistic circles. But, who are these people? They have such strong opinions, some of them, and yet they seem so ill-informed about the paper.

"We're not getting enough information about what's happening in the Dallas business community," says a man in his fifties named Herb, who has described himself as a serious consumer of news who hates TV and listens to public radio.

A guy in a knitted shirt named Fred agrees with Herb. There's not enough space in the paper for business news.

Begging to differ, Files, behind the mirror, turns to the woman next to her, Berta Delgado, a religion reporter, and says, "We've got the biggest newshole in the country!"

But Fred isn't finished yet. Now he's saying he thinks the business section has no regular reporters, that it just uses interns. This elicits a gasp from Files, followed a couple minutes later by another when Fred, on a roll, says, "The business report, as far as I'm concerned, they might as well delete it."

Delgado leans over, in sympathy, and says, "You're getting hammered."

Files isn't the only one. Walt Stallings, the assistant managing editor for metro news, is also in the doghouse. Nearly all the focus-group participants have complained that the local report is "unbalanced," that it has too much gruesome crime news and not enough "good news." This, they feel, is because "good news doesn't sell" and "the police blotter is easy to report."

"There are a lot of kids out there, they never see anything good. They need that," says Fred.

"Role-model stuff," says a fortyish woman named Jenny.

"Yeah," says Fred, "role-model stuff."

They egg each other on. When Cherie Sion, the moderator, an energetic woman in dark slacks and blazer, asks what kind of good news they're talking about, someone mentions a story he read about Eagle Scouts. Someone recalls a small business that succeeded against the odds. Someone else mentions a feature story about the zoo.

Jenny steers the conversation to politics. She wants more opposing points of view in the paper's election coverage, and more about the schools, and the state reps, and the city council. She wants her council-woman interviewed, and not just when sensational issues or scandals arise but on a routine basis. "No one's covering city hall, I feel."

This energizes Fred, who declares, "The *Dallas Morning News* has never, ever challenged the established authority. Mayor Kirk could rob a bank and I guarantee you, you'd never hear about it in the *Dallas Morning News*." He is waving his arms as he says this.

A guy named Mike, who rates the paper's local coverage a "four" on a scale of one to ten, says the Metro section "does a pretty good job of covering lots of special areas of the community. Not enough depth, though." He also thinks the Metro section lacks character. "It's a catch-all section," he says.

By now, in the gloom behind the mirror, people are loosening their ties and chewing on their eyeglass frames. Jennifer Files has emptied a pack of M&Ms on the desktop in front of her and is absentmindedly rolling them around. Eventually, gallows humor breaks out.

Stallings, the metro assistant managing editor, has a starched executive look—business suit, white shirt, conservative haircut—and a bone-dry sense of humor that's very effective in the present circumstances. "I'm going to work for Payless Shoes," he says. Then he wonders how he'll report this session back to his staff. He decides to tell them, "Metro is all the news that won't go anywhere else." This breaks up Steve Harris, an assistant metro editor.

Stallings says, "I'm going to do a story about some Eagle Scouts that start a small business."

Delgado says, "At the zoo."

Through the looking glass, people continue to complain. If anyone in the focus group disagrees with the prevailing sentiments, he keeps it to himself. In fact, as the evening wears on, the voices of Fred, Mike, and to some extent Jenny seem to grow more dominant.

The talk turns to a recent scandal involving the mayor's wife, who allegedly profited from a new $230 million sports arena. At least half the members of the group think the *Observer,* Dallas's alternative weekly, covered the stories about it better than the *Morning News* did. In Fred's opinion, the *News* didn't write about it at all.

Yet, as Stallings reminds everyone behind the mirror, "We broke all those stories."

A S THE DISCUSSION draws to a close, Cherie Sion invites the *News* staffers to come out and meet their critics, for a few minutes of Q&A. The group members are excited at the prospect of this, and initially it's a lighthearted little scene. A couple of people commend the journalists for having the spunk to show their faces in the lions' den. When Jennifer Files introduces herself as a business reporter, somebody asks, "Are you an intern?"

The journalists press for more particulars about what they've heard. Mike says he wants more news about his neighborhood. When Stallings names some stories the paper has run recently, Mike says, "I want more. I want more."

Finally, Stallings gets to the issue that's obviously sticking in his craw. Addressing the whole group but looking at one particular participant, he says, "Fred said earlier that we didn't cover the arena. If I'm not mistaken, then you mentioned the story about Mayor Kirk and his wife profiting on the stock options."

Fred jumps in and takes it from there. "I don't even recall that being covered in the *Morning News,*" he says. "Maybe it was. I remember seeing Kirk on TV and nobody challenged him on this." Fred holds forth for another half minute or so, recounting the financial elements of the story in rather impressive detail.

"We worked on that story for literally three months," Stallings informs him. "And we broke the story on the front page of the *Morning News,* the story about Mrs. Kirk getting the options. . . . So, for some reason, you guys aren't aware of that or didn't notice it or—that's what I'm trying to figure out. Like, we're trying to get stories that have impact and show that we're trying to cover both sides, and yet it doesn't seem like you're picking up on those stories."

Fred is unregenerate. "Well, why did you let him get away with it?" He launches another filibuster, longer than the last one.

Nobody in the focus group says, oops, we didn't realize you'd covered this thing as well as you have. Instead, Mike begins praising Laura Miller, a columnist for the *Observer* who wrote impassioned accounts of Dallas politics and then ran for city council and won.

"I think the election of Laura Miller is a totally black eye on the *Dallas Morning News,*" Mike says. "For someone to come from a small local newspaper that doesn't have the money behind it like the *Dallas Morning News,* to not only get citywide recognition but to win acceptance and then to run for political office—to me, this was a glowing thing. I was so happy."

Files says, "But we don't want to be politicians. We want to be journalists."

"I understand that," says Mike. "I don't think she wanted to either. But . . . she felt that she had to step up. I admire her for that. To me, that's a black eye. How could the *Observer*'s reporter get more attention for what she's doing than what the *Dallas Morning News* is?"

Stallings: "We don't want our reporters to get attention. We don't work that way."

Mike: "Well how did she get attention? By covering stories that we wanted to know about."

Stallings: "I would take exception with that. I think she got attention by putting her viewpoint in her stories, which is what we don't do in the newspaper."

On and on it went, and it didn't stop until Cherie Sion's husband and business partner, Berrien Moore, entered the room and said, in his courtly Georgia accent, "Excuse me for interrupting. The people outside, who run this facility, they say they've got to go." Everyone laughed.

Afterward, Stallings, Files, Delgado, and Harris held a little debriefing session with Barbara Quisenberry, the *News'* research director, who had organized the focus group. Stallings wondered what to make of the fact that the *News'* own readers didn't know the paper had investigated the arena. All the other media in town had picked up the story from the *News*. "And radio," Delgado said, "they just read our stuff right off the page."

"Does the *Dallas Morning News'* reporting just get to be part of the landscape?" Stallings wondered.

"Or," said Delgado, "do they forget they learned it from us?"

Files noted that when Channel 5 had an investigative report, the station promoted it. Maybe the *News* should do more of that.

Everybody was disturbed, too, that the group hadn't understood the paper's journalistic values—that people admired the *Observer*'s reporter for being so partisan. Here was the *News* trying to keep its reporters free from bias, and here were readers, it seemed, demanding bias. At one point, grasping at straws, Stallings said, "If people don't like the paper but they read it, that's not all bad."

Later, standing over by himself against the wall, he mused, to no one in particular, "I wonder what they meant by good news."

THIS WAS ONE of a set of six focus groups Barbara Quisenberry organized in October of 1998. While the group with Fred and Mike and Jenny was by far the most cantankerous, each group was problematic in its own way. If there was a common thread, it was that local news means so many different things to different people. Cherie Sion began every session by asking group members to define local news and give examples. In the first focus group, a woman said "local" meant the state of Texas. Her example was coverage of the floods then occurring in South Texas, about 250 miles from Dallas. To another participant local news meant "Dallas and the suburbs." To one it meant Dallas and Fort Worth, while to another it meant Dallas but not Fort Worth. One man said any news about the corporation he works for was local news. Others mentioned real estate ads, news about brides and marriages ("to see if any old high school classmates got married"), news about garage sales, news about telephone rate increases, news about the oil business, about the zoo, about "what local community leaders are doing." One woman said she didn't think of "local" as a geographic term; "local" was whatever affected people she had common interests with.

Such a dizzying array of answers is not unique to Dallas. It's an article of faith in the newspaper business these days that people want more local news—all the surveys say so—but it's also true that the term is nebulous and ever-changing.

"It used to be that local news was pretty much defined by geographic boundaries," said Tony Casale, president of American Opinion Research, based in Princeton, New Jersey. "That's not true any longer." When people think about what's local, he said, "they'll think about what affects them and their families. . . . My wife got Lyme disease a couple of summers ago. That became a local story for me."

A recent report by the Newspaper Management Center at Northwestern University spoke of the Internet's impact on all this. On the World Wide Web, the report said, people "are able to find others who share their interests and backgrounds, which is redefining the term 'community.'"

Vivian Vahlberg, director of journalism programs at the McCormick Tribune Foundation, is concerned about the perennial problem of declining newspaper readership, and about why newspaper executives don't do very much about it. As she explained it to me, there are probably things the industry could do to reverse the declines in circulation, but publishers don't have the confidence to carry them out. Partly, she said, it's that the research findings still aren't convincing enough.

"For example, research study after research study says local news is the key," she said. "But can you tell me for sure that anybody knows what we mean by local news? That you really know enough to go out tomorrow and change a newspaper by giving people local news? There's a feeling that we need to understand more deeply what we mean by local news. For someone who grew up in El Salvador but lives here now, local news might be news about El Salvador."

It will be a long time before focus groups settle this issue, or any other major issue. Although an entire industry has grown up around the focus group—there are businesses that recruit participants, other businesses that rent out rooms with the see-through mirrors, and others that provide moderators—the reliability of the focus group is highly suspect.

The modern focus group evolved during World War II as a way to test the effectiveness of films and radio programs used for training and morale. Soldiers watching the films would be asked to press a red button on their chairs when anything evoked a negative response, and a green button for a positive response. The buttons were wired to a set of fountain pens on a primitive polygraph machine, which recorded the ups and downs of the soldiers' responses across a timeline. After the film was over, an interviewer would question the group as a whole, asking why they'd reacted as they did.

The researchers found that they needed both kinds of input. The polygraph record had the character of a controlled experiment. It was "quantitative"—the squiggles could be toted up and studied in a statistical way. The "qualitative" interviews added human detail to the bare-bones polygraph records. But since the qualitative comments lacked scientific rigor, they had to be used as hypotheses for further study. To leave out the quantitative step and just rely on the soldiers' recollections would have been inadequate.

One of the researchers on those early projects was sociologist Robert K. Merton, whom many now consider the father of the modern focus group. After the war, he saw the use of focus groups explode when the method was embraced by market researchers for the business sector. But he also saw it come under attack, because so many people tried to draw conclusions based on focus groups alone, without the corroboration of other, more "scientific" methods. In 1989, when Merton was invited to speak at a New York meeting of the American Association of Public Opinion Research, he seemed disappointed at how his brainchild had turned out. "I gather that much focus group research today . . . does not involve this composite of both qualitative and quantitative inquiry," he said. "One gains the impression that focus-group research is sometimes being mercilessly misused."

Here is a smattering of the criticisms lodged against focus groups over the years:

- "Focus group interviewing . . . has not generated any significant body of research concerning its reliability and validity."—Albert E. Gollin of the Newspaper Association of America

- "The focus group is the most abused research technique in all phases of market research."—Daniel T. Seymour, a consultant to industry and higher education
- "People who can be enticed [into a focus group] do not always represent a true cross-section of potential customers . . . and loud-mouths can dominate and sway the discussion."—Leo Bogart, the veteran newspaper researcher, as quoted by Robert Merton
- "Samples are invariably small and never selected by probability methods. Questions are not asked the same way each time. Responses are not independent. Some respondents inflict their opinions on others; some contribute little or nothing at all. Results are difficult or impossible to quantify and are not grist for the statistical mill. Conclusions depend on the analyst's interpretative skill. The investigator can easily influence the results."—William D. Wells, in *Handbook of Marketing Research*
- "Because of the persuasiveness of the technique, unsophisticated clients may believe they have witnessed The Truth, and may make precipitous decisions on slender evidence."—Jane Farley Templeton, author of the book *The Focus Group*

In spite of all this, focus groups remain very much with us—and not just because they're quicker and cheaper than other research, although they are. One of the weaknesses of the formal "quantitative" survey is that people with strong, insightful opinions may never get to express them, because the interviewer isn't asking the right questions. As far back as 1931, a social scientist named Stuart Rice was complaining about this problem. He wrote that the results of an interview "are as likely to embody the preconceived ideas of the interviewer as the attitudes of the subject." In theory at least, a focus group strips away the straitjacket of the formal survey and lets people just speak their minds.

Another point in favor of qualitative research—the kind that comes from focus groups—is that newspaper people find it easier to understand than a survey. Even if the participants in a focus group are full of bull, which is often the case, what they say is more accessible than the tables and statistics of a quantitative research study. Belden's Deanne Termini told me that newsroom people "are very suspicious of the quantitative stuff sometimes."

And they should be. One crisp autumn day I visited the Princeton University library, hoping the social science journals could shed light on those perplexing contradictions in Orange County. Maybe something was wrong with the questions they were asking out there.

The day was an eye-opener. One of the most confounding documents I came upon was a report in *Public Opinion Quarterly* about the wording of comparative questions. In 1995, in a poll conducted in Germany, the authors asked people whether they found tennis more or less exciting than soccer to watch on TV. Thirty-five percent judged tennis more exciting, while 65 percent judged it less so. Then the authors reversed the wording, asking people whether they found soccer more or less exciting than tennis. This time, only 15 percent found soccer more exciting, down from 65. Seventy-seven percent found it less exciting, up from 35. And while 0 percent were undecided on the first wording, 8 percent were undecided on the second. Which sport these people would really rather watch, God only knows.

The authors conducted two other, similar experiments, and in both cases the order of the words again changed the outcome. When they asked, "Would you say that news reporting in your newspaper is better or worse than the news reporting on television?" 52 percent said the reporting in the paper was better. When they asked, "Would you say that news reporting on television is better or worse than the news reporting in your newspaper?" only 43 percent thought newspaper reporting was better.

Another journal article, from 1992, examined the wording of questions in a national health survey. In seven out of sixty cases, people had trouble understanding the question. When asked how many times a week they ate butter, many people didn't know whether to count margarine as butter. When asked how many "servings of eggs" they had "in a typical day," many didn't know what was meant by "a serving of eggs" (does a single egg count as a serving?) and others didn't know what was meant by a typical day. Asked whether they exercised or played sports regularly, many didn't know whether to count walking as exercise. And when asked whether their last consultation with a doctor took place at an HMO, many didn't know what an HMO was. None of these misunderstandings had been foreseen by the people who designed the survey.

A 1995 study found that often, when people don't know the answer to a question, they guess. Asked, for instance, about U.S. policy toward Nicaragua, a respondent who knows nothing about that policy may nonetheless form an opinion on the spot. In one classic case from the 1950s that has since been replicated, large percentages of people expressed opinions about the Heavy Metals Act, even though no such act had ever been passed, debated, or proposed.

A study in 1994 found that survey questions often contain unstated assumptions about people. "How long does it take you to drive to work?"

assumes that the person has a job. These unwarranted assumptions "are pervasive in all forms of social intercourse, including standardized surveys," the researchers wrote.

People are typically asked how intensely they hold some attitude or belief—"How important to you is protecting the environment?"—before it's been established that they hold any such belief at all.

A possible way around this kind of bias is to precede the main question with what's called a filter question. "Is protecting the environment important to you?" would be the filter question, and if the answer comes back yes, then you follow up with the main question, "How important is protecting the environment?" In this example, though, the filter introduces another kind of bias, known as socially acceptable response bias. How many people want to come out and say they don't give a damn about protecting the environment?

When the authors of this report ran experiments using the same questions with and without filters, they got different results. In three out of four cases, the use of a filter question doubled the percentage of respondents who said they were "not concerned" about a problem. In other words, without the filter, this survey would have been tainted with the opinions of a lot of people who really didn't care.

Surveyors have another basic problem: getting people to cooperate. Increasingly, people don't like to be bothered by pollsters. In two-career families, it's hard for telephone surveyors to catch anyone at home. When they are at home, people may suspect that the survey is one of those telephone-solicitation scams in which a caller poses as an opinion pollster but turns out to be a salesperson.

Accordingly, the "response rate"—the number of people who cooperate with phone and mail surveys—has been going down and down. Newspaper researchers say it's very hard now to get a response rate higher than 50 percent, which used to be considered the lowest acceptable number. The problem is that as response rates fall, a self-selecting bias is introduced. The people most likely to answer a survey questionnaire and mail it in, for instance, are those who feel most strongly about the issues in the survey. People who feel less strongly just pitch it. Two Ohio State professors, writing about nonresponse bias in *Public Opinion Quarterly,* felt moved to warn, "Trusting the results of a mail survey is like lowering yourself into a dark pit in search of treasure and trusting that you won't be bitten by a snake."

You can raise the response rate by paying people a cash incentive, usually from five dollars to twenty dollars, to return the questionnaire. But this can overweight your sample with people who need the five bucks.

Yet another kind of bias seems to have been created by the use of tele-phone answering machines. Households that screen nuisance calls with these machines tend to have higher than average incomes, more young people living there, and a higher level of education. Such households also tend to be urban or suburban, not rural. David Neft, Gannett's chief researcher, told me he foresees a time "when we're going to pretty much lose the phone as the basic mode of interviewing." He isn't sure what will replace it, although the Internet comes naturally to mind.

"ANY GOOD SURVEY is only as good as the questions you ask," says Tony Casale, the Princeton-based researcher. "There's a lot of bad questions asked on a lot of surveys."

Casale is a hands-on guy, not a scholar. He started out as a reporter for Gannett, then was an editor at *USA Today* for a while, and then he became the company's director of news research, where he got to see a lot of the work done for newspapers by outside vendors. Finally, with the formation of his own company, he became an outside vendor himself. So when the talk turns to built-in biases, leading questions, and misinterpretation, Casale has seen it from all sides.

"I saw this in a survey once," he says, "this exact question: 'What do you believe in most—radio, television, or large, prestigious newspapers such as the *New York Times* and the *Los Angeles Times*?'

"What they're saying is, 'Well, whaddaya think, moron?'"

Most of the problems Casale encounters are more subtle than that. He says he's noticed some questions get different responses when you ask them on the phone than when you ask them in a survey booklet mailed to people's homes. Questions about columnists, for instance. If you ask about a newspaper column over the phone, people may say they haven't read it, but if you show them a picture of the column with the logo, they'll remember that they did. "The visual awareness helps get more accurate data."

How did Casale learn that? I ask. "A lot of mistakes," he says. "Believe me, a lot of mistakes."

A typical modern survey has two parts—a telephone interview and then a follow-up mailing that contains questions in a booklet. "Things in need of probing we do on the telephone interview," he says. If people tell you in the mail survey they don't read the paper because they don't have time, you're stuck with that vague answer. "On the telephone interview, you can say, 'What do you mean you don't have time? Is it you really don't have time? Is the paper not worth your time? Is it not delivered early enough?' So the probing type of questions we need to put in the telephone interview."

It's also possible, theoretically, to correct for "order bias" in a telephone survey. In the case of the tennis-soccer question, for instance, one could reverse the order of the terms with every other respondent, so the built-in biases balance out. In theory, at least.

"Question order is an absolute art form," Casale says. "Once when I was at Gannett, a vendor gave us a survey. He'd asked about ten minutes' worth of questions about his local newspaper. 'What do you read in it? How much do you like it?' And then he says, 'OK, what's your primary source of local news and information?' Well, you've already sensitized him to say that the local newspaper is. So you have to put that earlier in the questionnaire, before the sensitizing."

Another general rule is to save the purely factual questions—those about people's interests and activities—for later in the questionnaire, because these are less subject to question-order bias.

On the other hand, a person's patience starts to wear thin after too long on the phone. "If you go past thirty minutes," Casale says, "people start giving you answers that they think you want to hear, just to get you off the phone."

One of the most common mistakes of all, in Casale's opinion, is to ask people to speculate about how they might respond if a newspaper changed the way it presents the news. "I've seen too many times where people would say, 'If we put five more stories on page one would you read it?' And the increased story count didn't have any effect. Or the advertising question, 'How likely are you in the next twelve months to buy a new car, a major appliance?' Well, most people don't buy a major appliance until theirs breaks down, let's face it. But you'll get 40 or 50 percent saying they're going to do it. And then when you ask the question on the survey, 'During the past twelve months have you done it?' it's really like 15 percent. . . .

"Questions like, 'Is the paper better or worse or about the same as it was two years ago?' I've just seen paper after paper after paper where the answers are the same every single year, no matter what they do."

G IVEN ALL THIS, it's easy to understand why pollsters have such trouble predicting the outcome of elections. Or why so many television programs, after being vetted by focus groups, fail in the market. The focus group and the sample survey are blunt instruments at best. Unfortunately, they are just about the only basic tools market researchers have.

In his book *Focus Groups: A Practical Guide for Applied Research,* Richard A. Krueger explains how the focus group and the survey can be used in such a way that one complements the other. He cited a study of morale problems among student volunteers at the University of North Carolina. The first step in assessing this problem was to survey the volunteers with a short questionnaire. The key question was: How satisfied are you with your volunteer position?

[   ]   5. Very Satisfied
[   ]   4. Satisfied
[   ]   3. Neither Satisfied nor Dissatisfied
[   ]   2. Dissatisfied
[   ]   1. Very Dissatisfied

The analysis showed that one subgroup of the volunteers, those with the most experience, had an average score of 1.7—a cause for concern. The second step was to interview the students in a "qualitative" way, asking them to explain in their own words why they were satisfied or dissatisfied. This produced a more complete picture than the bare statistics.

Although the North Carolina experiment stopped there, it could have been taken further. One could have made a list of the issues the students raised, written those into a formal questionnaire, and then asked everyone to rate their relative importance. This is the same dialectical, back-and-forth approach Robert Merton and his colleagues used with the soldiers in World War II.

It's also, in a general way, what has been happening in newspaper research with the issue of local news. First, newspapers discovered that readers rate local news very high in surveys. Next, probing this finding in focus groups, they found that the term "local news" is extremely vague. Now, in surveys, many researchers try to use more specific language, asking not about "local news" but about "news of your neighborhood" or "news about your city."

At the *Philadelphia Inquirer,* because readers gave local news such a high rating on surveys, executives wondered whether the paper should play more local stories on page one. So in 1997, they produced six front-page prototypes and showed them to focus groups. The prototypes were:

- The *Inquirer's* actual front page for June 26, 1997, which had three local and four national and foreign stories, sky boxes (prominent graphic keys to inside stories) at the top, and a dominant photo taken at a Phillies game

- A page with only one local story, all national and foreign stories above the fold, but three local sky boxes
- A page containing mainly "soft news," with an informational graphic as the dominant piece of art
- A page with only five stories, two of which did not jump
- A page on which all but one of the stories were local
- A page containing only four stories, plus an expanded index

After running these prototypes through ten focus groups, Tom Holbein of Belden Associates concluded that *Inquirer* readers liked the existing front page—the one with a mix of local, national ,and foreign stories— better than any of the other samples. True, these readers wanted plenty of local news, but they were happy to have it back in the local sections. If a local story made page one, they thought it should be important. In fact, any story that made page one was expected to be important. They didn't want any fluff out there.

Holbein's report said readers objected to photo features displacing more substantive news on page one, that they preferred six or seven stories out front rather than four or five, that they found sky boxes helpful, and that they followed the jumps but wanted them to be clear and easy to find.

"Basically, people expect the *Inquirer* to be like the *Washington Post,*" Holbein told me. "It has that national and international prestige, and essentially they want a mix of news on the front page."

This is not the conclusion one might have drawn based solely on the mail and telephone surveys, with their high ratings for local news.

IN OCTOBER 1990, with considerable fanfare, Knight Ridder totally and radically revamped one of its small papers, the *Boca Raton News*. As Tony Ridder, then the chain's president, explained to *Mediaweek,* "What we decided was to make a new newspaper from the front page to the last. We tried to find out as much about the people of Boca Raton as possible, how they led their lives, what they were thinking, what they did, what interested them. And then we tried to design a paper we thought would work for them."

CEO James Batten (who died in 1995) called the South Florida paper "a weapons lab designed to investigate and test new approaches to making newspapers work better for younger readers."

After all the market testing that went into it, the new paper wound up looking like *USA Today,* only more so: Short stories. Glitzy layouts. A flamingo-pink nameplate. No jumps. A color weather map. Extensive use of calendars, indexes, and briefs. Extensive use of labels and large body type to make the paper "more scannable." How-to features. A daily good-news feature called "Today's Hero." A downplaying of political and government news, which was considered too boring. Greater emphasis on personal health and fitness, personal finance, consumer news, parent-and-child relationships, and "reader-empowerment" features. The redesigned paper was the centerpiece of Knight Ridder's "25/43" Project, which was intended to reshape newspapers for readers in that age group—a population much coveted by advertisers but less loyal to newspapers than previous generations had been.

By the time the refurbished Boca Raton paper was launched, it was hardly unique. Lee Enterprises and other chains had adopted many of the same graphic flourishes and quick-read features.

The interesting thing about Boca Raton was not that it failed in the marketplace—most observers agree the paper probably would have in any case, sandwiched as it was by two powerful competitors, Fort Lauderdale's *Sun-Sentinel* and the *Palm Beach Post*. (Its precariousness was one reason it was selected as the "lab" in the first place.) Knight Ridder's chief researcher, Jenny Fielder, says the Boca experiment actually did succeed in raising readership in the twenty-five to forty-three age group, "but some of the older people didn't like the changes we were making in their newspaper." As it happened, half the people in Boca Raton were fifty-five or older, and they constituted the paper's most loyal audience. Offending them was a mistake. At the time of its 1990 makeover, the *Boca Raton News* claimed a daily circulation of 38,000, although it was unaudited and its competitors said heavy discounting and giveaways inflated that figure; a year later the circulation, now audited, was just 22,300. When Knight Ridder finally sold the paper to Community Newspaper Holdings Inc. in 1997, circulation was 15,000.

Ironically, given the way demographics are changing, the U.S. population twenty years from now may look something like the population of Boca Raton in 1990. According to a recent report from Northwestern University, 43 percent of the population will be fifty or older by 2010, and 47 percent will be fifty or older by 2020. "How do newspapers handle the paradox of an older readership base with disposable income and advertisers who want to target eighteen-year-olds?" asks Michael Smith, associate director of the Newspaper Management Center at Northwestern.

This is part of a larger dilemma for newspapers, the dilemma that Boca Raton illustrated so well: The kind of at-a-glance newspaper tailored to lure the elusive younger reader can be off-putting to older, more serious readers—the core audience that will probably be newspapers' bread and butter for decades to come.

In 1991, ASNE published a readership report called "Keys to Our Survival." It identified three main groups of readers. The first was the loyal newspaper reader, the kind who loves news and picks up the paper every day. The second type was the "at-risk" reader, who looks at a paper from time to time but has no abiding interest. The third was called the "potential" reader, who wants more information than the newspaper is providing.

The at-risk reader, the report said, could probably be lured into reading more if papers offered a diet of short, easily digestible tidbits of information—nothing very intimidating. However, the "potential" reader could only be lured by a paper with more depth and intelligence.

Each of the two groups accounted for an equal portion of the newspaper market, about 13 percent. And they stood at opposite ends of the spectrum, which meant if a newspaper wanted to increase readership it had to go after one or the other.

The problem with going after the at-risk group was that, in making a paper more superficial, it might offend its loyal readers, as in Boca. The problem with going after the potential reader was that, to do so, a paper had to beef up its coverage. It actually had to spend money and get better journalistically.

The ASNE report recommended the cheaper, easier route—going for the at-risk readers. And by and large, this is what the newspaper industry has done in the 1990s, even though logic suggests that you can please more readers (that is, two out of the three above-named groups) by investing in better, more substantive journalism.

On this very basic issue—"dumbing down" versus smartening up—ASNE has sent mixed messages. In a foreword to Ruth Clark's 1979 study —the one calling for newspapers to become more lifestyle-oriented—ASNE officers warned that it would be "exceedingly risky to cut back on hard news to emphasize soft features." And an introduction to a 1990 ASNE research report warned, "As we reach out to these occasional, distracted readers with clearer headlines, graphics, color, summaries and other devices, we risk turning off our base of regular readers."

In slicing and dicing the responses from surveys in its circulation area, the *Los Angeles Times* recently concluded that people with a high commitment to news and newspapers constitute 47 percent of the local market. Those with a medium commitment make up 26 percent, and those with a low commitment 27 percent. The *Times* also found that a high commitment to newspaper reading correlates with high interest in national and world news. People who prefer a quick and easy read over in-depth coverage, it found, have a lower than average interest in national and world news. If this is the general pattern in other markets—and the *Times'* findings do seem to track those of other metro papers—then newspapers make a mistake by emphasizing the quick and easy while downplaying national, foreign, and other serious news.

No research has been able to calculate just how much a paper can skimp on substantive news before it starts to drive away its core of loyal readers. But clearly, papers like the *Boca Raton News* or, on a larger scale, the now-defunct *Arkansas Gazette* have paid a price by going too far in that direction.

A 1998 Associated Press Managing Editors report contained this advice from researcher Christine Urban: "News coverage needs to be better and more intelligent. News is the primary reason people buy the paper. . . . On the continuum from easy to hard, the industry stays too much on the easy end. [It] employs concepts like teen magazines borrowed from other newspapers. These don't cost much time and don't upset many apple carts. By definition, they'll have little impact, which fuels the engine that we can't do anything about readership."

The pressure to give readers less substance doesn't just come from the so-called at-risk readers. It also comes from Wall Street. Miles Groves, the former head of market and business analysis for the Newspaper Association of America, said an investor pulled him aside at a PaineWebber Media Conference and asked why papers couldn't run more wire copy and get by with even fewer reporters. And in a 1998 report on Knight Ridder, analyst Lauren Rich Fine of Merrill Lynch commended the company for putting less emphasis on quality journalism. She told investors, "KRI's historic culture has been one of producing Pulitzer Prizes instead of profits, and while we think that culture is hard to change, it does seem to be happening."

With many publishers unwilling to invest much in better journalism, consultants and research companies try to make recommendations that won't cost much. Belden, for instance, has developed what it calls the "Belden Decision Model for Newspaper Content." This model divides all the content categories—metro news, pro sports, college sports, the arts, business news, and so forth—according to whether readers have high or low interest. Then it asks readers whether their newspaper does a good or a poor job covering each category.

When readers say they have a high interest in a category but don't think the paper does a good enough job covering it, Belden recommends the paper "expand and promote" its coverage. But if a category is of limited interest to readers and the newspaper is thought to be doing a poor job with it, Belden suggests the paper "evaluate" its coverage—that is, consider cutting back on it.

"This is a directional tool," Tom Holbein told me. "If certain subjects land over here [in the 'expand' box] and the research indicates they should be increased, and you have no budget and no space in order to do that, and you want to respond to the research, then the first place to look for opportunities to cut back, or not to add resources, is over here [in the 'evaluate' box]."

Many research firms have a similar construct—a way of saying, "Here are things you can cut back in order to beef up these other, more important things." The trouble with most of these schemes is, it's very hard to find categories to cut back. Readers just don't want that. In the Belden Decision Model, for instance, the "evaluate" box contains such popular items as the arts, college sports, high school sports, local obituaries, restaurant reviews and listings, and personal-finance and investment information.

GANNETT HAS PIONEERED one newspaper trend after another. It revolutionized design, the use of color, and the use of graphics. It proved that a newspaper company could raise earnings quarter after quarter in defiance of economic cycles. And it was the first major chain to really preach the gospel of giving readers what they say they want. So what Gannett does is always worth watching.

Recently, New Jersey's second-largest newspaper, the *Asbury Park Press,* got a dose of Gannett's reader-driven philosophy, both as it's preached and as it's practiced. On October 24, 1997, Gannett concluded its purchase of the *Press* and proceeded to change the paper's character from top to bottom.

The *Press* covers much of central New Jersey, and for its circulation size—159,000 daily and 225,000 Sunday—it may have been one of the best papers in the country for local news. It had a newsroom staff of 240. The capital bureau in Trenton had six full-time reporters; no other paper in America of the *Press*'s size had more.

Its final year under private ownership had been an especially good one. The *Press* had undertaken a detailed examination of the problems of poverty, corruption, and real estate fraud in its namesake city, Asbury Park. Jody Calendar, who was the deputy executive editor, said that initially the paper detached a half-dozen reporters for the project. In time, others were brought in, including a business reporter, a state reporter, and two specialists in computer-assisted reporting.

The paper's investigations resulted in a number of criminal indictments, along with civil actions and a federal racketeering suit alleging a conspiracy to defraud $24 million from a mortgage company.

The stories won numerous prizes—a National Headliner Award, a Scripps Howard Public Service Award, a Gerald Loeb Award, the Clark Mollenhoff Memorial Award for investigative journalism, the National Press Club's consumer journalism award, a Garden State Association of Black Journalists award, and more. And as a big red cherry on top of the sundae, the paper's editorial cartoonist, Stephen Breen, won a Pulitzer Prize for his work that year.

Then came Gannett, with what it said was a plan to transform the paper in accordance with what the readers really wanted. As it happened, in the year before Gannett took over, the previous owners had hired Cambridge Associates, a Chicago-based firm, to do some $500,000 worth of readership and market research. And Robert Collins, whom Gannett installed as the new publisher, told me that in revamping the paper he had taken advantage of that extensive research.

One of the company's first moves was to announce that within a year the newsroom staff would be slashed by a fourth—from 240 to 185 people. The newshole would also take a significant hit. Overtime pay, which had been generous under the previous owners, was halted, and individual workloads increased.

People watched in sadness as some of the paper's best talent packed up and left. Business reporter John Ward, who had worked on the Asbury Park investigation, jumped to Newark's *Star-Ledger*. "I was made a very attractive offer," he said. "That was the biggest component of it, but certainly the fact that Gannett owned the newpaper. . . . I knew the newshole was going to shrink dramatically, and that the staff was going to be reduced by attrition."

Indeed, many of the people who had worked on the award-winning Asbury Park investigation resigned. Besides Ward, these included the project's leader, Calendar, who became managing editor of the Record in Bergen County, and reporters Larry Arnold (who went to Washington for the Associated Press) and T. J. Foderaro (who went to the *Star-Ledger*).

Arlene Schneider, the *Press*'s highly respected Sunday editor, took a job on the national desk of the *New York Times*. In Trenton, capitol reporter Herb Jackson moved down the hall to the *Record*'s statehouse bureau. Eventually, five of the six reporters in the *Press*'s capital bureau left the paper, as did the state editor. The statehouse reporters were replaced, but instead of working exclusively for the *Press* the bureau now supplies coverage for all seven of Gannett's New Jersey papers. Other reporters in Trenton say they don't consider the Gannett bureau a serious competitor.

Beyond the cutback in regular staff, the *Press* eliminated many of its local stringers. These were the people who had kept track of developments in the region's many townships and school districts. Not only did readers learn less about their communities now, but depleting the local bureaus made it harder for the editorial writers to keep up with local events and comment on them. Gannett also saved money by reducing the number of locally zoned editions from five to four.

The new publisher, Collins, imposed Gannett's trademark strictures on layout and writing. He made a rule that at least one story per day would not jump off page one. On the local-news front, two or three stories a day, and sometimes more, no longer jump. Story lengths in general were cut, and reporters were instructed to localize their copy, whenever possible, by putting a quote from a local resident somewhere in the first five paragraphs. Herb Jackson told me that often, to get these local quotes, reporters first had to explain the story to people on the street, "and in doing so you'd kind of be shaping their reaction."

"We got quotes saying, 'That's really interesting.'"

In August of 1998, newspapers everywhere reported that stock markets in America and around the world had taken a dive—the Dow fell 357 points—due to panic over Russia's economic turmoil and the impotence of Boris Yeltsin's government. "Boris on the Brink" and "Dow Sees Red," the New York tabloids screamed. The *Asbury Park Press* took note of these developments too, but its approach was to rewrite an AP story to give it a soft, local lead. The page-one story began, "John E. Ekdahl, a stockbroker in Shrewsbury, had a hectic day yesterday." Where the AP had quoted sources from Wall Street and overseas—people with real knowledge of the day's events—the *Press* replaced them with remarks from local stockbrokers in Monmouth and Ocean Counties.

In another policy change, the *Press* began charging for obits. As Collins explained it to me, the first eighteen lines of an obit are free, the next ten lines cost $45, and each additional line is $4.50. "The funeral directors write the obits," he said. "They provide the information pretty much exactly as the family wants it, which is exactly as it should be."

Soon after this policy took effect, an obit appeared for Joseph F. Murray, a former mayor of Manchester, New Jersey. It was one hundred lines long, which by Collins's formula would have cost the Murray family

$369. According to the obit, Murray had been an Eagle Scout, a member of the Veterans of Foreign Wars, a ruling elder in the Presbyterian Church, a past exalted ruler of the Benevolent Protective Order of Elks, a trustee of an ambulatory-care center, and, of course, a former mayor.

The obit neglected to mention that Murray had also been involved in one of the largest municipal-corruption scandals in the state's history, that he had been among those indicted for conspiring to loot the township treasury of more than $2 million, and that he'd been convicted and sent to prison. That information was buried in a five-paragraph item that ran toward the bottom of another page, under an inconspicuous, one-column head: "Ex-mayor accused of corruption dies."

The *Press* also seeks to profit from obituaries of its readers' dogs, cats, birds, and other pets. For $45 it will print a picture of your deceased animal companion along with up to fifty words of tribute, written by you, the reader. This feature, "Pet Memorials," is part of a new weekly section called "Critters," consisting of a pet-care column written by a veterinarian, a photo of the "stray of the week," a light feature story that is staff-produced, a calendar of animal-related local events, three or four color snapshots, mailed in by readers, of their pets—at no charge, so long as the animal isn't dead—and ads for pet stores and pet supplies.

When I asked Collins what improvements he had made in response to reader-research findings, he mainly cited the paper's new features sections. He cited "Whatever" as an example. "Whatever" is a six-page section aimed at teenagers that appears once a week. It contains original poems, drawings, and essays submitted by area youths, a smattering of photo features, an advice column called "The Chat Room," a letters column, and a "Pop Quiz" for teens (sample topic: How well do you get along with people?). The section reads very much like a high school newspaper, but with less news.

Besides "Critters" and "Whatever," other new weekly sections include "Health & Fitness," "Out & About," "People," "Techworld," and "Learning Curve," which runs soft features about people in the local schools. Many of the new sections rely heavily on syndicated and wire copy, especially from Gannett News Service.

Collins said that after the first year the paper had regained most of the newshole it lost when Gannett first took over. An analysis of the newspaper's content bears this out. Furthermore, by shortening stories, the *Press* has been able to increase story count. But the news report seems thinner, especially in the areas of business, politics, and government. The paper seems far less inclined to ask probing questions. Certainly, it is less inclined to explore Asbury Park's continuing political and economic problems.

I asked Collins what was the relationship between research and all the changes the *Press* had made. "Research plays a significant part in what we do here," he said. He went on to say that the paper's research had found "that the readers want more local news. That wasn't an earth-shaking finding, but it just got us to focus more with an intensity that should be brought to that commitment."

When I told him of my perception that local news had been reduced, not expanded, he said, "Your perception is incorrect," and that day in and day out "we are giving people more hard news than ever before."

I said I was nonplussed by his statement and wondered if, in some way, he had redefined the meaning of local news.

"The readers have defined what local news is," he shot back. "We don't define it."

On January 13, 1999, Collins was named Gannett's manager of the year. Richard C. Clapp, a senior vice president of the company, praised Collins for transforming the *Press* "into a decisive, results-oriented enterprise."

A T ASNE'S ANNUAL CONFERENCE in 1997, a panel composed mostly of editors was discussing the impact of marketing issues on editorial judgment. Ed Jones, the managing editor of the *Free Lance-Star* in Fredericksburg, Virginia, admitted that, "like most editors, I certainly have a case of angst."

"Five years ago, ten years ago, my focus could be solely on content," he said. "Now, instead of the key question being, 'Is this a good story?' very often the key question is, 'Is this a good story that a significant chunk of our readers, especially single-copy buyers, will somehow connect to?'"

When the token reporter on the panel, Doug Pardue of the *State* in Columbia, South Carolina, was asked for his thoughts, he said, "What I really regret is that we no longer publish the newspaper every day to piss people off."

The moderator, William Boggs of Synectics Corporation, a consulting firm, seemed not to understand what Pardue was getting at. "Is that right?" Boggs said. "We're publishing this thing, and we sincerely hope it has no connection whatsoever to your life and furthermore that it irritates you?"

"No, I think you missed the point again," said Pardue, who had just won a National Headliner Award for stories about women in the military being raped and sexually molested. "It's the watchdog aspect. It's not, 'Let's go out and find out what Mr. Suburbia wants to plant in his garden, and write about pretty things that *Southern Living* writes about.' That's not journalism. It's denial of reality."

In his 1996 book, *News Values,* Jack Fuller, president of the Tribune Company, faulted researchers for not delving deeply enough "into the real appetites that newspapers fill." He wrote, "I have seen no adequate explanation why columnists like Mike Royko can attract huge and loyal audiences by repeatedly provoking the very people who read them. . . .

"Unfortunately, most market research has taken little interest in the deeper needs a newspaper fills, the very things the journalists worry are undervalued in the marketers' analysis. There is, for example, every reason to believe that readers expect newspapers to be courageous and bold, to challenge conventional wisdom and question authority."

In 1957, when Arkansas governor Orval Faubus defied the federal government by refusing to integrate Central High School in Little Rock, the *Arkansas Gazette* not only covered the story comprehensively, but it editorialized in favor of school integration. The community responded with hate mail, telephone threats, cancellation of subscriptions, and an advertiser boycott. What, one wonders, would the *Gazette*'s readers have said if a research firm had gone in and surveyed them? "I don't think there's any doubt that most people in Arkansas would have said they wouldn't have wanted so much coverage of civil rights," Richard Cole, dean of journalism at the University of North Carolina, told me. "I think most of the readers would have said, 'You're giving us too much of this.'"

And yet, after the *Gazette* had won two Pulitzer Prizes and gained international praise for its journalistic courage, it not only recovered its lost circulation and advertising, but it became an icon of community pride for decades to come. Only in the 1980s, after it was purchased by Gannett and turned into a softer, less serious paper, did the *Gazette* start to lose the loyalty of its core readers to its hometown rival, the *Arkansas Democrat.* The *Gazette* folded in 1991.

The *Washington Post* also made enemies in the 1970s by exposing the Nixon administration's Watergate crimes. But in the long run, says Sharon Warden, the paper's research director, Watergate "was very good for the *Washington Post* because it set a standard, and a reputation nationally. So that now we are the premiere resource for national political news in the country. And people trust us and go to us for that kind of information. Even our local research tells us that people in the Baltimore market want to read the *Post*" for national political news.

On the morning of October 29, 1991, Lois Wark, a special-projects editor at the *Philadelphia Inquirer,* showed up for work and found a crowd of people blocking the front entrance. "I couldn't get in the building," she said. "It was like a movie theater, and they were lined up down the block."

Two of Wark's reporters, Donald Barlett and James Steele, had just published a project that was almost ridiculously long (nine days, twenty jump pages) and complex (it dealt with government economic policy). Yet as the huge series came to a close, people were pushing their way into the *Inquirer*'s front lobby to pick up additional copies, so they could mail them to out-of-town relatives and friends. In the days to come, as parts of the series were reprinted in more than fifty papers around the country, the *Inquirer* was swamped with requests for reprints. They came from union leaders, company presidents, teachers, students, psychologists, truck drivers, lawyers, and readers with names as familiar as Ralph Nader and Gregory Peck. Eventually, the paper distributed nearly four hundred thousand reprinted copies of the series.

"We set up a hotline for people to call, and their comments were tape-recorded," Wark said. "The first day there would be, like, 60 calls, and the second day there would be 120 calls." Eventually, the newsroom had to recruit typists from every other department of the paper to work a couple of hours overtime each night, either transcribing the tapes or mailing out reprints. "We had a little factory going here, shipping out reprints," Wark said.

The series was called "America: What Went Wrong?" Its point was that the concentration of corporate power, abetted by Washington's rules on international trade, taxation, deregulation ,and other complex issues, had produced massive job layoffs and a shrinking of the American middle class. This thesis was documented in detail and illustrated with example after example of Americans who had fallen victim to government policies they could barely understand, let alone influence.

The series more than met Doug Pardue's journalistic standard of pissing readers off.

"I don't think I've read anything recently in any publication that has captured my attention like your series," a man in Holland, Pennsylvania, wrote. "I found myself blurting out things like, 'No wonder,' 'That's why,' and 'Those bastards' while reading your article."

Hardly any readership surveys try to measure the impact of this sort of classic watchdog journalism. One of the few that did was the 1997 ASNE study by Clark, Martire and Bartolomeo. It asked readers if they were interested in the "investigation of important issues." So how many said they were "extremely" or "very" interested?

Seventy-two percent.

6 | Follow the Money

The following piece endeavored to describe business and sports coverage as it appeared to most observers in 1999.

At that time, driven by the go-go climate of the 1990s, financial pages were booming. Newspapers had expanded business coverage because, with so many ordinary Americans invested in the markets, subjects once relegated to thin business sections now had an impact in every corner of every community.

In hindsight, however, critics have rightly noted that much of the expanded business coverage in American newspapers was naively uncritical of the extreme efforts then being made by many business and financial people to pump the markets artificially, sometimes even fraudulently. Many critics now see journalists as having been part of the general cheerleading that led so many innocent people to trust the misleading claims of Wall Street analysts, auditing firms, and corporate executives. Following the market collapse, the bankruptcies, and the scandals of 2001 and 2002, Joe Nocera, the executive editor of Fortune *magazine, said that "in the business press there is some sheepishness at the way we have lionized some of these guys."*

Also during the 1990s, the passion for sports was rising as fast as the stock markets, and newspapers responded with expanded sports sections and deeper coverage. The salaries paid to leading sports writers were enough to make a dedicated metro reporter think about throwing in the towel.

By Lewis M. Simons
ORIGINALLY PUBLISHED IN NOVEMBER 1999

THE YEAR WAS 1925, Calvin Coolidge was sitting "tranquilly," as he liked to say, in the White House, and Americans basked in the mellow glow of peace and prosperity. On January 17 the president loosened that famously buttoned lip just long enough to pronounce one of the few terse Coolidgisms that would survive him. "The chief business of the American people," he asserted in a Washington speech, "is business. They are profoundly concerned with producing, buying, selling, investing and prospering in the world."

Much less remembered is that Coolidge delivered this nugget to the American Society of Newspaper Editors, then but a three-year-old toddler.

What, if anything, the editors in the audience that day responded went unreported. But evidently they missed Silent Cal's point. For in those contented times, with Black Tuesday and the Great Depression still four years down the road, if Americans were "profoundly concerned" with business you certainly couldn't tell it from their newspapers. Indeed, scant and naive business coverage was later cited as one reason so many Roaring Twenties investors were in over their heads. For the mainstream press it would be another half a century before business news was hardly worthy of the name.

Whatever the case was in 1925, there is no doubt that in 1999 the business of America is business. We are transfixed by it, gripped by it, seeing our lives and culture changed forever by it. Cab drivers check their portfolios, and grocery clerks want in on the latest dot-com IPO. And this time there is no question that America's editors are all over the phenomenon.

In recent years business news has been, far and away, the fastest-growing editorial segment in the nation's newspapers, if not in all media. At a time when many papers are reducing coverage of traditional mainstay areas, from statehouse news to international affairs, the buildup of business coverage has reached explosive proportions, sweeping the field from the metropolitan giants to the most introspective of hometown dailies.

Once almost the exclusive realm of the *Wall Street Journal* and its weekend cousin, *Barron's,* business news is now the arena where mainstream editors say they test their mettle against the competition. Business stories appear regularly and prominently on front pages and throughout the paper, having slipped the bonds of their own sections the same way business itself has infiltrated every nook of society. Today "business" could be the page-one takeout (on a global monetary crisis) or a sports report ($800 million for the Washington Redskins!) or a lifestyle piece (is it gauche to compare stock options at a cocktail party?).

"Business coverage is leaping out of the old ghettoized system," says *Washington Post* columnist David Ignatius, whose reporting and commentary focus on business and the way it is transforming society. "Business is now a subject that's changing our lives so much that it shows up regularly in op-ed, and it's included more and more in the mix with policy."

Along the way business is transforming the cultures of newspapers themselves, something you see clearly if you travel the country and talk to editors and writers about the business movement, as I did in 1999. You notice how the *San Jose Mercury News,* having consciously set out to make itself the "paper of record" for Silicon Valley, infuses the entire editorial product with high tech. How down in Austin the *American-Statesman* wants to do the same for its burgeoning Texas "technopolis." How in Portland, home of Nike, the *Oregonian* is digging into sneakers and tracking the elusive french fry. And how two national giants, the *New York Times* and *USA Today,* are devoting an enormous amount of thought and resources to staking out respective corners of the crowded business field.

Changing right along with the newspapers is the reporter culture. Where the business desk once was Siberia, now some of the best and brightest young journalists—reporters who a generation ago would have had their sights set on Washington or overseas assignments—are opting to build careers covering the sexy new world of commerce. *Wall Street Journal* managing editor Paul Steiger, who joined the paper in 1966 after studying economics at Yale, claims that today people with his background aren't qualified to be hired. "The young people we get now have awesome talent," he says. "They can write a page-one story immediately, and they want to cover business."

The new business culture is no secret; you can't pass a corner newsstand or go online without having it slap you in the face. But the statistics nicely reinforce the impression. A content survey of ten mainstream regional dailies, conducted by writer Carl Sessions Stepp and published in the September 1999 *American Journalism Review,* reveals that in the past generation the percentage of newshole devoted to business news has more than doubled, from 7 to 15 percent. When you consider that overall newshole also has doubled, it means that the space devoted to business stories has actually quadrupled in the past three decades. Meantime, the Associated Press reports that more newspapers are using more business agate (stock listings, mutual-fund tables, and related data) than ever. Stepp's data confirm that; he found that space devoted to business agate is up nearly fourfold. And at the nation's largest papers, which were not included in Stepp's survey but which have plowed tens of millions of dollars into additional staffing and space, the increases would be even more significant.

How obsessed are Americans with business? Ask CNBC, MSNBC, or TheStreet.com. Talk to the folks at Bloomberg News. A decade ago the service didn't exist, but now it fields more than 1,100 full-time print and broadcast reporters in seventy-eight bureaus around the world, and Bloomberg's terminals are ubiquitous in the nation's newsrooms.

Consider the stories we're writing, and the people we're writing about. Once upon a time, how many regular folks could identify the chief of the Federal Reserve or the Treasury secretary, much less discuss their monetary philosophies? But look at the ink spilled on Alan Greenspan and the recently retired Robert Rubin. And Bill Gates! Every other magazine cover seems to feature the Microsoft genius with his bad haircut. By now he's known as much for his incredible wealth as for how he spends it—on his forty-thousand-square-foot house, on his charitable contributions (most recently $1 billion for scholarships), on his tenuous golf game. Or take the Gates wannabes. The feature about the nouveau riche twenty-something exchanging his battered Hyundai for a Porsche when his company goes public has become such a newspaper staple that it's already a cliche.

Then again, who can blame us for being so interested? These entrepreneurs and their businesses change so quickly and create such surprises that anyone with a shred of curiosity must be enthralled. Firms start up out of nowhere, go public, go global, acquire other firms, spin off still others, get swallowed themselves—all at warp speed. In the process the fortunes made and lost simply defy mortal comprehension.

It's a dazzling display, and just maybe one of those instances where newspapers seem right in tune with their readers. And why not? In this business environment, editors understand they have the ultimate reader involvement. Today, virtually everyone out there (journalists among them) is a business "player"—if not a direct investor then by dint of their company pensions or 401Ks or employee stock-ownership plans.

Or their mutual funds—especially mutual funds, the basic instrument through which even the least likely or least knowledgeable investor can move money into the stock market. At least 7,500 mutual funds exist today—or existed yesterday anyway, since the number grows constantly. Some 77 million Americans, which translates into 35 million households, are invested in these funds. In 1990, investors had pumped a mere $1 trillion into funds; today that number has exploded into an absolutely staggering $6 trillion. (This happens to be about $1 trillion more than the total national debt, principal plus interest.)

The funds have ridden a stock market whose trajectory in the 1990s has looked like a bottle rocket. Toss in the Internet explosion and the mind-boggling volatility of tech stocks, and the effect has been addicting. If business used to seem a dusty, cobwebbed affair, it's not anymore. Checking out the roller-coaster stocks in your personal portfolio packs all the thrills of a sudden-death playoff—with considerably more at stake. Compare the dash of an Intel with the staidness of a Kellogg's, a Compaq with a Ford; can there be any wonder why journalists who once fled business editors are now running after them? Says the *Post*'s Ignatius, "Business news has gone from broccoli to dessert."

Of course, you can make a strong case that this fascination is really nothing new. "The economy has always been the big story in America, even if newspapers didn't treat it as such," contends the *Oregonian*'s technology editor, Mike Francis. "I'll bet the typical newspaper reader has always cared a lot more about the economy—and his place in it—than about Cold War politics, or even the Vietnam or Korean conflicts. Most newspapers simply failed to recognize it."

Ironically, when they did recognize it, many newspapers were busy whittling away at staff and newshole in other areas, such as foreign news. But determined editors managed to get the money they needed for business expansion. No doubt this was due in part to the fact that business is one subject publishers and general managers are inherently interested in. But more likely this was a case where the business side recognized an opportunity —that the percolating U.S. economy could open up whole new revenue streams (in such areas as high-tech and mutual-fund ads) if there was compelling editorial to surround it. Nor did it hurt that at a time when the industry was preaching the gospel of local news, editors pegged their business-expansion plans to covering what was happening close to home.

"By having a strong business section focused on local news, we can give our readers something that no one else can," explains Hank Klibanoff, business editor of the *Philadelphia Inquirer*. "I'm not competing with the *Wall Street Journal* on the big national story, and I'm not competing with the *New York Times* on the big international story. I'm competing only with local press, and, not to dismiss them, it's on something where I know I can win."

For all the *gemutlichkeit*, however, the fantastic growth in business journalism has surfaced a darker side.

Take the murky area of professional ethics. Not surprisingly, in a world where the go-go entrepreneurs and the reporters covering them both tend to be young and ambitious, opportunity and its attendant temptation are rearing their heads. The fiercely debated demotion this summer of a technology columnist at the *Mercury News*—she profited $9,000 when a Silicon Valley firm went public—is but a case in point. It used to be simple: Journalists couldn't invest in the companies they covered. But most papers are realizing they are in no way prepared for the grayer, more perplexing world of mushrooming startups and nonstop IPOs. What ethics policies exist tend to be outdated or so vague as to be useless on this subject. And if the reporters are forbidden from investing, is it a double standard when the media conglomerates they work for do invest in those same companies, as is often the case today?

Then there's pay. Good business reporters at a first-class paper earning, say, $60,000 or $80,000 find that people of their own age and educational background are earning considerably more at online portals. Front-page glamor fades quickly under such circumstances, and most editors are powerless to compete. Even if some can muster bonuses to snag an especially talented business reporter, the pay differential can create bad feelings and morale problems around the newsroom. The difficulty compounds when these reporters are also the hardest to find, skilled in the intricacies of technology, finance, and economics, the most desirable fields in the electronic media.

Then there's the more subtle but very real problem of our business infatuation coloring all else. Already you can sense this in the reporting coming out of Washington. The capital press corps increasingly is populated by business journalists, and they are tackling more and more stories—from health care to welfare—that once were the purview of traditional news reporters. But if these stories are being reported through a business filter, is anyone asking the broader questions about government policy? Yes, a program might be in business's best interest, but what about the nation's? Is it fair? Is it wise?

Important concerns all, and newspapers coast to coast are grappling with them. Still, the problems are not so distressing as to wipe the smiles off the nation's financial editors. Ask them how's business, and you're apt to hear a lot of people sounding like Klibanoff, who tells me, "It's a great time."

THIS IS A DIFFERENT world indeed from the one in which many veteran business journalists still in harness came of age. There's no need to go back to Coolidge to recapture it. At all too many papers—including some as late as a decade ago, when the collapse of the Soviet Union and the stampeding of the Wall Street bulls really accelerated the business-news boom—the business desk was a kind of purgatory, the corner where editors exiled their problem children: the deadwood, the booze hounds, the old and weary. There, they rewrote—when bothering to do even that—press releases from the big firms in town. The rare interview with a company CEO, the reporter generously pre-lubed with drinks and eats, would inevitably come off as an exercise in fawning sycophancy, the hard questions left unanswered, if asked at all. Business news was, at best, little more than a weed-strewn patch in which corporate flackery waved in the dusty breeze. At worst, it misinformed and misled readers.

Alan Murray, Washington bureau chief of the *Wall Street Journal*, remembers this world. In 1977 he graduated from the University of North

Carolina and went to work as a general-assignment reporter for the *Chattanooga Times*. "In those days," he says, "business coverage at most metropolitan dailies was dismal." Chattanooga was no exception. A literature major at Chapel Hill, Murray had an "interest" in economics, a subject of less than passing fancy to most journalists at the time. "So, I offered to cover economics, and they made me business editor, at age twenty-three—which shows you how bad things were."

A year later he enrolled at the London School of Economics. Then, with newly bolstered academic qualifications, he spent the next four years career-building, in Washington at *Congressional Quarterly* and in Tokyo at the *Nihon Keizai Shimbun,* often referred to as "Japan's *Wall Street Journal.*" In 1983, he went to work on the Washington staff of the genuine article. He arrived just in time for the business boom—and as the *Journal* began to encounter serious competition on all sides.

The granddaddy of business coverage, the *Journal* still sets the standard for others to shoot at. But the improving marksmanship exhibited by so many "nonbusiness" papers has been extraordinary to watch. "We haven't changed drastically since '83. Rather, everyone else has changed to be more like us," Murray says. "As a result, where we used to have very little competition, we now have a lot."

So much, in fact, that the financial daily's circulation has remained flat for more than a decade. *Journal* numbers started slipping in the mid-1980s, from a high of 2 million to between 1.8 and 1.9 million, where they hover today, according to Peter Kann, chairman and chief executive of Dow Jones Company, the *Journal*'s parent. "Our circulation began to dip . . . as major corporations began changing direction and cutting back on staff," Kann says.

Exacerbating the problem for the *Journal* was the fact that at the same time, the sea change in the mainstream media's approach to business was well under way. The public, having lived through the harrowing inflation of the mid-1970s, had become increasingly concerned, and sophisticated, about how the overall economy affected them personally. The term "pocketbook issues" joined the political and media vocabularies. For newspapers, a pivotal event was the appearance in 1980 of "Business Monday" at the *Miami Herald* and a counterpart tabloid product at the *Washington Post,* a highly readable and profitable format that other metros quickly copied.

So began an inexorable process. Brigades of business reporters began to develop. The once-anemic "business report" emerged from behind the sports pages and got its own daily section. Specialty beats—personal finance, technology, Pacific Rim—arose. And the action wasn't just at daily newspapers. The *Business Journal* chain of weeklies took hold. Business and personal-finance magazines sprouted by the rackful. Cable television added business channels. Then came outlets providing real-time stock-market and related coverage, what Kann terms "the new multiplicity of sources for business news"—capped, of course, by the Internet, which by now has been almost entirely transformed from its beginnings as an academic resource to a virtual global marketplace.

From its perch the *Journal* watched it all, and it has tried to respond on a variety of fronts. Its online operation is one of the few genuinely profitable news sites on the Web, though that might be something of a mixed blessing: Of the three hundred thousand paying subscribers, two hundred thousand don't take the paper-and-ink version. The *Journal* has launched editions in the developing economies of Asia and in Europe, helping recoup the number of U.S. corporate subscribers lost in the 1980s, Kann says. In addition, in 1994 the paper began introducing vernacular inserts into major dailies throughout Asia and Latin America. The sections share the dignified, restrained appearance of the mothership—copperplate drawings, long gray columns, and all—but are written in such languages as Thai and Korean. The Latin American version, published in Spanish and Portuguese, is the most successful, with a total circulation of 2.3 million.

Then in September the *Journal,* which does not publish on weekends, launched a domestic variant of its overseas sections: the *Wall Street Journal Sunday.* This four-page package kicked off in the Sunday business sections of ten major metros across the country, from the *Orange County Register* to the *St. Petersburg Times.* Total circulation of these Sunday joint ventures exceeds 4.5 million. The *Journal* sells the nationally based advertising and splits the revenue with the host papers after subtracting a publication fee. An editorial staff of five produces fresh material for the Sunday inserts, which the *Journal* is still pitching to other metros.

While it's far too early to be able to weigh success, Richard Tofel, Dow Jones's vice president for corporate communications, labels the project a "win-win-win—the local papers, the [*Journal*], and the reader all get more."

In today's familiar marketspeak, the *Journal* is using its reputation and resources to sell "branded" product—as Tofel calls it, a "twenty-first-century approach to syndication."

It's also a prime example of competition driving creative marketing, and two of the *Journal's* most adroit competitors in the business-news field are the nation's two other national dailies—*USA Today* and the *New York*

Times. Both papers are successfully leveraging business coverage to extend their audiences, but with somewhat different priorities and approaches.

At *USA Today*'s offices in a pair of sleek half-moon towers across the Potomac River from Washington, D.C., business editor John Hillkirk II is discussing the lengths to which the paper has gone to make personal finance an anchor of its "Money" section—the one with the pointedly dollar-green logo. I mention that Alan Murray had told me that he and others at the *Journal* now rate *USA Today* among the leaders in that heavily trafficked field. "That's nice of him," Hillkirk replies with evident sincerity as well as evident satisfaction. "Not long ago we weren't even on their radar screens."

In 1999 Hillkirk and his "Green Team" were honored by the Society of American Business Editors and Writers for producing one of the four best business sections in the country, along with the *Boston Globe, Los Angeles Times,* and *Dallas Morning News.* The citation stated in part that *USA Today*'s "personal finance information is an integral part of the package, not something separate and apart. And while it's written in a reader-friendly way, it's never patronizing."

Hillkirk has been in charge of the "Money" section for the last nine years, but he's been with *USA Today* since 1982, when he was called in from Gannett's Rochester paper to help tend to Al Neuharth's newborn. "In those days this place was surreal," he recalls. "Know what I mean? We were supposed to be a national daily, but no one knew who we were. You'd call and they'd say, 'You mean *U.S. News?*' We wondered how long we'd last."

Now, of course, just about everyone knows the paper that made color graphics and brevity the sine qua non of the industry. Attending a news meeting, I see an entire wall of the conference room taken up with front pages from around the country, papers that had hit the streets the day after U.S. and allied forces began bombing Kosovo. At first glance I assume they all are Gannett papers. They aren't. Yet each, with its centered color photo of incendiary action and bold headline, looks like a blood brother of *USA Today.*

Back in his glass cubicle, Hillkirk excitedly ticks off for me recent signs of newfound respect. "Jack Welch at General Electric told us that he finds *USA Today* better than the *Wall Street Journal* for what's really going on in the country. The CEOs of Ford and Chevrolet have lined up to come in for interviews. . . . When Greenspan made his big Fed statement at the end of June, our guy in Chicago was allowed onto the Board of Trade floor—a real coup. And Citigroup CEO John Reed told our reporter that he has to read us because 'all my customers do.'"

Nevertheless, Hillkirk appreciates better than most his staff's limitations. "Look, the *Wall Street Journal* has, what, 250 reporters, all of them covering one thing—business. We have 35 in "Money." So, obviously we have to single out what we can do best, know what I mean? Our strategy is all about focus—to be first and to write it so ordinary people can understand. Whether it's interest rates or personal finance, we tell you what it means to you."

Thus, every Tuesday the section runs the popular "Your Money" column, and each Friday there's a full page of personal-finance features. In between, the staff is continually on the prowl for what Hillkirk calls "one big hit" each month, a major piece that breaks the no-jump norm with alacrity and even roves across multiple pages. The "Money" team is guided by a dictum summarized as BEATMAP:

Business travel
Economics/workplace
Automobiles
Technology
Markets
Ad marketing
Personal finance

Money staffers are issued wallet-size cards emblazoned with the catechismal exhortation, and blowups are taped to walls. The gimmicks are in keeping with the paper's founding philosophy. Says Ray Goldbacher, who edits the personal-finance matter, "From day one there was an emphasis on personal finance, because *USA Today* was intended to be a 'second read' for travelers. Then readers began asking for more news, including the big stories, and we turned our attention to that for a number of years. But in '94, we returned to our roots: back to an emphasis on personal finance. We've found that it's what people really want and need."

Goldbacher, who came to the paper in 1986, assembled what he calls a "talented team" of four and began putting an emphasis on mutual-funds coverage. The market was running at full bore, and people who'd never owned a share of stock were pouring their savings into mutual funds. Many people who understood little or nothing about Wall Street saw them as a safe way to invest. *USA Today* seized the opportunity. "One message we started getting from readers, and it continues today, is that unlike their parents they now have to handle their own money," says Goldbacher. "They find it hard and confusing. They feel there are millions of ways to invest—not just through the bank or a broker—and they welcome our ability to filter tons of information and make it digestible."

Doubtless the *New York Times* desires to perform the same service for its readers. But as the paper continues a decade-long beefing up of its business coverage, it has come around to a distinctly Timesian, big-picture approach to the subject. This is in keeping with the evolving worldview of the paper's executive editor, Joseph Lelyveld, a Pulitzer Prize–winning foreign correspondent before he crossed over into management.

"Throughout the '90s, we've said that the Cold War was over and we wanted to look less at the fate of political regimes," Lelyveld says. "Sure, you look at Angola because it's a horror. But you don't care about it in the same way as you did in the days of the Soviet and Cuban involvement. Every change of regime in Ethiopia or Somalia is no longer major news for our readers. But economic policies around the world mean more than they ever did."

Lelyveld, a career Timesman who ascended to the top job in 1994, focused almost immediately on improving the business report. He hired John Geddes back from the *Wall Street Journal* and made him business editor. At this point the paper's efforts went into mining the realm of personal finance, but in time Lelyveld decided that the emphasis on individual investing had been overdone.

"That's not what readers turn to us for," Lelyveld tells me in his small, pin-neat office. Instead, Lelyveld says, the *Times* is concentrating some of its heaviest fire on a different target: the confluence of global politics and business. The *Times* reporter first assigned to this target, and the one whose name comes up most often among others in this field, is David E. Sanger. "The quintessential modern reporter," Sanger's boss, business editor Glenn Kramon, calls him.

Formerly the paper's Tokyo bureau chief, Sanger has been on the international-business beat in the Washington bureau for the last five years. Over a nostalgic bowl of soba at a popular downtown D.C. lunch spot called Oodles Noodles, Sanger says that while he still misses the more varied life of a foreign correspondent, he has no doubt that he is covering "the most important story in the world. When I left Tokyo and came back to the States, I had to explain to people that what I was covering was the intersection of international news and economics. I don't have to do that anymore. People, certainly in Washington, understand it intuitively now."

One ex-Washingtonian who understands is former treasury secretary Rubin. Sanger, recognizing early on Rubin's keen insights into financial markets, assiduously cultivated the mild-mannered multimillionaire trader. This relationship helped him produce stories on his own beat, as well as on other facets of the Clinton administration, that have earned him accolades from colleagues inside and outside the *Times*. The *Wall Street Journal*'s Alan Murray, in describing the *Times* as the *Journal*'s foremost competitor, gives Sanger the kind of unadorned compliment one journalist most appreciates from another: "He's really good."

While Sanger concurs that the rise of the everyman investor is the basic explanation for the recent torrent of business news, he says globalization runs a close second. He cites the meltdown of the Russian economy, the tanking of the Hong Kong market in October 1997, and the Thailand-led Asian collapse in 1998 as three occasions in which Americans couldn't help but see how they were directly affected by events in once-distant lands. Overnight, it seemed, plumbers, bus drivers, dentists—people who'd never been sure just where Thailand was, who might've supposed the *bhat* was something used to play cricket—suddenly knew all about the international crisis caused by the Thai currency. "This shows that while Americans typically don't care much about foreign news, they do care when they can see the effects on their own lives and, in particular, their pockets," Sanger says.

In order to handle the kind of stories generated by such complex economic developments as those Sanger describes, several news organizations, including the *Times* and the Associated Press, have set up procedures to school new foreign correspondents in the dismal science before they head overseas. AP has written a textbook for its fledgling foreign reporters and has an accountant tutor them in Econ 101. The *Times* assigns them to its business desk for a month. Indeed, while the bulk of the paper's foreign correspondents report to the foreign desk, some overseas-based staffers and stringers report directly to business.

To help fill the business newshole, expanded twice in the last year, Kramon recently hired five reporters to be based in key business centers around the world: London, Moscow, Singapore, Toronto, and Sao Paolo. In addition, editors have instructed the paper's forty or so foreign correspondents already posted to blend their coverage cocktails, traditionally based on politics and culture, with a stiff shot of business and economics. Not surprisingly, the new demands for stepped-up business contributions from correspondents long considered the exclusive property of the foreign desk don't always go down smoothly. Turf struggles arise. In an effort to improve relations between foreign and business, Lelyveld established the position of international business editor, who sits on the foreign desk.

The very intentional effect of all these moves has been to blur the lines between what some reporters still call "regular" news and business news. "We've recognized that every story is a 'business' story," says Kramon.

Want proof? Take the August 29 *Times,* a Sunday, as an arbitrary example. The front page carried a story on how contributions from tobacco companies were embarrassing the Gore and Bush campaigns. On the front of "Sunday Styles" was one piece about New York's "Silicon Alley" developing its own cachet and another on how the beauty business was moving online. The lead of the "Money & Business" section was on how DNA researchers were becoming entrepreneurs, a story that in an earlier day may have landed on the science page. And "Week in Review" led with an earthy piece on one-world fallout—a feature about French farmers who, infuriated by high tariffs imposed on foie gras and other delicacies entering the U.S., were retaliating by staging guerrilla raids against that most ubiquitous symbol of globalization, McDonald's.

WHILE THE MAJOR PAPERS have most of the resources and get most of the attention, a case can be made that the true revolution in the industry's coverage of business is occurring not in New York or Washington but at many of the nation's regional papers. The best of these are combining heightened professionalism with distinctly local perspectives to create some of the most compelling journalism now on view.

Sandra Mims Rowe, the highly regarded editor of Portland's *Oregonian,* articulates this spirit. "I care about it passionately," she says of her paper's business coverage. "Business has everything—power, influence, sex, drama—and our job is to pull back the curtain: That bank merger last week? Who got screwed? Who came out on top? This is what really happened. Business news should be handled as finely crafted drama; it's got substance and great meaning.

"Business should be the backbone of the newspaper," she continues, the edges of her voice only slightly rounded by a soft Virginia drawl. "And what readers think of your business report creates a halo effect: If business leaders and opinion leaders think your business stuff is consuming, then so is the rest of your paper. And now that the definition of business has expanded, you get into things that affect people's lives—everyone's life."

During my visit to Portland in August, the *Oregonian* produced a smart example of what Rowe was talking about. The centerpiece of a Sunday business section was a story by its top investigative reporter, Jeff Manning. It recounted the tale of a shoe designer at Nike who had developed a new, gorgeously hued sneaker, the Air Tuned Max. Brilliantly illustrated with photos and drawings, the story could easily have run in the slick pages of *Sports Illustrated,* yet it had a nice business edge.

Needless to say, global giant Nike, headquartered in a Portland suburb and one of the Northwest's major employers, "is a big deal to us," says business editor Mike Hester. "Here, we talk about the 'Nike footprint' and the 'Nike psyche.'" In other words, the paper values stories that get beneath the company's glossy veneer, as Manning's did. A sports approach to the same story might have focused on the shoe's technical qualities—"feather-light, air-cushioned, reduces shock"—but Manning chose to emphasize how Nike had struck an unusual deal with the financially troubled Venator Group, granting their Foot Locker stores, the largest athletic-shoe chain in the country, exclusive rights to the new design. The result: huge sales for Nike and Venator and unbridled fury from competing retailers.

Not many years ago a story like this, if it had been produced by a business writer at all, most likely would have been a stylistically arid affair. But here was Manning's appealing lead: "Sean McDowell, a young Nike Inc. athletic footwear designer, returned to Beaverton from a Florida vacation in October 1997, his mind chock full of images of white beaches and languorous purple sunsets. Little did he know his tropical daydreams would help revitalize the industry's largest retailer, let alone generate a full-blown political brouhaha among the rest."

In tackling the vagaries of the athletic-shoe market, the writer's prose, while businesslike, still managed to be vivid enough to attract readers who might normally toss the Sunday business section aside. "The shoe's wild success—and its marketing fallout—shows how an elusive combination of cosmetics and technology can still generate intense demand from young sneaker aficionados," he wrote. "It also demonstrates how marketing strategies that seem deliberate and smart when they happen are often the result of internal politics, shifting corporate alliances and just plain luck."

The *Oregonian,* like other top metros (its daily circulation is 356,000), concentrates its resources and abilities on stories that hit close to home. Amanda Bennett, the paper's managing editor, is responsible for introducing a more inviting style into business stories, and redesigning the business pages was her first assignment upon joining the *Oregonian* a year ago. Business is a subject she knows well: She worked at the *Wall Street Journal* for twenty-three years, most recently as its Atlanta bureau chief.

Energetic and determined, Bennett says she quickly found that the best reporters at the paper were on the business staff. At the same time, she saw that they were muffling their talent, having bought into the canard that "you had to be deadly dull if you were going to be taken seriously." Too, there was confusion among the reporters covering the region's high-tech industry. "There was no concept of the page," Bennett says, "and the question out there was, 'Who're we writing for, the business community or civilians?'"

Bennett's response? That it's a nonissue. "You write sophisticated stories in a way to capture both," she says. As for the dullness problem, she launched a campaign that she sums up as "pushing every story to its limit." At an early Monday meeting with the business staff, she singled out Manning's sneaker story as having achieved this goal.

Of course, covering the hometown colossus so tied to your readers' lives and financial well-being is always challenging and often uncomfortable. In the *Oregonian*'s case, it has aggressively reported from Vietnam and Indonesia on allegations that Nike was exploiting workers making sneakers, overworking and underpaying them. In 1992, well before the issue came to national prominence, the paper dispatched to Southeast Asia a business reporter who wrote an overwhelmingly negative piece. According to Hester, Nike founder Phil Knight—intriguingly, the son of the former publisher of the *Oregon Journal,* since subsumed into the Newhouse-owned *Oregonian*—"hated" the story and "retreated into a deep hole" as far as future contacts with the paper were concerned.

Two years ago, Jeff Manning returned to the region and produced what Hester termed a "far better-balanced piece." This story related how life had improved for most Nike workers; how most of the cultural clash was between the workers and their supervisors, who were Korean; and how Americans, given their elevated standard of living, couldn't comprehend the willingness of people in some countries to work under conditions that simply would not be acceptable here. Though this wasn't the paper's motivation, the piece had a salutary effect on the *Oregonian*'s relations with Nike. (And having spent thirty years covering Asia myself, I can add that Manning's nuanced report also had the benefit of being true.)

After the news meeting, Bennett and I have coffee in a shady park near the paper, buff joggers doing their thing on a lovely day. "It'd be hard for any newsroom to be up to the standards of the *Journal*," she says. "But when I began here I found that there was needless anxiety over bifurcating the audience. So I had to convince [the staff] that all you need to do is look at the quality of the story. If the story is sophisticated, compelling, and interesting enough, you'll have no problem with who's going to read it. Everyone will."

Rowe concurs. A primary reason for hiring Bennett, the editor says, was to finish a job Rowe began back in 1993 when she arrived at the *Oregonian* with a writ to improve a decidedly underachieving paper. Instinctively, she turned first to the business desk. What she discovered was discouraging:

reporters and editors who lacked commitment and interest in their work and who, in turn, doubted management's commitment to them. Some, she quickly recognized, knew little or nothing about business, nor cared to know. They were moved to other beats. "In business reporting," Rowe says, "if you can't write with authority, you're lost."

Rowe says her other great news passion is explanatory journalism; no surprise, given that this year the *Oregonian* won its first Pulitzer in four decades—for explanatory journalism. Business and explanation were fused beautifully in the award-winning series entitled "The French Fry Connection." The series was produced by Richard Read, who bears the heady title of international business writer. Employing as his vehicle the humble french fry, Read was able to tie the currency implosion in Asia to everyday lives back across the Pacific. His editors explained the unorthodox series to readers with this note: "Anyone can relate to a french fry, but not everyone can stomach detailed explanations of Asia's financial crisis, even when the fallout claims lives, jobs and businesses. We decided to trace one batch of fries back to its Pacific Northwest potato patch and then to follow it to the Far East. The point was to explain Asia's economic meltdown and its effects on the Northwest, the nation and the world. We never imagined the range of people and cultures we would encounter."

Read, who already had extensive experience reporting from Japan and Southeast Asia, and staff photographer Kathryn Scott Osler tracked the potatoes, twenty tons worth, step by step—from a technologically advanced farm in neighboring Washington run by members of the Hutterite sect, to a processing plant which prepared them for McDonald's outlets in Indonesia, to a ship sailing out of Tacoma, to Hong Kong, and from there to Singapore. They followed the fries to Jakarta, hitting town just in time to cover the economy-sparked riots that resulted in the overthrow of President Suharto. Then it was back to Portland, where people were by now feeling the crunch from Asian consumers cutting back on restaurant meals.

What could have been a mere curiosity was transformed into a tour de force that revealed eye-opening glimpses into the $286 million potato-exporting industry: the Amish-like Hutterites who, surprisingly, employ some of the world's most advanced agricultural techniques to produce bumper crops; religious sensitivities among Muslim Indonesians about prepared foods imported from the United States; charges of American cultural imperialism, with fast food high on the list; the disastrous effects of sudden economic reversal on poor Indonesian children; and, finally, how the inability of one Indonesian to pay for a Big Mac and fries ripples all the way back to the wallets of prosperous Portlanders. The region, Read wrote climactically, "hangs in the balance, caught between the resilient U.S. economy and teetering Asian countries."

IN A JULY 1999 report on business coverage, the Freedom Forum's Media Studies Center said that the press's daunting task really boils down to this: Cover a far more complicated universe and make it intelligible to far more people than ever before. The *Oregonian*'s french-fry opus was an example of a story that worked. For one that didn't, stunningly, the Media Studies Center report cited AP's coverage of the 1929 stock-market crash. Here was the lead from the wire's main story that fateful October 29: "Huge barriers of buying orders, hastily erected by powerful financial interests, finally checked today the most frantic stampede of selling yet experienced by the securities markets, which threatened at times to bring about an utter collapse of prices." Jim Kennedy, a former AP business editor, observed that almost no one other than a market professional could have made heads or tails of that.

But in the market meltdown of October 1987, AP assembled all the data its reporters could put their hands on. Interpretation, including a glossary of market terms and charts of the Dow Jones average over a period of years, made the story comprehensible to almost any reader. Kennedy, who now runs AP's multimedia operations, says he remembers too vividly the knots in his stomach back then, wondering whether his troops were up to making sense of the crash. But they got the story out and onto the front pages of thousands of papers around the world. And, says Kennedy, they've never looked back. "It was a truly defining moment. In essence, the story—the business story—has been on the front page ever since."

While the business-news phenomenon has been developing for several decades now, it was the exponential rise in stock investing beginning in 1989 that truly revolutionized business coverage, packing on new muscle and integrating it as never before in the total news package. On the eve of the 1929 crash, only a handful of Americans were investors. Anyone else with a little something left over at the end of the week salted it away in a savings account. In 1965, investors numbered just 10 percent of the U.S. public; most Americans were still savers. In schools, banks handed out imitation passbooks with little slots in which we kids stuck our nickels and dimes; my mother deposited five dollars a week in a Christmas Club account. Today, conventional saving is passé; half the entire population invests.

And how do they follow their money? On the business agate pages. Marvels Philadelphia's Hank Klibanoff, "Among baby boomers, there's as much excitement in the stock tables as there is in sports agate."

Indeed, one of the more arcane but telling indicators of business coverage in recent years is what has happened to the stock tables, mutual-fund listings, and related financial data, all printed in page after page of eye-straining agate.

Carl Stepp's content survey found that, in the 1960s, the ten regional papers he tracked had published on average four news columns' worth of business agate, or two-thirds of a page. Now they publish fifteen columns, or two-and-a-half pages. *USA Today* prints five pages or more of the stuff daily, the *New York Times* ten.

The power of business agate might be intuited from the *Times*, where a few years ago editors decided to beef up the Saturday business report, which they considered thin compared to the rest of the week. Beyond adding extra space for stories, they enhanced the section's business agate and augmented it with material that had been running on Sundays, such as commodities and metals reports. One motivation was the fact that since the *Wall Street Journal* and *USA Today* don't publish on Saturdays, an unusually thorough agate report might appeal to readers around the nation. For whatever reasons, Saturday became the fastest-growing day of the week for the *Times*; since 1990 sales of that day's paper outside its greater New York circulation zone have risen four times faster than the weekday edition.

At the *Washington Post*, David Ignatius, who had been recruited from the Journal, took over as assistant managing editor for business in 1993. At the time the paper had cut back severely on agate, deeming it "a waste for a paper like the *Washington Post*." But Ignatius determined that this was "a terrible mistake," because, he says, the tables "are essential to the mission." He succeeded in restoring them, with some tailoring for the Washington audience. Today the paper publishes more than five pages of comprehensive listings daily.

But the jump in agate is most telling at small and medium-sized papers, many of which once ran either no listings at all or barebones versions —say twenty-five or fifty stocks of local interest. Overall, according to AP, which provides the listings, usage has nearly doubled in a decade.

"We've never had more papers run stock agate in our history—over nine hundred, compared with five hundred [a decade] ago," said AP business editor Randy Picht. That represents nearly two-thirds of all the daily papers in the country. "That flies in the face of all conventional wisdom because the tables have been considered problematic ever since the newsprint crisis [of the mid-1990s]. But advertisers love 'em; they plant their ads in the middle of the tables, and so editors keep asking for them."

About a third of the client papers print an abbreviated setup daily—one-third or one-half page, which amount to 800 to 1,200 stocks in the no-frills format—and about half of these expand to a multipage listing on the weekend. The other six hundred papers run one or more pages every day, Picht says.

Not surprisingly, he says, mutual funds are especially popular, utilized in some fashion by 75 percent of the overall nine hundred user papers.

Contributing to the agate boom is the computer technology that enables AP to customize tables for each paper, whether its preference is for long or short lists, focused or broad. This is particularly true at smaller papers, which must make the most judicious use of limited space. AP helps them assemble the tables of their choice, often guided by where they want the ads placed, and from then on it's a simple matter of downloading the data with a few mouse clicks.

"What really lies at the heart of this," says Picht, "is that readers want the data. You have readers calling up their local paper and asking for 'that fund that we have in our 401K down at the plant.' The editor reacts to that. And we react to the editor."

There are days, of course, when what the editor really wants is a life preserver, because you can easily be pulled down in this sea of tiny type. There are so many stocks on the major exchanges that only the *Journal* and the *Times* print them all (*Investor's Business Daily* comes close), and new companies turn up constantly. Editors who don't get the extra space to accommodate burgeoning tables must either cannibalize their main news-hole or, more often, run listings that only include the most active stocks. That in turn irks readers, who, increasingly sophisticated about stocks, expect to find even marginal companies in their daily paper.

While AP may be pleased with its leadership in agate, neither Picht nor his staffers hedge about having lost ground to brash competitors in some broader editorial areas. Reuters, Bridge News (formerly Knight Ridder's financial service), and, most of all, Bloomberg News are bones lodged in the throat of the grande dame of Rockefeller Center. "The fact is that Bloomberg is so comprehensive that they've hurt us," Picht says. "They supply stuff that we just don't offer, and business editors feel they need Bloomberg, even to help them cover local news."

Bloomberg, which only a few years ago was desperately giving its service away in exchange for usage, has made itself indispensable at business desks around the country. A paper in Colorado, for example, uses Bloomberg's mining report to put its own local stories in context; a paper in Indiana turns to the agency for its daily "steel briefs." Editors report that Bloomberg turns up stories in their backyards that they themselves hadn't heard about.

Nevertheless, no matter what service it derives from, at bottom it's just data and information; individual papers and editors still have to make sense of it for readers or lose them to more responsive competitors—be they other papers or, more likely, the up-to-the-minute TV business programs and up-to-the-nanosecond online sites. Nearly all the editors I spoke with consider it their primary job to sift through this incredible cache of material, filter it, interpret and explain it; in essence, paint the big picture for harried readers.

ACCELERATING IN HIS red Porsche roadster through a steeply climbing curve, Rich Oppel is taking me for a spin around Austin and up into the West Texas Hill Country, putting the throaty machine through its paces with measured nonchalance. Suntanned and white-haired, Oppel acquired the car a few years back to mark his simultaneous arrival at midlife and a new life, as editor of the *American-Statesman.* He wheels into the parking lot of a casual chic techie hangout, pulling his sporty little car to a stop between two absurdly stretched limos, one black and one white. Inside, our dinner entrees arrive in volcano-like peaks, a style a West Coast friend later informs me is known as "tall food." This, of course, is yesterday's news in Silicon Valley.

Like other emerging high-tech hubs, such as those found around Boston and in the Northern Virginia suburbs of Washington, Austin is echoing to the shot first fired a generation ago in California's Silicon Valley. As recently as the mid-1980s, Austin was still best known for sheltering the state capital, the University of Texas, and a melange of aging activists, causists, dropouts, musicians, and other social border-dwellers. Now suddenly it's hot—103 this particular afternoon—but we're talking business climate here.

The Austin revolution began fifteen years ago when Michael Dell started up the eponymous computer company now known around the world for its market-beating low prices. Not yet out of his teens at the time, Dell was treading in the footsteps of those who had emerged from the middle-class garages around San Jose. And today, like those other members of a super-elite fraternity, Dell lives in the requisite $21 million, stadium-scale mansion in the dramatic, stone-strewn hills above the city.

Because of Dell and the corporations and entrepreneurs who flocked here in his wake, Austin is no longer a funky, eccentric burg but one of the world's tech capitals—a veritable "technopolis," to borrow a phrase from Oppel's *American-Statesman*. In fact, "Technopolis" is the name the paper has given its new weekly section devoted to business, high tech, and lifestyle. Previewing the section for me—it wouldn't launch until October—Oppel promises it will "look at the culture of technology. . . . How technology is changing people's lives in this place, and making Austin a 'technopolis,' a place as unique as this section's going to be."

Oppel is ex–Marine Corps, ex–AP and ex–Knight Ridder. He left a job running that chain's Washington bureau to edit the Cox-owned Austin paper, which has a daily circulation of 190,000. Part of the appeal, he admits, was the fact that his son was then based in Austin for the *Dallas Morning News,* covering high tech. At age thirty, Richard A. Oppel Jr. left Texas for New York and the *Times.* "The quickest and surest way for a young reporter to make it these days is through business," says the proud father.

Oppel comes by the enthusiasm honestly. "It's a special place at a special time," he tells me, meaning both the city and the paper. "There's high growth, an interesting collision of very different people—'60s slackers and go-go entrepreneurs—a liberal Southern city, a place where good writers want to live. So we can attract them, as well as mature editors. We're growing both in circulation and ads. About the only downside is that it's getting expensive to live here."

Oppel's managing editor, Kathy Warbelow, represents some of the new blood infusing Austin. Until 1996 she was at the *Detroit Free Press.* Having left behind a rusty community built on iron and steel for one being built on silicon, Warbelow is a true believer. Back in Detroit, she says, "the core city is broken. Here the story is all about possibilities, and the newspaper can play a significant role in that."

The "Technopolis" section was born of that brio. Oppel had invited a task force of staffers to come up with ideas for a new way to cover the specifics of Austin-area business life. "We quickly moved away from gadgets and gimmicks and focused on how technology affects life—society, community, individual attitudes, all of that and more," he says. "The closest sister we found was the weekend section of the Friday *Wall Street Journal,* which talks to readers about how they live."

"Technopolis" is overseen by assistant managing editor Melissa Segrist and edited by Gretchen Heber. The section, which debuted at a prosperous twenty-four broadsheet pages, is staffed by a business reporter who specializes in personal technology, a general features writer, a designer, a photographer, a graphics artist, a part-time copy editor, and a part-time clerk. "This is the first time in quite a few years that we've had this kind of growth around here," says Segrist.

With the region's economic expansion, the paper's circulation has been ticking up nicely at about 1 or 2 percent a year. But a readership analysis shows that penetration is low in the community's Hispanic precincts. Since advertisers here pitch to the upscale end and reporters tend to worry about the deprived, staff meetings have seen questions about whether "Technopolis" will ignore the lower socioeconomic classes while catering to the wealthy. "These are, obviously, highly legitimate concerns," Oppel responds. "But we mustn't disparage the high end, because that's the end that makes everything possible. Bluntly, yes, there is an emphasis on the high end, but that strengthens our ability to do better journalism."

While Oppel expresses only praise for the editorial freedom he receives from Cox, it's clear from this and other of his comments that he is under pressure to raise ad revenues. "An editor's shrewdness about where to take a newspaper provides the way for that newspaper to grow in the next ten years," he says. "We've got to figure out ways to build alliances with advertisers and circulation. But we don't prostitute ourselves."

The concerns of Austin's staff are of a piece with other touchy areas arising from the business bonanza. Yes, the boom has created new opportunities for revenue generation, promotion, and corporate partnerships, but what is a paper's rightful role? When a newspaper gets too cozy with the businesses it covers, the potential for conflicts can rise dramatically. Take newspapers' sponsorship of investment conferences, something popularized by the *Los Angeles Times* and spreading nationwide. These can be lucrative—the papers typically sell sponsorships to companies in exchange for ads and exhibit space—but they are rife with potential pitfalls.

In October 1999, for instance, the *Philadelphia Inquirer* held its second such conference, drawing upwards of 4,500 participants. At other papers, editors have told me privately they're not sure enough steps are being taken to ensure journalistic probity where these programs are concerned. But in Philadelphia, business editor Hank Klibanoff says he has taken pains to construct "high brick walls" to separate his journalists from the paper's advertising staff, which organizes and promotes the affairs. "We [journalists], not the ad people, provide the content ideas," he says. "And even the invitations aren't handled by the ad people; they're issued by a third party, Morningstar."

Despite the precautions, Klibanoff acknowledges being nagged by a sense of "mushiness" about the fact that corporate sponsorships of the conferences have enabled the *Inquirer* to launch a Tuesday investment section. Although he praises the section as being "smart, sophisticated, yet not above the eye level of the average reader," he admits that it wouldn't exist without "our knowing that companies out there would advertise in it."

The ongoing argument between editorial staff and ad sellers is as old as newspapers, and it has never been resolved to both sides' satisfaction. But it has become more acute, especially in the wake of the technology boom, as business sections metamorphosed into significant revenue earners. Business pages are particularly attractive draws for certain types of ads. One is the so-called tombstones, often full-page announcements placed to herald the offering of new securities. These ads—understated, heavy on white space, with just a few lines of names and numbers plus a corporate logo—represent leading profit-earners in the business pages. Another strong category is advertising for mutual funds. A third and fast-emerging sector is the dot-com ads for Internet-related companies.

And then there are the "island" ads, for broker services or banks, say, which float in a sea of agate stock tables. Island ads were highly controversial when the newspaper industry advocated their adoption in the mid-1980s, many editors considering them an unprecedented breach of news content. To this day such major papers as the *Journal, Times, Post,* and *Inquirer,* among others, still won't run them. But they are in the minority, and you scarcely hear the practice even debated anymore. Island ads are now so standard that they appear in countless other top papers, among them the *Atlanta Journal and Constitution, Baltimore Sun, Denver Post, Miami Herald,* and *St. Louis Post-Dispatch.*

Like other editors I talked with about this issue, Oppel happily acknowledges the earnings potential of the fledgling "Technopolis" section, but emphasizes the paper's insistence on editorial integrity. "Publishers stand accused of not using their papers as a public trust, while editors are guilty of not recognizing them as businesses—which they've always been," Oppel says. True enough, and as you drive about a community like Austin, where development hits you like the heat, squarely between the eyes, you want to applaud a paper that recognizes and capitalizes on the phenomenon. At the same time you hope its writers and editors are up for what is surely the greater challenge: Caring about, and covering, not just those who are enjoying this boomtime ride, but those who are left behind.

IN CRANKING UP "Technopolis," the *American-Statesman* turned for some pointers, not surprisingly, to the *San Jose Mercury News.* Once the *Merc* was a sleepy daily in an even sleepier town thought to lie somewhere south of San Francisco and known primarily for apricots and prunes. Today San Jose is the unofficial capital of Silicon Valley, itself the unofficial capital of the digital universe. And the *Mercury News,* its unofficial voice, tells the story of the place, the products, and the people in ways that excite the envy of countless other news organizations.

Two decades ago the *Merc* pretty much had to invent high-tech coverage, since at the time practically no one in daily journalism knew much about the burgeoning industry. Columnist Jim Mitchell recalls that when he joined the paper in 1977, the business department had a staff of three. Now it has forty, not counting dozens of other employees at *Mercury Center,* the paper's online extension that itself specializes in the tech realm. "We were very weak," Mitchell says. "Today, we're the best in covering electronics—and probably all technology—as we certainly ought to be."

Executive editor David Yarnold, who succeeded Jerry Ceppos to the top job in May 1999, says that tech coverage has come to distinguish and differentiate the *Mercury News* brand. Certainly there's little question that the paper and its owner, Knight Ridder—which in 1998 moved its corporate headquarters from Miami to San Jose, a clear sign of where it believes power lies—will continue to grow the business report. "It's one of the most important stories in the world and it's happening right here," says Yarnold, pointing out that two years ago Silicon Valley led the United States in exports, and last year ranked second.

More than that, the paper has excelled at doing precisely what Austin says it wants to do, which is go beyond conventional news reporting to convey the feel and pulse of this dynamic place, in every venue of the paper. Considering how thoroughly the *Merc* has achieved this integration, it's hard to imagine how close it apparently came to missing out on its own story.

Ceppos, my old boss and now Knight Ridder's vice president for news, recounts this from the deck of his home, perched amid disappearing wineries in the Los Gatos hills. By 1995, he says, the paper was covering high tech, of course, but more or less in the rote way that it might handle education or the courts. It had become complacent, and just maybe a little myopic: The high-tech story was happening at such close proximity that the *Merc* wasn't seeing the broader ramifications. Then outsiders began slipping into the paper's backyard, setting off alarm bells. In February 1996, for instance, *Time* published a cover story on Marc Andreessen, the twenty-four-year-old programming wizard behind Netscape. Seeing it, Ceppos says he felt violated. A week afterward, he summoned the news staff to a slide-illustrated speech in which he told them that they "were on the verge of missing . . . the full story of the people who make Silicon Valley unlike anywhere else on Earth."

He credits former assistant managing editor Jonathan Krim, who during sixteen years with the paper edited both its Pulitzer Prize winners, with "drawing the map" that guided the *Mercury News* through the resulting period of growth and improvement in its business coverage. That plan focused heavily on what Ceppos has called "the modern-day Medicis" of the valley. As a result of the changes, the paper emerged "ahead of the curve, but only by a hair, and just managed to avoid having our lunch eaten," says Ceppos, merrily mixing metaphors.

Simultaneously, the paper was building its Internet presence. *Mercury Center* debuted in 1992, and with its spinoff sites it has grown right along with the Web even as it has covered that growth. Today Knight Ridder is moving aggressively to parlay its many newspaper Web sites—already linked in the RealCities network—into portals, which are megasites that provide a variety of services to users and steer them to myriad other news and commercial links. At the same time, the company is exploiting the *Merc*'s unique position and expertise in a bid to become the authoritative address for high-tech information online as well as in print. Hence the advent of Siliconvalley.com and other tech-oriented sites.

In some ways the *Mercury News* may have succeeded too well. The paper has become a spawning ground for high-tech reporters who, once they're trained and polished, are snapped up by the *Times,* the *Journal, Fortune,* and, in the newest wave, by Web sites like TheStreet.com. One such notable is Adam Lashinsky. For a reported $250,000 salary plus options, the young reporter evidently found it easy to walk away from the rambling, warehouse-like building on Ridder Park Drive to write a Silicon Valley column for TheStreet.com.

Indeed, Lashinsky's case raises the specter of money—big money—which is unavoidable in Silicon Valley and which poses increasing problems for the paper in a host of ways.

First and foremost is the high cost of living, the flip side of the Silicon Valley dream. Prunes have pretty much disappeared from the landscape, and the orchards that once flourished across the flat countryside have been seeded with college campus–like complexes housing hardware, software, and everything-in-between-ware companies. Not far from the work sites as the crow flies, but an hour or more as a BMW negotiates the ever more sclerotic "freeways," nothing-special houses cost a million dollars and more.

Real estate has breached these stratospheric heights because of the overabundance of new wealth. At the same time, the San Jose area is heavily populated by recent arrivals from Asia and Latin America. Some are finan-cially well off; most are not. How, the Austin people were curious to know, does the *Mercury News* tell their story while covering the broader setting of a cultural and economic flowering that Ceppos has likened to Renaissance Florence?

I ask Evelyn Richards, a prize-winning business reporter with whom I'd worked on several stories when she was covering technology from San Jose and I was based in Tokyo. As we chat alongside her paper-heaped com-puter terminal, she and some other writers are just winding up a yearlong project on what she half-jokingly refers to as "the rich, the super-rich, and the obscenely rich—meaning anyone with $8 billion and a sixty-thousand-square-foot home." But truth is, tales of such excesses no longer drop jaws around here. So Richards and her colleagues are using the area's stunning wealth as a vehicle for relating the largely ignored lives of those who are not only left out but, ironically, suffer even more because of the wealth sur-rounding them. "Not everyone shares in the high income," she explains, "but everyone shares in the high costs."

That includes newspaper staffers—who, while they live substantially better than many others in Silicon Valley, increasingly must look further and further afield for houses they can afford. Still, established writers on the business staff typically earn $10,000 or so more than their colleagues on other beats, as is the case at many other papers, because reporters who understand the intricacies of business—particularly specialists—are quite hard to come by. And to attract them to expensive spots like San Jose requires some sweetening of the pot.

Even so, no amount the *Merc* or any other paper might summon can begin to compete with what business journalists can snag if they make the leap from print-on-paper to print-on-glass. Skilled reporters who have gone to TheStreet.com, for instance, not only are paid salaries well beyond $100,000 ($70,000 for beginners), but they're eligible for options in the site's stock, potentially worth millions. The *New York Times,* which owns 15 percent of TheStreet.com, even now is confronting a management problem in seeing this kind of remuneration continue while its own staffers receive much less.

The big money and fast fortunes commonplace out here create other problems, too. Consider the well-chewed case of Chris Nolan, which for months has fueled an online debate about what constitutes journalistic ethics in the Internet age. Over the summer the *Merc* exiled the former tech-biz-buzz columnist after the *Wall Street Journal* reported how she had profited $9,000 when a local company went public. Nolan had purchased shares in an online automobile-supply outfit at the urging of the company's CEO. Nolan maintained that the CEO was an old friend and that she didn't cover the company; the *Merc* contended he could be considered a source and that the transaction violated journalistic ethics. Nolan quit the paper after being stripped of her column.

The Web has been rife with arguments, pro and con, about Nolan's case. They take up not only the fuzzy particulars of her case—e.g., did asking her boss about the purchase constitute adequate clearance?—but its broader implications. Is it time, some wonder, for the industry to revisit such longstanding commandments as "a reporter shall not invest in a company he covers"? Can today's business journalists be expected to be monklike in their investing when they have the brains and opportunity to better themselves and their families? And isn't what's good for the goose good for the gander? After all, one reason Knight Ridder relocated to San Jose was to be closer to the tech action, and the company has been a serious investor in a variety of startups.

In a day when celebrity journalists can exceed their base salaries with lectures and TV appearances, business reporters too are encountering ways of making more money. As Nolan told the *Journal,* "We don't take vows of poverty and chastity when we go into the newspaper business." And as Yarnold unhappily conceded in an explanation to readers, "It's only human for a journalist covering technology to be tempted by the vast wealth in this valley, and that's an argument for ongoing and clear discussion about what's permissible and what's not."

Meantime, the *Mercury* has its ethics policy under review with an eye toward updating it. The paper hopes to issue these new guidelines by early next year.

I T'S NOT THE *Mercury News'* job to peddle new IPOs, of course, any more than it's the *American-Statesman's* job to help sell Dell computers. But a lifelong newspaperman can't help but derive some perverse pleasure in the fact that, at a time when people are questioning the relevance of ink on paper, the business pages, at least, are clearly packing a wallop.

I saw that firsthand back in Portland. The day after Jeff Manning's piece about the new Nike sneaker appeared in the *Oregonian,* I dropped into the Nike showroom in downtown Portland to get a peek at the purplish/pinkish/yellowish Air Tuned Max and see what all the fuss was about. The showroom, really a cross between a museum and a shrine honoring the sneaker deities, occupies a prominent block near the core of Portland's crunchy-clean restored downtown. "Read that article in the paper?" asks the clerk, in his shorts-and-T-shirt uniform. I nod. "You're probably the fiftieth person to come in today looking for those shoes," he says. "We don't have a single pair left."

I smiled. Even Silent Cal might crack a smile. The business of America, indeed.

*   *   *

Follow the Ball

YES, SPORTS FANS, everything really is bigger in Texas, including the bait a newspaper will dangle in front of a prize catch. Fully a year after top sports columnist Randy Galloway bolted the *Dallas Morning News* in 1998 for the competing *Fort Worth Star-Telegram,* I found envious and incredulous staffers in both newsrooms still buzzing about the affair. Galloway, for thirty-two years a magnet for sports readers in the two-city area known as the Metroplex, had been the highest-paid writer at the Dallas paper, says *Morning News* executive sports editor Dave Smith, earning "well into six figures." But the rival *Star-Telegram* apparently landed him with a Texas-sized raise. Published accounts put his current salary somewhere between $350,000 and $500,000. Beyond that, the popular Galloway enjoys lucrative broadcast tie-ins, just as he did at the *Morning News.* When I ask Fort Worth's executive editor, Jim Witt, about these reports, he teasingly replies, "The published figures I've read have not been accurate— which you can take to mean that he's being paid more . . . or less."

Either way, prices sure have gone up in the Toy Department.

For writers who have a special knack with words, a love of games, and a willingness to mix it up with equally fanatical fans, the biggest bucks in newspapers today are in sports reporting. In 1996, *Cincinnati Enquirer* sports columnist Tim Sullivan observed in the *American Journalism Review* that the staggering salaries athletes now command were driving a wedge between players and the writers who cover them. "You can't say to a guy making $3 million a year, 'Hey, can I buy you a beer?' It would just seem ridiculous," Sullivan said. But the day of the millionaire sports columnist— a journalist who can go mano a mano (well, financially speaking) with the player he's writing about—may be approaching, if it isn't here already.

The high cost of buying marquee sportswriters like Randy Galloway is just another sign that sports, like business, has become one of the hottest, most competitive, and sometimes even contentious fields in newspapering. Beyond the salary budgets, you can see it in the sheer increase in volume that virtually all U.S. papers are giving over to sports coverage. According to a Project on the State of the American Newspaper analysis of ten top regional papers, the percentage of total newshole devoted to sports jumped from 16 to 21 percent in the past generation. And since overall editorial space doubled in that period, sports' increase in real terms is even more dramatic. Sports agate alone has risen from an average of two columns to two pages. And in sports-crazy markets like the Metroplex, the space devoted to sports today is nothing short of cavernous.

Clearly, the sports department has come a long way from being a haven for a newsroom's cutups and Peter Pans.

Unlike the concurrent explosion in business news, which is fairly easy to grasp as a dollars-and-cents phenomenon, the reasons for the growing appetite for sports are more ambiguous. Ask around and you'll get a lot of valid explanations—that sports have become big business, that franchises are more iconic of their communities than ever, that these ball-yard entertainments are among the few things that bind increasingly transient populations. Then there's television, and the "ESPN-ization" of the nation. (In fact, ESPN's various TV, radio, and magazine outlets regularly feature some of the best—and best-paid—newspaper sportswriters, such as Mike Lupica of the *New York Daily News,* Mitch Albom of the *Detroit Free Press,* Bob Ryan of the *Boston Globe,* and Tony Kornheiser of the *Washington Post.*)

Dave Smith is a legendary sports editor, having emigrated to Dallas two decades ago from the *Globe,* itself a sports powerhouse, by way of the late *Washington Star.* While in Dallas I asked him to take a stab at an explanation. "It's an escape, and it can be a healthy escape," he tries for starters, figuratively scratching his head. Then: "The more troubled the times, the more people attend sports events. Well, yeah, these aren't troubled times, but we have a lot more time and money to spend, and sports is the outlet." And finally: "A large percentage of men will always be little boys."

Well, yes, but what about the fact that girls are on board too—as athletes and, increasingly, as readers (and writers) of the sports section? The popularity of the World Cup–winning U.S. women's soccer team and the WNBA attest to the fact that our fascination with sports has definitely crossed the gender line.

We'll just say that, like business, sports is a genuine cultural phenomenon. And regardless what is fueling it, America's newspapers are happily riding the boom—in different ways in different cities, and for very different reasons.

R ANDY GALLOWAY'S upper lip is swept by a graying, Texas Ranger–style (we're talking lawmen here, not baseball players) brush. Still fun-loving as he approaches sixty, Galloway has about him the smoky air of a good ol' boy, a persona that goes down well around here with readers and journalists alike. It's hard to overestimate the shock of his defection, so identified was the columnist with the Morning News. "Even Randy Galloway's 81-year-old mother, herself a lifelong journalism veteran, couldn't believe it when he told her the news," wrote the weekly Dallas Observer.

Witt, pleasure shining in his eyes, recalls ushering Galloway around the Fort Worth newsroom on his first day. "He pumped everyone up. When I introduced him around, it was like meeting a big rock star."

Still, charisma per se isn't why he's worth the kind of money Fort Worth is paying him. Galloway is the biggest shot yet fired in the battle between the *Star-Telegram* and the *Morning News,* an entertaining scrap that is largely and fittingly being waged on the field of sports. He's the kind of talent that pulls both readers and advertisers. Says Witt, still enjoying himself, "To steal their number-one asset was a big thing. And it was fun. It says something about our commitment to do what we have to."

"Is Randy Galloway God's gift to sports columnists?" asks Gary Hardee, a *Star-Telegram* editor instrumental in attracting the writer. "No. But in an age when every media outlet is trying to bring attention to itself, Randy Galloway is a lightning rod. If a reader has only fifteen minutes a day, why, he'll turn to Galloway. He says something outrageous and people love it. You could spend hundreds of thousands more and still not get what he brings you. Like a fishing buddy of mine told me, 'When you got Galloway, you became legitimate.'"

While sports coverage has taken off all over the country, the Dallas–Fort Worth arena is in a class by itself. The newspaper sports war here is especially ferocious, the fans especially voracious. Texans' well-documented obsession with sports runs from the pro and college levels down to junior high. If one paper doesn't satisfy their near-insatiable craving for more and better sports stories, photos, columns, and stats, they're tempted to look elsewhere. So the *Morning News* and the *Star-Telegram* go to great lengths to win sports fans. When Rangers pitching star Nolan Ryan was inducted into baseball's Hall of Fame in July, both papers put out fat commemorative sections. Fort Worth commissioned high-priced graphics artist Robert Silvers to create a photomontage of Ryan for its cover, and the special section was printed on heavy stock. Dallas went to similar extremes.

To truly grasp the role of sports in this state, however, you have to look at the high schools and understand that Texans never seem to break their links to them, especially where football is concerned. "I'm forty-four," says Hardee, a native who left San Antonio for the Metroplex twenty years ago, "and I still look at the paper every Saturday morning to see how my high school and my wife's high school did [in football] the evening before. I'm already going to games at the high school my son will go to when he gets old enough."

Weigh these numbers: The *Star-Telegram,* with a circulation of 250,000 on weekdays and 350,000 on Sundays, fields a full-time sports staff of ninety. And of that impressive figure, fully one-third is devoted to high school sports. The *Morning News,* with a circulation more than double its competitor, maintains a similarly sized sports staff. Both papers run in the range of 120 to 125 columns—more than twenty open pages—of sports coverage on Sundays, and roughly half that daily. Declares Jim Witt, as though awed by his own contemplation, "That's incredible!"

The competition is particularly fierce in the epicenter of the Metroplex newspaper war: Arlington and surrounding Tarrant County. Here the *Star-Telegram* assigns a full-time reporter to each of the area's thirteen high schools. The paper publishes, in addition to its regular daily sports pages, a daily eight-page section on prep sports. At the start of football season, both the *Star-Telegram* and *Morning News* put out one-hundred-plus-page special sections. "There's nothing like it anywhere in the country," says Witt, "except Dallas."

With that depth of coverage, parents of Arlington-area jocks may expect to find something written about their kids in at least one of the papers at some point in the season, even if they've never gotten off the bench. And that, say editors, makes a huge difference. "If your kid's team wins on a Friday night, even if you get home delivery, I guarantee you'll be down at the corner box Saturday morning, scooping up extra copies to send to the grandparents," says Hardee, who oversees the *Star-Telegram* edition zoned for Arlington.

Adds Witt with unintended drama, "Sports is king here. So this is where we fight the war."

I met with Witt and Hardee in the sun-baked single-story building the paper acquired in 1996, when it more than doubled its editorial staff in Arlington to seventy-five (and boosted its marketing, advertising, and business ranks) in response to the Dallas paper launching the *Arlington Morning News.* Now it houses the *Arlington Star-Telegram,* essentially the Fort Worth paper with its own replated front page and banner and zoned editorial. "After the [Dallas] *Times Herald* collapsed, we decided that we just couldn't lose Arlington to the *Morning News,*" says Hardee. "Our circulation here is fifty thousand daily, seventy thousand Sunday. A paper of this size in the boonies somewhere might have a sports staff of four or five. While school is in session, we have twenty-two staff people, including a separate editor, devoted to covering the local schools."

Hardee, Witt, and others I spoke with in Fort Worth say they, as well as the paper's owner, Knight Ridder, consider the money being spent on Galloway, high school coverage, and other sports initiatives a sound investment. For validation, they point out that this year's sports section was cited as one of the ten best in the country. While Dallas regularly wins this accolade from the Associated Press Sports Editors, it was a first for the *Star-Telegram.*

The *Star-Telegram* people make no bones about the size of the battle against the respected and influential *Morning News.* Over a quick lunch in a downtown Fort Worth pizzeria, deputy sports editor Mitch Krugel marvels at what he called "Dave Smith's incredible sports machine."

But over in Dallas, *Morning News* executives barely deign to concede the existence of a serious rival. When I raise the subject of "your fierce competition with Fort Worth over sports coverage" with Bob Mong, the Dallas paper's president and general manager, he replies with the equivalent of letting the air out of the ball. "Sports has a strong readership, but it's not number one," says Mong, who came up on the editorial side of the *Morning News.* "It's part of a larger package—different people pick up the paper for different reasons." He goes on to praise his paper's Mexico coverage ("more than anyone else"), its regional section ("larger than anyone else"), and its increases in foreign, science, and technology news. "The goal is always a complete newspaper, and we've become more sophisticated in everything we do," Mong explains. "We don't rely on one section to drive the paper."

Still, he acknowledges that when the Dallas Cowboys win, there's a ten-thousand-paper jump in Monday morning's circulation.

And sports editor Dave Smith says his staff's travel budget "is as much as all the other departments combined."

IN LATE 1989, the *National,* a high-flying daily that wanted to be to sports what the *Wall Street Journal* was to business, burst onto the print landscape with a buzz that hadn't been seen since the launch of *USA Today.* In large part that was attributable to the *National's* conspicuous recruiting of top sportswriting talent and its flamboyant check-writing to pay for it. Eighteen months and $100 million later, the elegantly written sports daily was dead. For many still-disgruntled newspaper publishers and editors, its only lasting accomplishment was the inflated sports salaries (some would add egos) they are still coping with.

Meantime, the much-derided *USA Today* kept plugging away. Not only would it outlast the *National* and countless detractors, but it would come to influence contemporary sports coverage more than any other paper in the country.

Few could have predicted anything like that when Gannett's Al Neuharth sprang his pet project on a dubious world in 1982. A heavy emphasis on sports coast to coast was a key part of the Neuharth formula. This approach might well have backfired, given that so much of a typical sports fan's passion is local, but *USA Today* had little choice. As Monty Lorell, the current managing editor for sports, puts it, "We have to take a national focus because we have no hometown team. Every team is our home team."

But the paper made that philosophy a strength rather than a weakness, one of many ways it changed the assumptions and the rules of sports journalism.

For instance, *USA Today* was one of the first papers to acknowledge that it was time to join, rather than try to beat, TV in the business of covering sports. The paper's attitude may be best symbolized by columnist Rudy Martzke, who from the early 1980s has been America's proto–sports junkie. Martzke's job is to watch sports on television, then write about anything he finds interesting—not so much about the games themselves but about the commentators and the broadcasts and the experience, as shared by millions of people around the nation.

And clearly, says Lorell, TV has been the unifying and revolutionary force in the sports explosion. To cite some figures: In 1979, TV aired 2,100 hours of national sports. Two decades later that soared to a staggering 41,000 hours. In 1979 there were six networks televising sports; now there are seventy-nine. In 1979 there was no such thing as all-sports radio stations; by 1999 there were 251. People may be "inundated" with sports, as Lorell says, but "it seems they just can't get enough."

Recognizing that passion, *USA Today* decided early on that it must come across as being as timely as the broadcast media. That meant, at minimum, printing late sports scores—a lifelong nightmare for Eastern papers saddled with West Coast games. But owing to *USA Today*'s unique printing arrangement—more than thirty sites around the country crank out three editions nightly—it managed to have most of the late scores when the papers hit their TV-inspired newsracks. That timeliness made more than a few metro papers look bad and has inspired them, with faster presses and later deadlines, to do better, at least where their own teams are concerned.

Perhaps even more influential has been *USA Today*'s widely imitated colorizing of the daily grind. "Since sports has always been one of the drivers of our paper, it's benefited perhaps more than other sections in the use of color," says Lorell. But the paper did pioneering work at the other end of the gray-scale, too. From the beginning *USA Today* jammed its sports section with pages and pages of agate: detail-packed box scores, a page of team-by-team stats for baseball and football twice weekly, and a page of basketball and hockey once a week. Sports geeks, especially the nation's millions of fantasy baseball and football enthusiasts, simply can't get enough of the tiny type, and newspapers around the country have followed suit.

Lorell was at the launch pad—Rosslyn, Virginia—when *USA Today* took off in 1982. In 1996 he moved from being managing editor of the front page to head up the ninety-one-member sports staff. "It's the best job I ever had," he says without hesitation. "I get to look at sports all day and then I tell my wife I've been working hard."

MEANWHILE, ACROSS THE Potomac in Washington, D.C., where most grandstanding takes place outside stadiums and the players wear dark suits instead of polychrome spandex, an interesting experiment is underway. The decidedly number-two paper in town, the *Washington Times,* has focused on sports in the longshot hope of making inroads against its dominant rival, the *Post.*

Sports would seem an unlikely hook for the *Times,* with its deeply conservative take on the world and its Unification Church affiliation. "Our franchise has always been, is now, and always will be politics," affirms editor in chief Wesley Pruden. "That hasn't changed. But sports are on the rise around here and we decided to try to ride the crest."

The *Times,* with a daily circulation just under one hundred thousand, felt it had to do something dramatic in its combat with the *Post,* which has eight times more readers. Worse, on Sundays, unlike most other papers, the *Times'* circulation actually goes down. "We're only eighteen years old, while the *Post* has been here forever," says Pruden. "We're a teenager and the *Post* is a nine-hundred-pound gorilla."

So in the summer of 1999 the *Times* reconfigured its Sunday sports section and began wrapping it around the rest of the paper. Sections on art, entertainment, comics, and TV were moved out of the high-volume Saturday edition (which consistently outsells the Sunday paper, owing to its heavy dose of features, including a very popular continuing series on the history of the Civil War) and transferred to Sundays. This rearranged paper was then folded inside a newly designed and somewhat fattened sports section, et voila!—something new with brunch.

Pruden, a short, chunky son of Little Rock, nattily attired in a blue and white seersucker suit and black and white perforated wingtips, admits to having mixed feelings about what he terms "the sports obsession in this country." Nonetheless he tells me his original inclination for the Sunday makeover was even more daring: Turn the day's entire paper into a sports journal. "But the more we considered it," he says, "the more we realized that would shortchange readers who don't take any other paper, and we certainly didn't want them to go to the *Post.*"

The paper has been "quite heartened" by response so far. "We've had some complaints from readers who don't like sports, but I expected that," Pruden says. According to one *Times* editor, newsstand sales received a whopping 40 percent initial bump from the change. The *Times* had done almost no promotion for the new product during Washington's notorious dog days, using the slow season for a shakeout cruise and launching a concerted promotional campaign with fall's football season.

Although politics is, of course, the game in Washington, once you toss in the outside-the-Beltway Maryland and Virginia suburbs, with their heavy preponderance of middle-class families who have real jobs and lives, and then stir in Baltimore, only a short spin up Interstate 95, you have the makings of a pretty lively sports scene: NFL, NBA, NHL, WNBA, Orioles baseball, major league soccer, and half a dozen major college programs.

Of course, it ain't Texas. "We don't cover high school sports at all," says Pruden, although the *Post* does somewhat. "I'd love to, but there's nothing imminent." And the *Times* doesn't pay its columnists half a million dollars —or, for that matter, anything above the high five figures. "This is a Ford," Pruden says with a sniff and a shrug, "not a Lincoln, and certainly not a Lexus."

With a sports cover on Sundays, the *Times* has been slipping more sports stories onto the front page during the week. Editors, let alone readers, can be ground down by a steady page-one diet of politics, war, riots, hurricanes, and crime, so those at the *Times*—and the sports reporters— welcome a break in the sturm und drang. The paper still prides itself on fronting more hard news each day than the *Post,* but sports seems to be providing the narrow end of a wedge that eventually will push more features outside.

With the newly invigorated sports section have come three new writers and three new editors, all hired from outside. Gary Hopkins, the assistant managing editor who directs the *Times'* sports coverage, is delighted with his heavied-up firepower. "I don't know of any other sports section in the country that's doing what we are," he says. "I think it's the most interesting, most dynamic section in the country, and I'd stack it up against any other, anywhere. I'm expecting the *Post* to respond soon and then we'll be slugging it out, trying to break stories and beat each other out. That's what sports is all about, isn't it?"

7 | Fear.Com

The following piece was an attempt to capture a moment in the fast-moving world of the Internet and to predict where online newspapers might one day fit into the grander cyberscheme of things. It was a bit like sketching a still life with Ferris wheel from a spinning seat on the Tilt-a-Whirl. And in the ensuing years, things only became more unpredictable.

"Fear.com" appeared in June 1999, a time when the soaring valuations of new online companies that had never shown a profit put the fear of obliteration into established and respected news organizations. Major media players invested hundreds of millions of dollars in a variety of online strategies to stake out turf in a world that you could not touch.

There was a whiff of desperation in the air as people whose careers were dedicated to delivering bundles of inky newsprint to your doorstep grappled with the idea that an increasing number of readers were getting their news online. More frightening was the realization that they could get their classifieds on the Web, too, and that advertisers would spend top dollar for banner ads on sites with heavy user traffic.

Some papers tried to charge Web users to read their product online, while most gave the news away, sometimes going so far as to build virtual communities around their online editions, offering free e-mail accounts, dining and leisure information, and weather updates. But as soon as they thought they had a clear vision of this brazen new world, their seats veered and Up was Down again. All perspective was lost.

The phrase "irrational exuberance" was as irritating as a cell phone at the opera. Wall Street was still showering gold on bold entrepreneurs whose balance sheets were smeared with red. Mergers were threatening to create media Leviathans that could provide their own content over their own cables to millions of homes. And in such an environment, newspaper executives were able to rationalize the money their online editions drained from their budgets. They held their breath and hoped that they would be smartly positioned when the world stopped spinning.

> *Within months of the publication of "Fear.Com," the engines generating the Internet's riches had begun to sputter, and it was not uncommon to hear the terms "New Economy" and "Tulipmania" uttered in the same breath. It would be some time before the vertigo subsided.*

By Chip Brown
ORIGINALLY PUBLISHED IN JUNE 1999

1. ROMANCING THE ABYSS

If you had canvassed the tenth annual Editor & Publisher's Interactive Newspapers Conference last February you would have been hard-pressed to find people eager to define themselves as relics of a lost age. Most of the 1,100 journalists who gathered for three days at the Hyatt Regency in downtown Atlanta worked for newspaper companies that were the bastions of what has long been called "Old Media." But these weren't clueless Old Media fogies and Luddite computer-phobes who wouldn't know a monitor-refresh rate from a URL. They had cool jobs, jobs not normally associated with the newspaper business. They were site designers, and online producers, and chat-room hosts, and directors of New Media-this and Interactive-that. The sort of work, in short, that put them in the vanguard of a frightened industry's attempt to reinvent itself.

And yet there were times in Atlanta when it seemed that even these most digitally sophisticated journalists were fated to spend the rest of their careers tottering on the threshold of a new world, wondering if there was a place in it for them. It was going on five years since they had been swept up (or in some cases blindsided) by the online era. And still the question was, were they nimble enough to survive? Or would they be remembered as the woolly mammoths of the information age, too shaggy, too slow, too complacently wedded to business as usual to do anything but blunder inexorably toward the abyss?

It was this question that accounted for the worried air, the whistling-past-the-graveyard bravado, and even the occasional outbreaks of hand-wringing. You had to feel especially sorry for some of the older journalists in the crowd, the graybeards trying to get up to speed. They had begun their careers when the "web" was the ribbon of newsprint that rushed through the presses. Now the Web was—well, if you had to ask; if you didn't know; if you weren't really at home in that pell-mell, hydra-headed cyber-scape of frames, sites, portals, links, search engines, chat rooms, banner ads, HTML, Perl, Cold Fusion, streaming video, e-commerce, day-trading, personalized stock portfolios, and underage porn stars; if it had somehow escaped your attention that this virtual frontier, with its unimaginably vast and invisible traffic of ones and zeroes, was gathering new users at the rate of seven people per second and producing new competitors almost as rapidly —well, it was probably too late, you were hopelessly behind. The bromide about time on the Web was no joke: A few months were the practical equivalent of a year; a few years, a virtual eternity.

For three days the graybeards and their junior colleagues attended seminars and speeches and workshops. Dutifully they scribbled notes on pads supplied gratis by RegionOnline.com and tried not to flinch under the barrage of blunt advice and bitter observations:

"Round one is over and America Online has won."

"Newspaper journalists love words too much."

"The Web is about speed, not accuracy."

"Young people, who grow up with interactivity, get as much value getting information from each other as they do from editors and writers."

"You have to stop thinking of yourselves as newspaper people and start thinking of yourselves as 'information utilities.'"

During breaks they milled among the booths in the exhibition hall, listening gamely as baby-faced sales reps rhapsodized about "Internet platform solutions" and "local portal functionality." In the eyes of its most evangelical advocates, online technology had spawned not just a new medium but a new culture with its own lingo and metaphors. You surfed, you linked, you drilled down. It had also created new ways of publishing, selling, and using information, and it was these last, practical developments that were causing panicked newspaper executives to fear for their franchises.

In a way they were under siege. On one side of the castle were their traditional competitors, the magazines and TV and radio stations, which had also begun to migrate to the Web. Old Media in all forms was feeling pressed to defend its brands in the new medium and stake out a share of the Web's enormous audiences and potential business. These organizations knew what was at stake because they'd all printed or aired stories about how the current total of 62 million North American users was expected to grow to 150 million by the year 2002, and how by the year 2006 some 90 percent of Americans would be surfing and linking and drilling down. A huge new audience lay at the far end of their servers. The *New York Times* alone had discovered that half the 3 million registered users of its Web site had never bought a copy of the paper. And a survey by the Pew Research Center found that the percentage of Americans getting news online at least once a week had tripled from 1996 to 1998 to over 36 million; in the lush demographic category of under-thirty college graduates, 47 percent were reading news online. And then there was electronic commerce, growing at a rate exceeding 200 percent a year. And online advertising revenues, which, while they represented less than one half of 1 percent of the U.S. ad budget, had nonetheless grown in a few years from virtually nothing to more than a billion dollars by February 1999.

And on the other side of the castle there was a freaky Star Wars horde of alien new rivals, companies that had grown up in the medium and were doing a lot better in it, as if possessed of some innate advantage, the head start of being "Web-centric" where newspapers were merely "Web-enabled." (Or disabled, as the case may be.) The superstars among these new organizations owned the lion's share of the ad revenues and user traffic: There were portal sites such as Yahoo! and Lycos, which were known as "content aggregators" and were threatening newspapers because they provided access to Associated Press and Reuters and Bloomberg wire-service news, and they ran classified ads too. There was the software giant Microsoft, which was molting into an information-services company, having created the Microsoft Network, *Sidewalk* city guides, and a high-profile Webzine, *Slate.* The company @Home had partnered with the portal Excite, and had contracts with cable television companies that promised blazingly fast, always-on connections to the Web. America Online had cleverly blended Web content into its proprietary, subscription-based online service and had emerged as one of the traffic kingpins of everything from e-commerce to New Media. Even the entertainment conglomerate Disney had forged an alliance with the portal Infoseek and cobbled together the Go Network, which featured ESPN's popular sports coverage. Hundreds of other sites threatened to usurp the social and commercial niches newspapers had traditionally occupied. They ranged from e-commerce giant Amazon.com and virtual auction house eBay to such community sites as theglobe.com and Tripod to specialty classified-ad sites devoted to jobs, houses, and cars.

The extent to which the newspaper industry was running scared and in the midst of some weird identity crisis was illustrated on Friday afternoon, when the organizers of the Interactive Newspapers Conference thought it would be a good idea to rally any flagging spirits with an inspirational speech. The morning before, business-information tycoon Michael Bloomberg had painted a bleak picture, telling the journalists, "If you mix the ink and chop the trees, you'll probably be put out of business," and furthermore that if they didn't find and publish information people wanted, they could just "forget about it," they were goners. He did concede that "serious people" would always value what journalists did, but it seemed more of a sop to get out of the room before everyone burst into tears.

So on Friday afternoon there was a full house as "anthropologist, journalist, mountaineer, adventurist" Jeff Salz bounded onto the stage like a golden retriever that had been waiting all day for a trip to the park. The lights went down, slides came up, and Dr. Salz launched on his theme, which was "the adventure of change." What he hoped to do, he said, was to pass along some "timeless certainties in uncertain times." Some were simple:

"Leap before you look."

"Aim high."

"Give it all you've got."

"Work some magic."

"Enjoy the view."

Some were more complex:

"People don't care how much you know until they know how much you care."

"If you always do what you always did, you'll always get what you always got."

Were things so bad that 1,100 men and women who worked in the daily rush of novelty and ought to be priding themselves for their part in writing the "first rough draft of history" needed a pep talk on the adventure of change? Wasn't the adventure of change their reason for being? And yet they sat there without so much as a rolled eye or an ironic "Hallelujah!" No one told the adventurist to go sit on a piton even when he repeated that bit about them being "information utilities," not newspaper people. What restraint! What civility! Were anxieties so high that any Pied Piper was welcome who promised to turn the prospect of oblivion into the Adventure of Change? Perhaps people would soon be bolting from their seats to shout, "When the going gets tough, information utilities get going!" The real question was what they would do after the fog of platitudes had lifted. Had they truly missed their chance? Had the future come and gone already and now they were all just marking time, romancing the abyss?

2. VANITY AND PANIC

In some sense the story of newspapers in the online era is a business story first and a story of journalism and cultural evolution second. It has so far been dominated by business themes, the nuts and bolts of margins, revenue streams, investment strategies, barriers to entry, technology headaches, accounting questions, e-commerce, and the still unclear issue of what's the best path to a profitable future. Is it to follow the tight, pay-as-you-go heading of the Thomson chain, whose shoestring online-newspaper operations netted a profit of $3 million in 1998? Or is it to take the loss-leading tack of the San Jose–based Knight Ridder chain, or Tribune Company in Chicago, both of which are investing tens of millions of dollars in a sort of Field of Dreams strategy? Or is the wisest course the one followed by Gannett, the country's largest chain, which has severely reined in its online operations, and in some cases, such as at the *Rockford Register Star* in Illinois, canceled the online news part of a paper altogether?

Gannett's notable exception, its major New Media extravagance, is the online version of its flagship, *USA Today,* a paper which may have finally demonstrated that even newspapers can undergo sex-change operations. *USA Today* is the Renee Richards of media properties. After years living a false life in a heavily subsidized, pulp-based body, and being criticized as the McDonald's of newspapers for conducting cutesy-wutesy but proto-interactive Q&A opinion polls, and running squibby Web-like stories before the Web even existed, the spirit of the paper has finally been liberated and found its true home in the twinkling palette of USA Today.com. It's one of the most popular news sites on the Web, and the company says it has been making a profit since September. The handheld version that comes off the presses seems more and more what it always was—a Web-site printout.

That's one paper, one company. Every media company has a different approach. In its latest annual report, Times Mirror, which publishes the *Los Angeles Times* among other estimable titles, timidly says that the company wants to wait and "figure out where the new medium is going." But then the company also boldly dumped $25 million into Web sites in 1998. Depending on who's talking, that's either too much or not nearly enough; either clueless extravagance or foolish penny-pinching. All these business decisions and opinions reflect a social context. It's important to remember that Old and New Media rivalries are shaped by cultural conflicts and aesthetic differences and generational tensions. Not long after my trip to Atlanta I received a promotional copy of *Min's New Media Report,* which contained this item in a column called the "Roving Eye":

"The puckish Eyeball thinks that E&P should rename its Interactive Newspapers Conference the Deathmarch of the Grey Bears. After repeated warnings from speakers that the Web will feast on their reticence to reimagine print news operations and embrace the new medium, crowds of fortysomething, white (but graying) male defenders of 'journalistic integrity' desperately latched onto Michael Bloomberg's fleeting reassurance that 'serious people' always will read newspapers. Sure, Mike . . . both of them."

What a buncha cards, those New Media kids! Or maybe they're just exasperated because the gray bears won't get out of the way. Pundits have been predicting the death of newspapers for more than one hundred years. In 1880, the assassin was supposed to be photography. In the 1920s, newspapers were going to be destroyed by radio; in the 1950s, TV was going to destroy newspapers and radio. In the 1990s the Web was going to destroy . . . well, you get the idea, and it is a misleading one because the main theme of media history is not extirpation of one form by another, but mutual accommodation among forms. Old Media has shown a remarkable resilience. As Roger Fidler, one of the pioneers of electronic distribution, observes in his book *Mediamorphosis,* even parchment scrolls, the preferred medium for five thousand years, are still used in some tradition-conscious religions.

So it's a safe bet the $54 billion newspaper business is not about to sink into oblivion tomorrow. By some measures the industry is the healthiest it's been in more than a generation. Ad revenue was up 6.3 percent in 1998. Circulation numbers have stabilized after two decades of steady decline: Yes, the numbers were down last year in seven of the top ten markets, but they were up in nineteen of the top thirty, and the bottom line, according to the Newspaper Association of America (NAA), is that "newspapers are still among the most profitable media companies."

Profitable, it should be noted, despite their infatuation with the Web.

In 1994 there were 20 newspapers online; within four years there were 4,925 worldwide, 2,799 of them in the United States. There's no ready figure for the investment such growth represents, but it's clearly in the hundreds of millions of dollars. "The U.S. Internet daily newspaper market has grown rapidly from a scant $21 million in 1996 to $203.7 million by the end of 1998," according to a Dataquest report by analyst Peggy O'Neill. With costs so high (newspaper sites were estimated to have lost more than $80 million in 1998), returns still meager, and success so uncertain—more than 100 online newspapers have already died in their cribs—some critics are starting to argue that newspapers have not been too reluctant to embrace the Web, but too eager. The reasoning goes that it's not their Old Media pasts newspaper people can't escape, but their penchant for pipe-dreaming about a New Media future.

THE SPIRIT OF spendthrift techno-romanticism goes back at least to the 1970s, when many papers were seduced into ill-advised ventures in audio- and videotex services. There were deals with cable TV companies, and by the mid-1980s many newspapers were hoping to cash in delivering their product by fax. That none of these gambits really caught the public's imagination didn't stop newspapers from piling into cyberspace. So why are they suddenly so eager to give away the content they used to charge for?

"Can you say fad?" asked University of Illinois journalism professor Eric Meyer.

Fad? For a phenomenon that encompasses more than 4,900 online newspapers?

"Maybe now that there's so many more newspapers involved, fad isn't fair," he conceded, "but what would you call it if you have all these intelligent people and they don't know why they're doing something other than because everybody else is doing it, and every day they're saying to themselves, 'If I don't do it, I'll get left behind!' And the venture is still just as shaky in terms of rewards because virtually no one is making money."

I had telephoned Meyer because for nearly twenty years he has been tracking the online fortunes of newspapers and has been making a census of the population, posting updates on AJR NewsLink, the Web site he operates with *American Journalism Review.* Lately he has emerged as one of the leading voices of the counterrevolution, wondering about the risks of the online gamble and questioning the claims of newspaper companies that say their Web sites are in the black. Last year there were notable declarations of online profitability from the *New York Times* and *USA Today;* recent surveys have reported that 24 percent of all newspaper Web sites are earning more money than they spend. But in Meyer's view most of these operations aren't taking into account the hidden subsidies, and the longer he looks at the great experiment the more he wonders how rational it is.

"Some newspapers like the *Minneapolis Star-Tribune* are making money doing design work. Morris Communications makes money hosting sites for churches and banks in Topeka, Kansas. Some papers have become Internet service providers. But I have yet to see any news sites that claim a profit being billed for the actual cost of putting out the newspaper. They're not paying for desks or supplies. They're not paying 20 percent of the city-hall reporter's salary. And they're certainly not going to turn a profit on banner ads. Banner-ad rates have collapsed. They started out at between $35 and $50 per thousand impressions, and now they're around $5, and some of the major national sites are getting around $2 per thousand hits. Subscription sales are the biggest bust of all. Nearly every news-

paper that has tried to charge for content—the *San Jose Me*
Colorado Springs Gazette, the *Hays Daily News* in Hay
stopped. The only ones I know are the *Wall Street Jou.*
Champagne News Gazette in Illinois, which charges $4.50 a month just read the sports pages. They have some columnist and everybody who went
to school at Illinois and followed sports likes to keep up with him."

For these reasons Meyer said he was beginning to think maybe
Gannett's conservative approach made a lot of sense. As a whole, the
industry was growing out of its "Gee Whiz" period and into what Meyer
called the "How Are We Going to Pay for This?" period.

"I would never argue that newspapers should do nothing," he said, "but
the future is very murky and I would argue that they should make only a
small bet, just to cover themselves. I said last year that it was going to be
last year and it wasn't, but I still think there's going to be a major player
that is going to cut way back—someone like Knight Ridder or the *Chicago
Tribune,* which has lost close to $100 million."

Happy as they might be about it, the bounty of free news online has
confused even some readers. The columnist Kurt Andersen, noting that he
used to cough up fifteen to twenty dollars a week for the *Washington Post*
and the three big New York papers—the *Times, Post,* and *Daily News*—
wondered why their publishers were suddenly willing to comp him on the
Web. "They justify the practice vaguely as brand protection and R&D," he
wrote in the *New Yorker,* "but the reasons look more like confused mix-
tures of vanity and panic."

The power of vanity should never be underestimated, but over the last
couple of years it is panic that has been the driving force. Simply put,
newspapers are spending money to keep from losing their classified-ad
base. Classifieds are the newspaper industry's lifeline, a $15 billion to $18
billion business. They can account for anywhere from 25 to 50 percent of
a given paper's ad revenue. A publisher's vanity might be piqued at the idea
of Microsoft or Yahoo! or America Online edging into the news business,
but the prospect of companies cutting into his base of classified ads
arouses nothing but mortal terror. And to make matters worse, the Web in
many ways is a much better medium for classifieds than newspapers.

The interactive functions of the Web enable users to move expeditiously
through massive databases in ways not possible in a pulp-based medium.
Why plow through all the ads for Buicks and Oldsmobiles if what you want
is just a red Honda no more than five years old with less than sixty thousand miles? Plug in the variables, hit "search," and presto! Classified-ad sites
such as Autobytel.com and Monster.com were springing up on the Web;

they offered faster and handier ways of posting and looking for anything you wanted—jobs, cars, apartments, houses, land in Florida, saxophones, and every thingamajig in grandmother's trunk. Even more excruciating for newspapers, the ads were often free. The current projections are that in the next five years classified sites will capture as much as one-third of newspaper classified-ad revenues, a loss of upwards of $6 billion.

"The classified ad stream is a goner in the coming years," said New York Times Electronic Media Company. President Martin Nisenholtz, speaking late last year in an online dialogue sponsored by the Webzine *Feed*. "That means taking the Internet seriously rather than treating it as a distribution channel." Or as *Washington Post* publisher Don Graham once famously said, explaining the decision to put his paper online: "There are three reasons —classifieds, classifieds, classifieds."

The newspaper classified-ad crisis is a classic variation on the leitmotif known as "disintermediation." Disintermediation is the Department of Media Studies word for the Web's potential to eliminate middlemen and directly connect producers or vendors with consumers. The prospect of being disintermediated looms over dozens of businesses. Why cut in Sotheby's if you can auction stuff on eBay or UBid? Why fork out fat commissions to a broker at Merrill Lynch when you can trade the same lot of stock at eTrade for fifteen bucks? Or shop retail when the same book is 40 percent less on Amazon.com? Why bother with mortgage brokers and car dealers and drugstores and travel agents? And why—cue extinction scenario—pick up a paper for its classifieds?

The industry has made some large if belated moves to meet the classified crisis. In December 1997, a consortium of newspaper companies including Tribune Company, Times Mirror, and the Washington Post Company launched Classified Ventures, a family of Web sites that now includes searchable listings for apartments, jobs, and cars. Cars.com was backed by Gannett, Knight Ridder, and the *New York Times*, but it was one of the last sites to arrive in an already crowded field.

The biggest push has been to stanch the hemorrhage in the employment portion of the classified market, which the NAA estimated in 1997 accounted for $12 billion, or 70 percent or more of the entire classified market. CareerPath.com, a network of newspaper job-listing pages begun in 1995 by the *Washington Post, San Jose Mercury News, L.A. Times, New York Times, Chicago Tribune,* and *Boston Globe* (with additional investments from Gannett, Hearst, and Cox), had eighty-three newspaper affiliates by 1999, boasting "the largest and most current database" of jobs on the Web, with more than 322,000 listings and, as of January, 8.35 million job searches per month. But the company is up against formidable competitors. Monster.com, owned by direct-marketing and yellow-page advertising company TMP Worldwide, saw a huge spike in its traffic after a hilarious Super Bowl advertising campaign that featured kids staring into the camera with deadpan expressions and confessing the ultra-modest prospects they faced without the help of a job-search site like Monster.com: "When I grow up I want to be a yes-man." "I want to be forced into early retirement." "I want to claw my way up to middle management."

Where panic has been checked, there is nevertheless a lot of anxiety among newspapers that they aren't gaining the audience they need, or competing well enough, or that their position is fundamentally untenable. "I think we're in a totally critical stage," said Larry Pryor, the former editor of the *L.A. Times* Web site who now runs the *Online Journalism Review* at the University of Southern California. "What's driving online journalism at the moment is e-commerce; that's more important than content. If publishers get too far into e-commerce retailing, they're going to tick off their retail advertisers. But if they continue to lag behind, defending their classifieds and deferring to retail advertisers and not getting into e-commerce, they're going to lose their financial base."

Among the stark statistics discussed in Atlanta, none was more sobering than the site-usage measurements developed by Media Metrix, the Nielsens of the Web. Media Metrix figures showed that in major metropolitan areas, newspapers were getting trounced in their backyards. No newspaper Web site cracked the top ten in its local market except the *Washington Post,* which was eighth.

But dwelling only on the business questions you'll miss the bigger picture. If newspapers lack some crucial understanding of the Web, of how it works not just technically but psychically, it may be because they don't really want to understand the Web. "Most traditional news organizations are hostile to new media," Pryor wrote in a recent issue of the *Online Journalism Review.* "Editorial pages and even news reports use every opportunity to attack the Internet as being synonymous with confusion, clutter, gossip and sensationalism. A shaky study on a link between depression and Web usage gets page one treatment. Pornography, hackers and all forms of cyber-crime receive prominent but often superficial and inaccurate coverage. Matt Drudge gets elevated to Net Whipping Boy." As Roger Fidler, a longtime critic of news-media myopia, put it: "People don't seem to grasp that we are in the midst of a tremendous transformation in communications. It's as historically significant as the development of the printing press in the 1400s."

If newspaper executives haven't fully grasped the extent of changes in communication or the opportunity the Web represents, then the story of online newspapering is as much about culture as business. Executives often seem handicapped by an almost mythic fear that their Old Media franchises will be devoured by their dot-com offspring. They forget how much more pleasant it is to be eaten by your own child than by someone else's. Web-centric companies (or Net-native, as they are also called) are at home in the language of interactivity that Web-enabled companies are still stumbling to learn; many have corporate metabolisms that enable them to move more quickly and imaginatively than Old Media organizations.

Take that January 1998 *New Yorker* column in which Kurt Andersen was bold enough to mock the "nutty" valuation of Yahoo!, then capitalized at $2.7 billion. Mocking Yahoo! and its ilk has become such a regular Old Media sport that the founders of the Motley Fool financial Web site use the volume of negative comment as a contrarian buy indicator for additions to their Rule Breakers portfolio. In May, fifteen months after Andersen's column, Yahoo! was worth $33.9 billion. Hey, maybe Yahoo's valuation really is nutty now. But grossly overvalued or not, the stock gave Yahoo! leverage to gobble up Geocities and Broadcast.com, thus creating new reasons for people—onetime stalwarts of the pulp-based world, perhaps—to check out the site.

Disintermediation respects no franchise and is as liable to overrun a social niche as an economic one. Which means that people who work for newspapers, bastions of mediation, confront the prospect that the Web may usurp their role as agenda-setters and news filters. The Web puts a cornucopia of primary sources within everyone's reach, and makes the stuff of which news is made available to anyone, raw and unprocessed, minus the contributions of reporters and editors, minus their judicious evaluation and careful fact-checking, but also minus their "family-newspaper" euphemisms, their pack-mentality blind spots, and their sometimes patronizing determinations about what is in the "public interest."

"The time when newspapers were the gatekeepers of information is over," said *Newsweek* columnist and media critic Jonathan Alter. "What newspapers are now becoming is the authenticators of information, the quality control instruments on a huge river of rumor—and for that you have to have reporters. Newspapers will continue to be the primary instruments of newsgathering, but when you have so many sources of information, any one pundit has less influence. Even if there were a Walter Lippmann today, he'd just be another guy with a link to the 'Drudge Report.'"

3. ALL THE NEWS THAT'S FIT TO FRAME

So you've finally got all the gear together, untangled that rat's nest of wires, and managed to get yourself jacked into a local online service provider, and now you're raring to go, ready to surf, link, and drill down, ready to roam the universe of the Web for . . . a newspaper?

Let me risk extrapolating from personal experience and say, not! And venture further out on a limb to say that the thrills of reading newspapers online aren't going to lure legions of people to the Web. Even with the financial incentive of an assignment, it took me two months to get my mouse pointed along the lines of duty. There were simply too many other things on the Web that were more interesting than newspapers.

Never mind the shrines devoted to cyberbabes like Pamela Anderson, or the usenet groups offering downloadable excerpts from the blue film career of Traci Lords. There were untold G-, PG-, and R-rated sites that could soak up days—months—of your time. Stock chat boards that promised day-traders quick riches or hard lessons. Sites for weather obsessives, and Tiger Woods fans, and devotees of curling, flatfish, and volcanoes. Sites for parrot fanciers and leather fetishists. Whatever you could imagine was no trouble to conjure with a search engine. Need something to riposte one of those smart-aleck exponents of disintermediation? Try the Elizabethan curse generator: "O thou pribbling skainsmate, thou beslubbering milk-livered clot-pole!"

The Web might be the world's greatest source of information, but its spirit is playful, informal, collaborative. Its anti-hierarchical, libertarian mindset was epitomized by Suck.com, whose bat-fowling canker-blossoms loved nothing better than to launch a bracing diatribe into the flanks of Old Media. Or the comedy news site the Onion.com, which offered mock reportage under headlines such as "Sudan Passes Campaign Reform: All Candidates to Be Limited to 500,000 Rounds of 7.62mm Ammo." Or: "Miracle Overpass Issues Mysterious Stream of Urine." The Web subverted authority with interactive functions that practically begged you to fool around. Would that I had the space in this claustrophobic Old Media forum to publish the results of my experiments using an Alta Vista program to translate the cracked-plate prose of *New York Times* columnist Abe Rosenthal into French and then back into even more sidesplittingly fractured English.

Suffice to say that this was the kind of thing many new Web users amuse themselves with during their first months in cyberspace. I indulged every juvenile vice available in a domain that seemed the digital equivalent of the global id, pausing once in a while between X-rated downloads, Elizabethan curses, and reprocessed pundit gibberish to wonder how newspapers could ever compete with a repository where every forbidden pleasure and irresistible fascination was a click away. There's an old *New Yorker* cartoon that shows two commuters sitting on a train, one holding a paper that says "Lots of Important Stuff You Have to Know" and the other a paper headlined "Rumors, Gossip and Wacky Stunts." The joke is that Lots of Important Stuff is peeking over at Rumors, Gossip and Wacky Stunts. In the online age, Lots of Important Stuff would be craning for a glimpse of his seatmate's laptop and all the frames of gossip and wacky stunts streaming in by wireless modem.

The voluptuarial recesses of the Web made all newspapers, even the mad-dog tabs, seem part of the nation's superego. Didn't most newspapers aspire to be civic-minded and socially responsible? Didn't they spend a lot of energy hectoring readers to vote, eat vegetables, cross at the corner, love the neighbors, and, if possible, refrain from flashing thong underwear at the president? Even when reporting on crime and depravity, they were mindful of their roles as gatekeepers—guardians of "family values" and "community standards." Whether they functioned as judicious filters or uptight censors or simple old-fashioned killjoys, newspapers seemed constitutionally misallied with the anything-goes spirit of the Web. As media critic Jon Katz succinctly summed up the dilemma in a famous 1994 *Wired* magazine essay, "How can a medium that censors Doonesbury cartoons thrive online?"

In Katz's notably untempered opinion—the headline of his piece was "Online or Not, Newspapers Suck"—the difficulty the Web posed for newspapers was not the technical challenge of grappling with a new mode of distribution but the cultural problem of attracting a generation of readers who couldn't give a damn no matter how you packaged the content. I caught up with Katz in the midst of a book tour in which he was trying to harness the promotional power of the Web by filing diary-style feeds to a literary site called Slashdot.com. Though his thesis about the alienation of the young is contradicted by studies showing that newspaper-phobic young people tend to become newspaper-friendly readers as they get older and buy houses and develop stakes in their communities, he didn't mince words.

"The time is getting short for newspapers to wake up, and I'm getting more and more pessimistic," he said. "Part of the problem is that newspapers have warred against the culture of the young. They attacked rock 'n' roll, they attacked Nintendo, and they attacked the Web. It's the medium of Old Fartism. We're at the point now where the debate about newspapers and the Web is dead. Young people have created their own information culture that's totally apart from the sensibility, form, and values of journalism. They don't like to be lectured to, which is the mainstay of newspapers. They're interactive, they're zappers and switchers, and the culture of objective journalism is not very interactive. Interactive basically means one thing: You give up power."

Amid the many Web-related milestones in 1998, the online publication of the Starr report in September offered the most spectacular confirmation of the power and reach of the new medium. Sites that published news on the Web saw their traffic surge more than 300 percent, and even the most inveterate Old Media ostriches had to pull their heads out of the sand. It's hard to describe the weird enchantment of a medium that enables you to sit alone in your home office and audit the bubbleheaded chitchat of Monica and Linda. It's also hard to describe the chagrin you feel that such magnificent technology should be turned to such consummately trivial ends.

When I finally got around to fulfilling my obligations, I started with newspaper sites that were ranked high on the "hot 100 newspapers," a scoreboard compiled by a clearinghouse called 100hot.com. (Some of the hot 100 newspapers were actually broadcast Web sites or news-search engines like Totalnews.com; some were mock newspapers, like the *Onion,* or Webzines like *Salon* and *Slate;* and some, such as the Pharmaceutical Information Network, weren't newspapers or news sites in the traditional sense at all.) Among the true newspaper sites were the usual suspects— such cyberpioneers and leaders as the San *Jose Mercury News, Chicago Tribune, Raleigh News & Observer, L.A. Times, USA Today, Washington Post,* and my majestic local rag, the *New York Times,* with its handsome screen version of the print edition's front page.

Some advantages to online news were immediately obvious: Most of the big sites posted the time with their content, meaning that they had broken from the once-a-day news cycle and were issuing updates like any broadcast-news operation. Most offered users the ability to search within the site. Many allowed links to sites outside their own.

Here and there, especially at smaller papers with younger editors, there were tweaks and innovations, and even some flashes of the Web's irreverent spirit. The *San Francisco Examiner*'s Webmaster raised a lot of Old Media eyebrows when he trained a Webcam on the newsroom and allowed users a peek at what was happening on the news-production lines. There wasn't much to see, of course, and if the innovation was more of a gimmick, and a sleepy one at that, it was nonetheless a gesture in the right direction. Hoping to attract Gen-X readers, the *Baltimore Sun*'s Web site, Sunspot, hired a nineteen-year-old columnist who wrote a wildly popular three-part series on what would happen if she drank Jolt cola every day for three weeks.

I was struck by the Web site of the *Newtown Bee,* not for the stuff you'd expect to find in a western Connecticut weekly—Emily Dickinson quilts, problems with the police chief—but for the "Internet Info for Real People" column, a terrific compendium of practical advice and interesting stuff about the Web. It's written by Bob Brand, and the archives include an account of a classic case of Old Media running afoul of the Web—this would be the story of how online users, abetted by publicity from Howard Stern, hijacked *People* magazine's "Third Annual Most Beautiful People" poll and ensured that a character known as Hank the Angry Drunken Dwarf buried Leonardo DiCaprio, 223,737 to 13,739.

"Hank has an inner beauty . . ."

"Hank is not afraid to show us the ugliness of alcoholism . . ."

Down south, at TCPalm.com, a site comprising six Scripps Howard newspapers and an NBC station along Florida's Atlantic Coast, content producer Brian Costello was trying to get some New Media zip in Old Media news coverage. At twenty-three, a recent graduate of the University of Illinois, he was unfettered by traditional Old Media protocol. Unable to get tickets to the Super Bowl in Miami, he cobbled together a bunch of reports called "Quarterback Sneak" about trying to crash the big game. During the hullabaloo over John Glenn's return to space, Costello and three fellow twenty-somethings took a recreational vehicle on a two-day interview-and-hijinks-filled gadabout to Cape Canaveral. They posted pages comparing the stats of Glenn's space shuttle, *Discovery,* with their Coachman Leprechaun RV. They filed digital photos and bulletins and conducted online chats. And while Costello's stunt probably won't endear him to establishmentarians, his decision to report on taking a leak at the Mercury launch site where John Glenn was first rocketed into space was definitely Web-wise: "T-minus 22 hours, 10 minutes: I find relief behind the weeds of John Glenn's launch pad. I exit the furry tundra with burrs on my shoelaces."

"I had just watched *The Right Stuff,* and there's a scene where Alan Shepard has an urgent need, and I somehow linked to that—we shared the same metaphysical need," Costello recalled.

Any casual surfer could see many papers were still straddling the Old and New Media divide. They were short on interactivity, reluctant to open themselves to readers. Many didn't provide for instant e-mail feedback or online chat rooms or live interviews. The *San Jose Mercury News* linked bylines to e-mail addresses, and you could instantly contact the reporters—but the *Washington Post* and the *New York Times* did not. Indeed, some of the bigger papers seemed more interested in fending off the public than reaching out to it. And many papers, both big and small, were still just shifting their print editions onto the Web—a practice known as publishing "shovelware."

After a while the aesthetic difficulties of reading online were impossible to ignore. It was giddy at first to be able to roam the world of news, gleaning dope about the Oscars from the *L.A. Times,* or discovering from the *Anchorage Daily News* that king-salmon anglers recently blocked the train tracks on the fishing bridge over Bird Creek and had to be ejected by state troopers. But that very freedom to carom from site to site meant it was no longer necessary to rely on one group of editors to corral interesting items under the typical newspaper sections of national news, metro, sports, business, living, style, arts, opinion, etc. You could edit your own newspaper, as it were—assembling a feed of news from your personalized list of "bookmarks" or "favorites." You might be the sort of person who would zip to CNN for breaking news, then over to the *Washington Post* for Capitol Hill stuff, to ESPN for sports, to CNET for technology coverage, to the *New York Times* for "Cybertimes" and reports from overseas and columns by Maureen Dowd. Then, for more opinions, you could go to *Slate, Suck,* or *Salon;* for financial information, the *Wall Street Journal* or the Motley Fool or TheStreet.com or CBS Marketwatch; for the weather . . .

Even if you stuck with one media company, the experience of reading news online often got weirdly disorienting, for the simple reason that you never had the satisfaction of finishing the paper—of knowing you were done and could proceed with the day. Each page might have tens of thousands of pages behind or below it. What at first seemed like a researcher's dream, a great luxury of information, could quickly become an unnerving sort of bottomlessness—an info overload, too much cyberspace yawning below your frame. It reminded me of those shivery moments when you're snorkeling in shallow water and the reef drops off suddenly, leaving you suspended above a lightless abyss.

I knew I had been surfing, linking, and drilling down too long when I woke one night from a peculiar dream, disturbed not by the content but by the way the scenes had changed; they had not unfolded in a horizontal flow, the movie-like montage of typical dream presentation, but had scrolled past, rolling up vertically from bottom to top. And my focus had shifted too, as if the inner observer were no longer located behind my eyes, but had been projected twenty-four inches forward, out of my body, a displacement roughly equal to the distance between my desk chair and the computer monitor. The conclusion was inescapable. I had become a mouse. Not even a mouse. A mouse indicator. A cursor.

Not an uncommon malady, I hear. Surf, link, and drill long enough and you will have an irresistible urge to break from the virtual realm into the so-called real world. Enough with e-mail! Enough with Web sites and New Media clot-poles pribbling about bandwidth and local portal functionality. I went online one more time to make some plane reservations, and thus aid in the disintermediation of yet another local business, and then I took my corporeal body west, to San Jose and the *Mercury News*, where a fair case can be made that the age of online newspapers began.

4. "How Is This Different from the Other Stuff Out There?"

You'd think it would be a simple matter to establish who was first to get a newspaper online, but it turns out to be one of those ambiguity-shrouded, headwaters-of-the-Amazon questions, because there are many kinds of "firsts," and nearly as many ways to define or qualify what it means to be "online." In the 1970s, "online" meant audio- and videotex systems accessed over telephone lines. In the 1980s and early 1990s, it meant shoveling content onto proprietary services like the Source, CompuServe, Prodigy, and the little dial-up service that eventually crushed them all, America Online. Different papers took different electronic paths, but in the mid-1990s, like tributaries in a vast watershed, they all began to converge, drawn together by developments in technology. First came the stunning advances in computing power. Then software engineer Tim Berners-Lee devised the coding that imposed the conventions of the World Wide Web on the domain of the Internet. And finally, from the University of Illinois (and subsequently Netscape) sprang the browser code that put pictures with text and made it possible to traipse about the terra nova of cyberspace in style.

A deft timeline of these developments has been posted on the Web by David E. Carlson, the founder of the Interactive Media Lab at the University of Florida and himself an online pioneer. The first online newspaper in the United States, by Carlson's reckoning, was the *Columbus Dispatch* in Ohio. In 1980 it offered an electronic version of itself via

CompuServe, which is based in Columbus. In that pre–IBM PC era, CompuServe had all of 3,600 subscribers, so the circulation was necessarily limited. When IBM introduced its personal computer the next year, joining the three-year-old Apple II, the age of desktop computing was secured for good.

And more than a few newspaper executives caught the first wave of New Media fever. By 1982, there were eleven U.S. papers making portions of their print editions available electronically on CompuServe. Among them: the *Atlanta Journal and Constitution, L.A. Times, Washington Post, San Francisco Examiner, San Francisco Chronicle,* the *Star Tribune* in Minneapolis, and even the *Middlesex News* in Framingham, Massachusetts. The trouble with the new distribution channel was that it cost a fortune. As Elizabeth M. Ferrarini noted in her 1982 book *The Electronic Newspaper: Fact or Fetish,* CompuServe charged five dollars an hour for access, and the state-of-the-art modems of the day could only download content at the paraplegic rate of three hundred baud per second, so all the news that would cost you about twenty-five cents to get in print would cost more than thirty dollars to get online. By June of 1982, this early round of New Media fever went into a fiscally induced remission.

Carlson, now forty-eight, had caught the bug himself in 1981 when he was working as a thirty-year-old energy and environment reporter for the *Gallup Independent* in northern New Mexico. "One day I got a call from the publisher's son, who was a noted oddball," he said last spring when I went to see him at his university office in Gainesville, Florida. "He said, 'There's a package for you at the bus station, go get it.' So I drove forty miles to the bus station and picked it up. It was a Radio Shack Model 100. And it had something called a modem, three hundred baud, and it came with ten free hours on something called CompuServe. I logged on, and I discovered that I could get the AP wire. I was working in a bureau and living sixty miles from Gallup in Bluewater Lake, New Mexico, and now I could read the AP news. It was as if I had discovered the future. I started dancing around the kitchen table and yelling, 'I've seen the future of newspapers!' and then my wife comes in to see what I'm yelling about. She looks at the Model 100, which has an eight-line screen, and then looks at me, and then she shakes her head and goes back to bed. But I have believed from that moment forward that the future of media was online and interactive."

By 1990 Carlson had moved on to the *Albuquerque Tribune,* where he spotted a notice posted on the "wailing wall" seeking someone to work ten hours a week on an electronic version of the paper. He volunteered. A lot of online gambles, most of them dial-up services that required special terminals or that asked users to punch in command codes on their telephones, had bitten the dust. They cost too much, and they failed to excite much interest. What had taken off, however, was the personal computer, and Carlson thought he could take advantage of the new technology. The *Electronic Trib,* as the service was called, was to be distributed to and accessed by readers from a PC.

"As nearly as we've been able to tell, it was the first multiline, PC-based online newspaper product," Carlson said. "All the earlier experiments were mainframe-based, and they were incredibly expensive because you had to develop special software. It occurred to us that PCs had become powerful enough to house an online system. We leased a 286 clone from a local store and customized some bulletin-board software and hooked it up to four incoming phone lines. The total cost was about $5,000. We did absolutely no market research, and we had no idea whether anybody would be interested or not. My boss said it would be incredible if we had four hundred users in a month. We had four hundred in the first twenty-four hours—it was so busy I couldn't log onto the damn thing to update the system."

They started adding more phone lines, and Carlson, who was a design editor at the *Tribune,* began to spend half his workday on the electronic paper. He created memberships—for $50 a year you could log on for three hours a day. The launch began to attract attention. After a three-paragraph story about the *Electronic Trib* appeared in *Editor & Publisher,* Carlson got a call from Knight Ridder. Then headquartered in Miami, Knight Ridder was arguably the Old Media company with the most severe case of New Media fever. It had poured more than $55 million into a videotex service called Viewtron before finally shutting it down in March 1986.

"There were three guys on the speakerphone from Tony Ridder's office, and I could practically hear them chuckling in the background that this hillbilly hick from New Mexico thinks he can make this electronic newspaper thing work when they spent $55 million on Viewtron. But we figured out a way to do it cheaply. There were no graphics. From 1990 to 1993 we had four thousand user accounts. We started the second wave of online newspapers."

Which is to say, as Carlson notes on his resume, the *Albuquerque E-Trib* was the first online paper to carry databases of public records, the first online paper to provide for e-mailing letters to the editor, the first to offer chat sessions with newsmakers, even the first to offer online pizza ordering. The *Trib,* according to Carlson, was also the first to make a profit, modest as it was.

And after that spasm of creativity the paper rested, and Carlson and the world moved on. It was only in 1998 that the *Tribune* got itself onto the Web, Carlson said. The great online milestones that followed the achievements of the *E-Trib* were left to some of those astonished suits in Tony Ridder's office, in particular to one New Media convert who happened to be editing the newspaper at the epicenter of the digital age.

WHEN I CALLED on Bob Ingle in San Jose, he was employed as president of New Media for Knight Ridder, the nation's second-largest newspaper chain. His group occupied the seventh floor of a downtown office building with a commanding view of the surrounding hills and many of the companies that had created the legend of Silicon Valley. The *Mercury News,* where Ingle had been the executive editor for fourteen years, was located about half an hour to the north, and in that stretch of land between the venerable Bay Area paper named for the mercury used in the gold mines of nineteenth-century California and Ingle's New Media headquarters, there seemed to be nothing but the new gold rush of tech companies: tech off the freeway, tech in the hills, tech in sprawling low-slung "campuses" and modest office towers. It's no wonder that just a month earlier, Knight Ridder, with its chronic New Media fever, had moved its headquarters from Miami to San Jose.

People waiting in the lobby for appointments with the New Media group have their choice of paging through the latest issue of the *Mercury News* or using the wall-mounted monitors to prowl Knight Ridder's RealCities Network, a constellation of forty-five Web sites mixing newspaper content, online classifieds, shopping, and entertainment services. Read a paper when you could surf, link, and drill down? I clicked around the Web version of the *Mercury News* for a while, and then when I thought I'd venture further afield and check my comatose retirement portfolio, the screen went blank with a zzztt sound like a blooded-up mosquito hitting a bug zapper. Thankfully the receptionist seemed not to have noticed; I slunk back to the couch and seized the crashproof version of the *Mercury News.*

When I finally reached his office, Ingle was on the phone, moving his feet around an old Viewtron terminal that was under his desk, still in its original box—a reminder of Knight Ridder's misadventure in electronic videotex. He was nearly sixty, a trim Midwesterner, born in Iowa, with a full head of brown hair. There was a melancholy light in his eyes that suggested some old, subterranean bereavement, like the death of a brother or something, but that apparently didn't indicate anything of the sort. (So much for first impressions.)

Ingle's position as head of New Media and his reputation as a "visionary" editor stemmed from a memo he had written nine years earlier. In early 1990, almost a year before David Carlson was uploading stories onto the *Albuquerque E-Trib*'s now laughably primitive computer, Ingle was one of five people on a Knight Ridder corporate-strategy committee. Everybody would jet in from various places and hole up in a Dallas airport hotel room to stare at charts, chew on metrics, and ponder Knight Ridder's response to the digital revolution. It had been frustratingly abstract work, especially for someone as pragmatic and blunt as Ingle—a man famous for his delicate method of separating wheat from chaff with lines like, "That is the stupidest fucking idea I've ever heard." So Ingle decided to put some specifics down on paper. One January day he poured himself a scotch and sat down at a Macintosh computer in the kitchen of his townhouse overlooking a San Jose golf course.

"I started trying to think what Viewtron and videotex had taught us," he told me. "We spent $55 million and what did we learn? The thing was completely wrongheaded. The technology was terrible. It was hard to navigate, you were never sure that what you saw was the most important content. There was no e-commerce, really. We were fulfilling a need that seemed not to exist."

Though four years had passed since Knight Ridder had written off its foray into videotex, Ingle was mindful that everybody involved still bore "deep scars from the premature effort." He was hardly one of the New Media evangelists in the company. He'd taken a dim view of Viewtron, and later at the *Mercury News,* according to Roger Fidler, who worked at Knight Ridder, he'd been reluctant to adopt the company's photo and graphics archive service called PressLink. (Fidler also remembers Ingle arguing that Amiga was a better computer than Apple.) But the numbers, if not the scotch, had emboldened Ingle. In Santa Clara County itself, home of Silicon Valley, backyard of his newspaper, analysts were projecting modem-PC penetration would rise from its 1989 level of 13 percent to 58 percent by 1995.

"It would be nothing short of criminal if the company that had the courage to launch Viewtron failed to seize the moment when the market turned," Ingle wrote. Over the course of two nights he drafted a twelve-page memo proposing Knight Ridder start an "experimental electronic service." The key question, he noted, would be, "How is this different from the other stuff out there?" The answer? Well, the focus of the new service would be local. It would be integrated with the *Mercury News,* unlike the online services then available in Atlanta and Fort Worth. It would encompass a range of media so that users could log on by computer or by phone, and could retrieve news as videotex, audiotex, or even as a fax printout. And the paper would push the hell out of it. Ingle came up with a working name: *Mercury Center.*

He insisted that *Mercury Center,* or *Merc Center* as it was quickly dubbed, would not replace the newspaper, and also that "for the most part the user could not expect to get current news from it." This last prediction was one of his less Delphic insights, given that breaking news would emerge as one of the main online attractions. Nonetheless, the memo as a whole was farsighted, and it went over well at the next powwow in Dallas.

"We wound up recommending the proposal to Tony Ridder, then president of Knight Ridder, and he said, 'Put together a business plan.' I thought, 'Sheesh, I'm a journalist, I've never put together a business plan.'" But nearly a year later, in December 1991, with the help of Bob Gilbert from Knight Ridder Technology, Ingle was knee-deep in ramp rates, computer traffic, PC-user demographics, and spreadsheets. Two months later, in February 1992, the paper got the go-ahead and started hiring tech people, editors, marketing experts, even a "community evangelist" who went out to school and civic groups to get people interested in the service. Ingle and his staff decided to piggyback the content on one of the big three online services, which were all vying for content.

"CompuServe had the interface from hell," Ingle recalled. "Prodigy looked like a goddamned ransom note. AOL was far and away the easiest to use." An artist designed the logo "Merky," a stick figure with an M-shaped body and four hair-like rays of yellow accenting the red "C" of a head. "It took a couple of tries," Ingle said. "The first looked too much like Kennedy's head being blown away."

The *E-Trib* had been going for a while, the *Chicago Tribune* had gotten some of its paper online the year before, but in May 1993, more than three years after Ingle's memo, *Mercury Center* galloped across the finish line on the back of AOL's proprietary service, thus making the *San Jose Mercury News* the first newspaper in the country to get its complete news content and classified ads online.

Awards and accolades quickly followed, but even faster came technological changes. Not seven months later, *Merc Center* general manager Chris Jennewein, now Knight Ridder New Media vice president for technology and operations, and Mike Deleo, then a programmer at the paper and now an employee of Sun Microsystems, gave Ingle a demonstration of the Mosaic Communications browser—what eventually became Netscape Navigator.

"They brought it up on the screen—graphics, text, data. I was blown away. It didn't take long to see that this was going to be a revolution. I was sold. I flew to Miami to see Tony Ridder, and basically I said that in the old online world there were a couple of people who owned the pipes—the phone companies and the online services. In the new world it's totally open, you're not the captive of anybody."

Ridder was sold too, which meant that all the work Ingle had done getting *Merc Center* up on America Online's proprietary service would have to be redone to take advantage of the open architecture of the Web. The *Mercury News* became Netscape's first cash customer, paying $50,000 for a co-development agreement that granted it access to anything the company came up with in the next year. Knight Ridder also took an equity position in the Silicon Valley start-up that in a few months' time produced a $40 million profit.

Ingle finally got *Merc Center* onto the new platform in December 1994, a quiet launch that coincidentally came on the same day Netscape released the first version of its landmark browser. The Web site's URL was printed in one-column filler ads in the *Mercury News*. A splashier launch was staged a month later after the sales force had rounded up some advertisers.

"Most newspaper companies in this period of time were not even conscious of the Web or its implications," Ingle recalled. "It's the magic of Metcalfe's Law. Do you know what Metcalfe's Law is?"

I thought about confessing that not only did I not know what Metcalfe's Law was but scarcely more than an hour ago I had crashed the computer in the lobby.

"Metcalfe's Law says that the utility of any network increases exponentially with the number of users."

Which meant that the more people used it, the more use there would be for it.

The *Mercury News* was the first of twenty-nine newspapers that Knight Ridder trundled onto the Web over the next two years. It was a busy time, with plenty of discoveries and rude awakenings. *Merc Center* offered live online coverage of the funeral of Silicon Valley pioneer David Packard. Site visitors could interact with fictional characters in a popular Silicon Valley novel. While at *Merc Center,* Chris Jennewein and Mike Deleo had developed two ambitious applications called NewsLibrary, which searched the paper's morgue for back articles, and NewsHound, which enabled users to dig up choice bones from various wire services; both proved to be new sources of revenue. But there was much resistance when, in 1995, *Merc Center* started charging subscription fees to access the entire Web site; usage dropped, and eventually the fee was abandoned.

In August 1996 the paper printed its "Dark Alliance" series about connections among Los Angeles–area crack dealers, Colombian drug traffickers, and the CIA-backed Contras. While the interactive aspects of the Web helped circulate and promote the story nationally and internationally, they also heightened the paper's embarrassment when then–executive editor Jerry Ceppos made a partial retraction of the story in May 1997.

For all San Jose's innovations, other papers were piling into cyberspace too, and it was harder for *Merc Center* to produce a good answer to the question, "How is this different from the other stuff out there?" Ingle and Bob Ryan, who became director of *Mercury Center* in 1995, constantly stressed the value of "integration" and the contribution print reporters and editors could and needed to make to the Web site. But that was partially of necessity, as the paper couldn't afford to hire a whole new staff. Ingle was aware from the start of the newsroom's curmudgeons carping about the project.

"It was tough going at first," he said. "In any newsroom there are a handful of geeky types, but to everybody else you have to preach the gospel. The business people were quick to grasp the online potential, but to the reporters and editors on the desk it was just one more goddamned thing to do."

Today it's still one more goddamned thing to do, but somehow in the general urgency of the wired world the extra work doesn't seem quite so puzzling or onerous, and at times, as some reporters have discovered, it's useful and even fun. Errors can be corrected quickly. New talents can be displayed. A sports reporter covering the U.S. Open filed hole-by-hole audio descriptions of the course. "Our front page is often the business page," said managing editor Bruce Koon. "On big stories the business section will file with us first."

Merc Center has twenty-two employees—online editors, producers, software technicians, designers, and managers. In the spirit of integration, its offices are just down the hall from the main newsroom. When I stopped by earlier this year, the masterminds were concluding eight months' work on what they hoped would be a brilliant new product.

"We've had a dilemma, and for the last two or three years we've recognized that we have to do something about it," Bob Ryan told me. "The dilemma is that we have two fundamental markets. One is demographic. It's the market defined by the size of the gas tanks on our circulation trucks. The other is psychographic. It's a nationwide, even worldwide audience that has been coming to read our coverage of Silicon Valley. Our fundamental mistake was trying to serve two very different audiences with the same product."

Ergo SiliconValley.com—a sort of Web site within a Web site. It's really an expansion of *Merc Center*'s popular morning summary of tech news, "Good Morning Silicon Valley." The new site enfolds all the technology coverage the *Mercury News* would like to be known for, including long reports, the paper's popular and influential columnists, and late-breaking stories. It has five daily "editions" and extensive service links. The idea was to create a product that would not only play to the psychographics but might be something the *Mercury News* could export to affiliates in the Knight Ridder RealCities Network or even other information providers. Executives were so intent on wedding the paper's identity to the industry that put San Jose on the map that they bought for a "modest price" the SiliconValley.com address from a local software engineer who'd had the foresight to register it in 1994.

Despite the innovations of SiliconValley.com, *Merc Center* is growing in the petri dish of Old Media, and there are intrinsic limitations. From Bob Ingle's point of view, it's a question of money. The *Mercury News* has not seen any substantial erosion in its classified revenues, but anything he wanted to do he had to do with real money—he couldn't use what he called the "Monopoly money" that Internet companies with gaga valuations can throw around. His New Media division will have revenues of $29 million this year, and expenses of $46 million—a loss of $17 million. He is hoping to break even next year.

One month after my visit, however, Ingle received a new assignment; he now runs Knight Ridder's investment ventures. The problem of breaking even would have to be solved by some other suit. "The time was right," he said. "I would have liked to have gotten us to profitability and to have expanded the RealCities network to include more than the Knight Ridder family of papers, but being president of New Media is a killer job. The pace is unbelievable."

And down in the trenches of the battle for cyber-news supremacy, in the streets—or perhaps we should say the bit maps—of the interface, money presents similar headaches for managing editor Bruce Koon. The salaries of some poky old newspaper with a flashy Web site didn't cut much ice in Silicon Valley. It was late in the day, and he sighed an Old Media sigh. "I lost two of my best editors to Yahoo!" he said.

5. "Give Me Sixty Days!"

Publishers and editors who think newspapers have been too hasty rushing into New Media, who prefer the so-called tail-lights strategy of letting the front-running spendthrifts show them what not to do, can't be very happy about the pioneering example of Derek Dunn-Rankin. At seventy-one, with his hair grayed and his face lined from a lifetime of squinting into the Florida sun, he certainly looks the part of an Old Media sea lion ready to haul up on a deck chair with a daiquiri and leave the next generation to grapple with all that agitas about the Internet.

But when he isn't in the middle of one of his two-mile swims across the estuary of Charlotte Harbor, Dunn-Rankin is busy showing what newspapers can do in the domain of New Media if they have the leadership and the zeal to plunge in. As the president of the Sun Coast Media Group, Dunn-Rankin is the publisher of three monthly real estate magazines, a twice-a-week paper in Venice, and his flagship, the *Charlotte Sun Herald*, which he bought in 1979 when it was a sixteen-page giveaway with four employees and offices in a storefront next to a laundromat. Now it has a daily circulation of 33,000 and comes in four editions zoned for the surrounding communities.

Dunn-Rankin is more computer literate than most of his peers. In leaner years, before he could afford the company's first Apple computer, he had programmed his HP calculator to do data processing. And the publisher had been surfing online early, paying long-distance rates to access Prodigy, CompuServe, and AOL. When the Mosaic browser came along it was as much of a revelation to him as it was to Bob Ingle.

Which brings us to a meeting of the Charlotte County Chamber of Commerce in early 1996.

Around that time, small Internet service providers were springing up all over the place. Several of these mom-and-pop ISPs had approached the chamber, offering to set up the organization's Web site for free on the assumption they could recoup the cost in publicity and business connections. The chamber had been weighing their proposals, but as communications director Ron Thomas recalled, "There was a lot of anxiety about the decision because most of the people on the committee had no idea what an ISP was." A meeting in Punta Gorda was attended by a dozen or so people, including Dunn-Rankin and three ISP owners, one of whom was based in Sarasota to the north, home of the *Herald Tribune,* which was battling the *Sun Herald* for circulation in outlying communities. Dunn-Rankin hoped to persuade the chamber to keep its business local, but he'd done nothing to get into the Internet game at that point.

The climactic moment, as Dunn-Rankin recalled it, came when one of the members of the chamber said, "Derek, this Sarasota entrepreneur is up and operating, and you don't have anything but an idea."

And Dunn-Rankin replied, "Give me sixty days!"

A lot of bigger newspapers didn't have their own Web sites, much less the equipment and expertise needed to provide customers with connections to the Internet. Dunn-Rankin's idea was to get the ISP established first, then start moving content online—mainly his monthly real estate listings and stories from the *Sun Herald* editions. With the clock running, he created an Internet division, Sunline. Looking for conscripts, he found the two key players on his staff. One was his daughter, Debbie Dunn-Rankin. The other was his city editor, Ronald Dupont. In the next three years Dupont and Debbie Dunn-Rankin, along with programmer Frank Wanicka and a handful of others, some hardly old enough to shave, created what has become arguably the paradigm for community-based newspaper Web sites.

Unlike the *Mercury News,* a regional newspaper that wants to be the national voice of Silicon Valley, the *Charlotte Sun Herald* and its sister publications are local papers, serving the retirement communities in Charlotte County. The story of the closing of County Road 74 can linger on the front page for days. Editors might volunteer to spend an hour reading Dr. Seuss at the local school.

The thrift and self-reliance with which the company secured its digital beachhead are among the most remarkable things about the success of Sunline and its Web sites. But just as notable, when money had to be spent, father and daughter went boldly to the checkbook. Debbie Dunn-Rankin wanted to provide unsurpassed ISP service; Sunline installed one modem for every seven or eight customers at a time when most ISPs had one modem for every thirty to forty. From the start Derek Dunn-Rankin took the long view, projecting it would take three to five years before the Internet division got into the black.

"We have spent a lot more than we planned," he told me when I visited the paper in March 1999. His doorless office lies off the newsroom, which is in a warehouse-style building a few blocks off Port Charlotte's unprepossessing strip. "We're just completing our third year, and at the start I thought we'd probably break even by now, or a little earlier, and I suppose we are—the ISP side of the business is profitable. But I look at the whole Internet operation more separately now. I knew from the start that we'd be in it forever. It's just a natural and easy way to get information, and we've never said we were in the newspaper business—we've always said we were in the information business."

"You don't feel you got into it too soon?"

"We should have done it six months sooner. We'd be serving two thousand more customers with our ISP."

The New Media nerve center—a stack of twinkling modems, routers, servers, and phone lines—is jammed into a big closet down the hall, just across from the lounge where *Sun Herald* staffers take coffee breaks and microwave their lunches. Further down the hall is the large open room occupied by the Sunline staff, which comprises seventeen people, including general manager Debbie Dunn-Rankin, current internet editor Jeff Roslow, site designers, programmers, ad sales people, and the young Mr. Fixits who man the phones of Sunline's tech-support service. One of them, eighteen-year-old Mark Powell, has been working for Sunline all through high school. One of his ninth-grade teachers in a "Life Management" course assigned him to write a resume. He shaped one for a job at Sunline.

"If we get a job interview, do we get extra credit?" he asked.

"Yes," the teacher said.

"And if we get the job?"

He got the job. Pretty soon he was known as Mark Powell from Sunline and was being called out of classes to help fix the high school printers.

"I always knew people were smart, but I never knew how incredibly creative they are," said Debbie Dunn-Rankin. "When we got started in February 1996, we didn't have chairs or desks. We wanted to get the real estate magazine up right away, so we bought a bunch of books over the phone: *Teach Yourself Web Publishing with HTML in Fourteen Days.* In the beginning people were always saying, 'Oh, it's too late, you can't do this, you're a woman, you don't know how to program a UNIX server,' but I just laughed. I was never afraid of the Internet. It always seemed like a huge library, and the library was always my idea of a place to go. This is a library that I can run and laugh and eat in. I'm a modern-day librarian, that's what I am!"

Sunline has nearly six thousand ISP customers who pay twenty-five dollars a month to access the Internet. Many of them make Sunline their home page, as do many users who come to the paper's Web site from other ISPs. Having all those modems may help, but the real reason is what they find on the site. And for that, much of the credit can be divided between Debbie Dunn-Rankin's modern-librarian crusade for "interactivity" and Ron Dupont's novel idea of creating a newspaper site that didn't have as much to do with the news as with some of the often-overlooked attributes of newspapers.

From the outset, the company's stated aim was to put the entire community online—for free—and then the newspaper. What emerged was *Our Town Charlotte*. A far cry from shovelware, it was an online newspaper only in the sense that it was a kind of village green, the cyber equivalent of the familiar malls and benches and boardwalks and other social intersections where people talked about spring training and remembered the days when they could play tennis without bottled oxygen.

To keep people stopping by their village green, the Sunline programmers developed a set of point-and-click tools that enabled even the biggest computer klutzes to create their own Web pages. In time the innovation generated an astonishing response—74 percent of the Sunline ISP customers built personal pages, loading their cyber storage bins with favorite poems, travel itineraries, pictures of their dogs and cats and ferrets. People started signing on just to check their site counters to see if they'd gotten any hits.

Not that Sunline wasn't devising other things for them to do. From the newspaper the Sunline staff took the horoscopes and movie reviews—color coded to reflect the reviewer's estimation of each film's merits. For the school-lunch menus, graphic artist Chris Exler made repeated digital scans of a baloney sandwich being eaten bite by bite. (He actually bit the baloney down to the last bite, but the bread dried out in the hot light of the scanner, and he had to tear it by hand to make it look as if it were being eaten.)

Boating and fishing news went into a section called "WaterLine." There was a page that enabled users to take the best photographs from the paper and send them out as cyber postcards. Debbie Dunn-Rankin saw the bromides on a box of Celestial Seasonings tea and got the idea for "Wit and Wisdom," a page where people post their favorite pithy sayings.

In the early days, Sunline staff discovered they had to do more than just provide people the means and the motive to go on the Web; they actually had to teach them what the Internet was and how they might use it. In 1996 they advertised a free Internet class and rented a room in a local cultural center for two hundred people. Five hundred showed up, most of them retired and elderly, belying the stereotypes of who was interested in cyberspace. Ron Dupont, who left Sunline in the autumn of 1998 to renovate the *St. Petersburg Times'* Web site, had to stand on a chair and shout, "There'll be another show!"

"What affected me the most," he recalled, "was a woman in her nineties who called up and said, 'Is this Mr. Dupont? I just want to thank you for introducing me to something I never would have seen without you.'"

After three years the company had nearly four hundred community groups online, including the Charlotte County government, which has a three-hundred-page Web site showing county job offerings and meeting agendas, and which can be updated directly by the county administration without the newspaper having to do anything. And Sunline's real estate service is among the most innovative in the industry. In other markets, companies like Microsoft have paid Realtors for listings, but Realtors are paying Sunline to use its service. Not only can prospective home buyers look at properties, but brokers with the proper password can access all sorts of behind-the-scenes market data. Sunline's software and design is considered one of the state-of-the-art packages, and the judges who awarded it the 1999 Eppy award for best shopping application—one of many such online awards the company has won—said that "Sunline continues to do amazing Internet work, considering its small size. . . . This online application beats the metropolitan newspapers' efforts hands down. A model for newspapers' relationships with Realtors in the next century."

If anything, the Sun Coast Media Group strategy of emphasizing community first and news second has succeeded too well. By November 1998, 10 to 15 percent of Charlotte County was signing onto Sunline every morning. Eighty percent of the traffic was going to the community pages and the personal Web sites; 20 percent was going to the newspaper sites. (The latest numbers show the newspaper traffic has increased to 36 percent.) To improve its margins, Sunline is now looking for ways to sell ads and sponsorships around some of the community sites, and to upgrade the news portion.

The ink-and-paper staff has begun to see the advantages of having a closet full of modems in the building and popular addresses like *Our Town Charlotte* and Sun-Herald.com in cyberspace. "When we first started the ISP, I thought there was something wrong about it, something unclean," said Jim Gouvellis, the paper's executive editor. "It was like letting the accounting department in the newsroom. Then I realized it's another way of distributing the news, and we own it. It's brought the paper closer to the people."

Gouvellis would like to get the Internet operation more involved in news coverage. Run longer pieces. Show the original documentation on the Web site. Think like a regional paper, maybe. "The truth is that nobody knows what the hell they're doing," Gouvellis said. "We're all just making it up as we go along. Community and local news is what brought us here, but ultimately I'd like to see the Web disappear as a separate department and be part of the paper."

That's the ambition of internet editor Jeff Roslow too—or, if not that exactly, then at least making the job more to do with news and less to do with the village green. "I believe that the future of our business is on the Internet," he told me. "I want to make Sun-Herald.com more useful, more timely, more interactive. But how do you make it more interactive? I have to approach my job totally differently than I have approached it for the last fifteen years. My readers are no longer readers—they're consumers."

The *Charlotte Sun Herald* for tomorrow will go up on the Web an hour or two before midnight. Jeff Roslow still has work to do inserting the "related links" on the story that he has designated "the hot topic." He spends more time than he bargained for tending that hydra-headed monster his predecessor Ron Dupont had created. It's a problem a lot of newspapers would like to have—a community so attached to the local newspaper's Web sites that five hundred people will turn out when the paper wants to muster a group portrait of its Internet class attendees. At day's end there are likely to be some unreturned phone messages on Roslow's desk, calls he couldn't get to from the ham radio club, or the Coast Guard, or the Chamber of Commerce, all wanting to update their sites. And then there's a flood of e-mail in his queue. . . . The future of his business may indeed be on the Internet, but it's hard to tell sometimes what it has to do with news, or exactly what kind of business it is.

6. "A Computer Game Converted to a Serious Purpose"

Before returning to the asylum of my computer, I had one last stop planned in the analog domain—this time a large paper, a venerable Old Media giant, whose pride has been stung over the years by some digital missteps, but which lately seems to be getting the hang of New Media and has emerged as one of the more prominent online successes. This would be the *Washington Post,* whose interactive offices are located across the Potomac River in Rosslyn, Virginia, in one of those glassy high-rises that are the bane of Washington's architectural traditionalists.

It's certainly a new kind of newsroom that has 180 employees and only one official "reporter." The Web hounds plastered to terminals at Washingtonpost.Newsweek Interactive ("suggestions for a new name are welcome," notes the company's annual report) work as producers, coders, technicians, and editors who must be versatile enough to write headlines, new leads, even a breaking story on the weather, and do layout, and understand coding and multimedia formats.

There's an insouciance about the newsroom that is easy to mistake for a lack of urgency (and at times it may in fact be a lack of urgency, or at least a lack of that atmosphere that used to be fetishized in the regular newsroom as "creative tension"). One of the persistent themes sounded by Don Graham, who stops by every month or two for get-acquainted-with-the-new-people lunches, is that the Web site should be less conservative than the paper. Graham also tells the staff that he doesn't want the Web site to lose its flavor—that mix of playfulness, informality, and attitude you see flashes of, for instance the self-deprecatory note with which *Post* "Style" reporter Linton Weeks welcomes site users to another "spine-tingling" edition of his Thursday "Navigator" chat sessions.

Some of the flavor, and the headaches, are part and parcel of having a young staff. Interactive newsroom dress tends toward sneakers and jeans and mercifully steers clear of that ghastly prep ensemble of blue blazer, khaki pants, and red Britches tie that is still de rigueur in the downtown newsroom. Interactive desks may be scattered with primitive examples of interactive technology, such as Pez dispensers, or sidearms that fire foam-rubber ammo. In the early days, when the computer-geek culture was at its height, there was always free candy and cheap soda to keep everybody jacked. Employees on the seventh floor could listen in on eighth-floor conferences via a baby monitor. You always knew who was editing the home page at any given hour because there would be an inflatable model of the space shuttle hanging over the desk.

"In the early days, we couldn't even get the cable service we wanted because we weren't a tavern," recalled Jody Brannon, the managing editor for breaking news who returned to the Web site after taking a leave to finish a doctorate in journalism. Brannon, and everybody else I talked to, was at pains to point out that the laid-back atmosphere is deceptive because there isn't one deadline a day, there's a deadline practically every hour, or more if events warrant. It can be like wire-service work, much in contrast to the *Post*'s vaunted in-depth journalism, and it creates high turnover. "I used to call it the minute-ly news, not the daily news," said former site editor Leslie Walker, who after nearly two years there returned to the *Post* to write a technology column. "Two years of that and I almost fell over."

"We're following a broadcast mode," said Chris Ma, the executive news editor of the Web site, who came over from *U.S. News & World Report*. "We do near real-time traffic updates and provide inning-by-inning scores of Orioles games. We do stuff off the breaking news. We're trying to walk a balance between breaking news and what the paper has certified as news the day before. We can't just republish the paper."

Most of tomorrow's *Post* is typically available on the Web site by 10:30 at night. The cyber version is not permitted to scoop big sister without consent. There have been a few occasions when the site has broken news ahead of the print edition—election results in the 1997 Virginia governor's race, the deaths of Mother Teresa and Princess Diana. "When the news broke about Diana, I was drinking a beer, watching TV," Walker recalled. "I set the beer down and went back to the office, and I didn't leave for seven days. That first night I changed how we programmed the home page."

But the story that more than any other put the *Post*'s Web site on the map was Monica Lewinsky's. The first scandal report appeared on the Web site around midnight, before any papers were on the streets. That week in January 1998 the traffic on the Web site, which the month before had been 25 million page views, jumped to 33 million. By April it had climbed to 40 million a month, and by the end of the year, after the Starr report, it was around 70 million. What all those page views mean, said Washingtonpost.Newsweek Interactive president Marc Teren, who came from Disney in 1997, is "an unduplicated audience of 2 million users a month, with an average of 300,000 a day." Because of the government, he said, "Washington has the highest percentage of Internet users in America—higher than Silicon Valley."

Monica's story fostered a new era of cooperation between the downtown newsroom and the Web site. "We began getting stories earlier, at nine o'clock," said current Web editor Doug Feaver, who joined the cybershop after nearly thirty years on the print side of the *Post* with the specific job of acting as a liaison between the two. "Reporters in the newsroom only got Internet access last year. They couldn't see what we were doing before that. Now the cooperation is getting better and better. [*Post* reporter] Peter Baker filed midday updates on the Lewinsky story. We did the same thing on the Microsoft trial."

In addition to breaking news, the *Post*'s Web site has pressed to extend other services. With CitySearch, *Post* producers developed and launched a comprehensive if underused entertainment area called StyleLive to counter Microsoft's local edition of Sidewalk. There's a shopping site called Marketplace and a D.C. visitors' guide. Sadly, no *San Francisco Examiner*-style Webcam is yet trained on the interactive newsroom, but in December 1998 the dot-com group introduced "washingtonpost.com on wheels," or as they like to call it, "WOW," a twenty-seven-foot-long version of a 1998 Lincoln Navigator equipped with six computers, a generator, and satellite Internet access, as well as a press release that could have been written by Deepak Chopra: "This super-cyber-sport utility vehicle is a fun, engaging symbol of the infinite possibilities of the Internet."

In keeping with the broadcast model, the *Post* site now offers five or six hours of live chat and other programs featuring *Post* reporters, critics, and sundry guests. Former restaurant reviewer Phyllis Richman's show routinely drew as many as two hundred questions. Even Don and Katharine Graham have signed on for interactive sessions with the public. The whimsy of the Web is positively contagious. Prior to one of his online appearances last January, executive editor Leonard Downie Jr. was challenged by his former managing editor, Bob Kaiser, to see if he could spot the question Kaiser planned to submit. Downie's conversation was ambling along when up popped the following query:

Washington, D.C.: How did a guy as good looking as you get sidelined into the news racket? Wasn't Hollywood your true calling?

Leonard Downie Jr.: Fortunately, I am a lot better looking than Bob Kaiser, who may have submitted this question, so I nosed him out for this job.

A short while later some haplessly uninformed foil from Greeley, Colorado, put in a question: Who's Bob Kaiser?

TO THINK PEOPLE would even have to ask! In Old Media circles Kaiser might be just another Russia expert and book writer, and maybe no one in Greeley could be expected to know he had recently ended a seven-year stint as managing editor of the *Post*. But in cyberspace . . . well, not many people knew his contribution there either. But the fact is, Kaiser was the godfather of the *Post*'s digital adventure.

In the summer of 1992, Kaiser had accepted an invitation to speak at a conference in San Francisco and he'd decided to make a side trip—his maiden voyage to Silicon Valley. Truth be told, he didn't know much about computers other than what sort of Elizabethan curses are appropriate when your PC eats chapter 1, but with the help of a *Post* correspondent and an old Yale classmate who ran a venture-capital company, Kaiser spent two days with such influential people as Andy Grove, the CEO of Intel, and John Sculley, then head of Apple. One thing led to another, and Sculley invited Kaiser to an Apple conference in Japan on the "future of multimedia."

There, Kaiser was "taken aback" by forecasts that before long computers would have advanced to the point where they had a billion bits of memory and would be able to process instructions and transmit data at the rate of a billion bits per second. These standards, which are now in view, were called the Three Billions, and they foretold major changes in the way people used and processed information, which meant they weighed heavily on the future of newspapers. "That trip changed my worldview," Kaiser recalled.

On the flight home from Japan, he composed a memo summarizing the new gestalt that had been sketched for him by the techno-futurists. Inevitably, perhaps, he posed the challenge it presented in negative terms—the *Post*'s online effort should be mounted in defense of its existing economic niche, not in pursuit of a new one:

> No one in our business has yet launched a really impressive or success-
> ful electronic product, but someone surely will. I'd bet it will happen rather
> soon. The *Post* ought to be in the forefront of this—not for the adventure,
> but for important defensive purposes. We'll only defeat electronic competi-
> tors by playing their game better than they can play it. And we can.

Kaiser proposed that the *Post* design an electronic classifieds section, as well as what he called, apparently unaware of the work under way at the *Albuquerque Tribune* and other places, "the world's first electronic newspaper." He envisioned a "series of 'Front Pages' and other devices that would guide readers the way our traditional cues do—headlines, captions, story placement, etc. And we could explore the feasibility of incorporating ads." Kaiser was outlining a service much more substantial than what the *Post* had offered CompuServe subscribers in the 1980s, but by today's standards it would be derided as mere shovelware. There was, however, a prescient passage in his memo in which the editor grasped the essence of the online experience that to this day has eluded many others in his profession:

> We tend to use new media first to replicate the products produced by
> old media—so early TV consisted of visible radio shows, for example. With
> this in mind, our electronic *Post* should be thought of not as a newspaper on
> a screen, but (perhaps) as a computer game converted to a serious purpose.
> In other words, it should be a computer product.

A *computer product.* There, in a phrase, was the gist of the new paradigm.

Kaiser's memo was a fascinating if contradictory amalgam of Old and New Media thinking. He circulated it to Don Graham, to the *Post*'s resident technology expert, Ralph Terkowitz, and a few others, and then he set up a committee to explore the ideas he had broached. Kaiser also tossed the memo to Mark Potts, a bearish staff reporter and self-described "problem child" who had covered technology since 1986, done a stint as a business editor, and was wondering that summer how to re-energize his career.

Potts couldn't believe what he was reading. Here was a *Post* editor sounding like one of his Silicon Valley sources. A senior *Post* editor who understood the digital future. A bow-tied Yalie, no less.

Potts had once cooked up an electronic version of the *Post*'s business section on his Mac PowerBook, and that August, on his own and unaware of Kaiser's high-powered committee, he decided to produce a full-fledged prototype. He called it PostCard. The design mimicked the print paper's section headings, typefaces, and logos. For photographs Potts used now-primitive clip-art files. To satisfy Kaiser's prophetic injunction that the electronic version be more than a paper on a screen, Potts devised animation and sound effects. Holding a microphone to his television, he captured some quotes from President Bush about Hurricane Andrew. He programmed the sound of thunder into the weather report. By the end of the weekend, Potts was satisfied that a first-time user could easily point and click his way around PostCard. When Kaiser saw it he sounded like Brigham Young entering Salt Lake Valley for the first time: "This is it!" he cried. "This is what I was talking about in my memo." He dragged Don Graham and some other executives down from the eighth floor. "This is great," Graham said.

Thus from the chrysalis of the "problem child" emerged the first New Media editor of the *Washington Post*. Potts started work January 1, 1993. "I remember that night before I started the job having no idea what I was doing," Potts recalled over lunch this spring, not far from his home in Falls Church, Virginia, where he now works as an Internet consultant to major media companies. "I was scared to death. I wondered, 'What do I do?' I had no idea what the job was." And despite his initial enthusiasm for Potts's prototype, Graham wasn't very encouraging. He summoned Kaiser and his new New Media editor up to his office, and, as Potts remembered the scene, he said, "I created the position but I don't really believe in it. We're not going to spend a lot of money on this thing. Don't get your hopes up."

"It was a very stern lecture," Kaiser recalled.

Graham's skepticism of New Media was well-founded. Caution had saved the Washington Post Company from the bath Knight Ridder and others had taken in videotex, but not from the red ink of a CD-ROM venture with *Newsweek* that was going nowhere. The *Post* had studied the possibility of becoming an ISP but had decided to leave that market to the heavyweights already in it. Potts was so uncertain of the relevance of his job to the *Post*'s future that when he went out to a meeting with Apple's Online group in Silicon Valley later that January, he asked Ralph Terkowitz, "Does Don Graham even know we're here?"

Graham must have, because that October the *Post* formally established an online newspaper operation under the name *Digital Ink,* a clever handle that ultimately proved counterproductive when the value of reinforcing an existing news brand in cyberspace became obvious. What turned out to be more expensive was the decision to base the proprietary electronic service on a Ziff-Davis software platform called Interchange, which was inconveniently sold to AT&T in the middle of development—and which was soon blindsided by the Web.

"Don Graham and I made the decision to go to the Web in the back of a taxicab in Chicago in November 1995," said *Post* president Allan Spoon. "We had 20,000 paying subscribers on Interchange at the time. The question was, 'Do we want to win the county track meet with 25,000 or 50,000 paying subscribers, or do we want to win the Olympics with millions?' We had a service that was clearly ahead of what users wanted in Washington, but we knew we were in it for the long haul."

Kaiser and Downie credit Spoon with persuading Graham to change horses in midstream. Add an assist from the bogeyman shadow of Bill Gates. "It was the Microsoft threat that got Don to support the electronic paper," Downie recalled. "He wanted to protect the classifieds and to promote the paper. What he never dreamed was of us becoming a national site."

For many years the *Post* has been dogged by the idea that it was a national paper without a national distribution, or a regional paper with a national and international franchise. How to reach those readers? The cost of far-flung printing plants was insupportable, and the *Post*'s *National Weekly Edition,* a digest of the daily paper with a circulation of eighty thousand, was a half measure. Its foreign reporting was mostly visible through its wire service and the *International Herald Tribune.* What Monica & Company revealed was that the *Post* did indeed have an international following and a way of distributing its news around the globe: the Web.

And though the Web has been much cheaper than buying trucks and building printing presses around the country, it was hardly a financial cakewalk. "I was nervous about spending too much money too soon, and I'm still nervous about it," said Spoon. "This year we're spending 10 percent of our operating income on the Web, and I don't know whether we're spending enough or too much. We're trying to fix ourselves in the galaxy of economic opportunity, but the answers aren't in yet."

Ten percent of the Post's 1998 operating income translates into a yearly investment of about $37.8 million. The company doesn't break out its

Internet numbers specifically, but recent annual reports make increasingly tense reference to the cost of Kaiser's bright idea—and cite losses in the interactive division that are largely, and sometimes entirely, attributable to the Web adventure: Web work added $13.5 million of red ink to the bottom line in 1996, $21.7 million in 1997, and $14.6 million last year. Moreover, it's too soon to tell if the measures the company has taken to preclude the feared hemorrhage in classified ads will be effective. The company's classified-ad revenues were up only 5 percent last year after increases of 12 and 13 percent the previous two years.

"I'd like to say I knew exactly when we would turn profitable," Marc Teren said. "But our focus is on what we're doing today for the long term. We're on the path to profitability, I know that by the number of advertisers, the size of the contracts, the renewal rates, the number of eyeballs and page views. And I know we're building brand value. Brand value is not only measured by profitability."

Financial pressure may eventually force the *Post* to reconsider its decision to set up its Web site as an independent operation in Rosslyn. It made sense at first to incubate the new business free of Old Media strictures. "We're trying to develop a new pattern of thinking and content creation and market outreach that are all marinated in the lingo of the Web," Spoon told me. "The newsroom is on a twenty-four-hour editorial cycle, and the Web site is on a broadcast cycle. We're not ready right now to ask the newsroom to serve two masters, print and electronic—every time I've ordered synergy, it's blown up in my face—but eventually the newsroom is going to have to learn to do both."

Leonard Downie, for his part, eyes the cyberchild with what seems a mix of chariness and awe at its power to reach people in ways that newspapers can't. "The Web site should be a separate operation," he said. "It's a different mentality and perspective. Bob Kaiser foresaw that they'd have their own newsroom, but I think that eventually we'll do more reporting for them on their news cycles. They may have a handful, or a dozen or so, of their own reporters to fill in the gaps. But I want a certain amount of separation between the paper and the Web site because I don't trust us to necessarily make the right decision for the Web audience."

7. FOLLOW THAT NEPHEW!

Was it a lot easier being in the news business a generation ago? Now it's not enough to do your job; editors and reporters and publishers are expected to master new trades. They have to reconfigure themselves as marketers and information utilities. They have to compete with TV stations and online services and Yellow Pages salesmen from metastasizing phone companies. They have to fortify their castles against New Media infidels while undertaking multimillion-dollar crusades of their own. They have to become merchants of books and videos and mail-order gingerbread, while staring into the mirror and saying, "Why didn't I think of Amazon.com? Why didn't I think of eBay?" And amid all the hand-wringing and frenetic to-and-fro, they have to gather and edit and publish the news, too.

Once they were proud of their ability to convert the codes of subcultures and the shoptalk of specialties into language a general audience could understand. Now it seems they have to find some way to accomplish something similar for their own profession—to tell the story of the central role of telling stories, and to translate the arcana of their specialty into terms that will demonstrate its value to a society that suddenly seems rather cavalier about their business. The adventure of change, indeed! But alterations of this order are not easily managed in an industry that has no history of research and development, and where any one organization pays a high, and sometimes ultimate, price for failure.

As I was riding the train back from Washington to New York, I kept thinking about a scene from my visit the month before to David Carlson's class at the University of Florida. Carlson had been through the media loop from Old to New, and had ended up in academia, and he was not hopeful about the future.

"Even as recently as two years ago," he had said, "there were an awful lot of publishers who believed online newspapers were a flash in the pan. At industry meetings people would ask questions that just proved they didn't believe it was important. I was a self-appointed evangelist. In my mind I believed I was trying to save newspapers. I still believe newspapers are doomed to extinction if they don't get with the program. I've been telling publishers if you don't think this industry is in trouble, find an eight-year-old and follow him around and see how he gathers information. I watched my eight-year-old nephew Chris for a day and saw how he related to TV and to computers, and to him interactivity was a natural thing."

Carlson listed the familiar gloomy facts: Networks like CNN and MSNBC had done a better job online because they were at home in multimedia. He ticked off the litany of changes looming: bandwidth, cable modems, digital subscriber lines—changes that were only going to exacerbate the problems of newspapers if they went unmet. "I love newspapers," he said. "I want to see them survive and improve. But at the rate they're going, I'm afraid the window of opportunity will close before newspapers get it. We really don't get it."

As I got up to leave, another professor brought a group of students into Carlson's interactive media lab. Carlson gathered them around a conference table beneath an enormous, wall-mounted, flat-screen computer monitor—a monitor an Old Media sourpuss might have called Orwellian, but which suddenly seemed much less the symbol of a dehumanized totalitarian state than the forum of a brave new world. "What we are doing here," Carlson began, "is trying to prepare students for a future that may or may not include newspapers."

A *future that may not include newspapers*. What sort of woebegone story would that make? Certainly not a tale to light a fire under the sleepy-heads in class that morning, who looked less ready to convert a computer game to a serious purpose than to convert a serious purpose to a computer game. Maybe the story would have to wait for somebody else, a fully interactive eight-year-old niece or nephew, perhaps. Aim high, kid, and work some magic, and ignore those pribbling clot-poles who say you love words too much, because some of us are counting on you to tell it someday, somewhere, in some medium or another.

Dot-com stocks that grew miraculously in 1990s began to wilt in the spring of 2000, but their decline had little effect on the flourishing economy until that fall. By year's end, the collapse of tech stocks was a terrific drag on Wall Street, and comparisons to the fortunes lost on Holland's seventeenth-century flower market after Continental tastes turned from the tulip no longer seemed outrageous. The Nasdaq, which had set a new high in March, fell by more than half. The pribbling skeptics now looked less like clot-poles than paragons of prudence.

At the dawn of the twenty-first century, pink slips were in bloom at high-tech companies across the land, and online newspapers and other media companies were not excepted: Knight-Ridder.com laid off 68 employees in December 2000. The following month, 69 workers were dismissed from nytimes.com and its subsidiaries; half the 450 online jobs were cut at FoxNews.com and FoxSports.com when Rupert Murdoch's News Corporation shuttered its digital media division; CNN let go 130 people at CNN Interactive. Earlier, Tribune Company laid off 34 staffers and cut 46 open positions.

These developments forced news executives to undertake an agonizing reappraisal of their situations. "The first era of newspaper experiments on the Internet, fueled in part by the fear that the Web would devour profits, is over," the New York Times declared in January 2001. "A new era of newspaper experiments on the Internet, fueled in part by the fear that the Web will not generate profits, has begun. Where will it lead?"

Many lessons were learned from the shakeout in tech stocks, and researchers even pinpointed the headwaters of the Amazon in the years following Chip Brown's exploration of cybernews. But the map to online success still led across terra incognita.

Online newspapers were worrying less about branding themselves for a national audience and more about turning a profit. Soon. They were shying away from the notion that their electronic twins should be separate entities with separate staffs and rethinking the synergies that could be created between existing news desks and online editors. While some saw this as the triumph of shovelware, others saw advantages in greater integration.

"Newspapers with established brands and capable news staffs are still in a position to dominate online news," said Larry Pryor of the Online Journalism Review. "Once their online staffs are integrated into core news operations, they'll be able to put up fresh content and get away from once-a-day publishing."

Several sites were still grasping for a handhold in the market, offering to build Web sites for people and partnering up with all manner of online and brick-and-mortar retailers. But in the aftermath of the tech-market crash, many analysts suggested that the keys to success online might just be the same traits found in successful newspapers: strong ties to the people and communities where they publish and the ability to churn out quality content day after day.

"The interesting sidelight to all of this is that it may throw some attention back onto the smaller, regional papers that do a credible, if not flashy, job in presenting news largely for newcomers and distant readers," said the University of Illinois's Eric Meyer. But no one was laying bets on what sort of shape online newspapers will be in when the carnival finally pulls out of town.

"Part of the reason why this is a difficult issue to handle is that it's not just technology, it's not just journalism," Meyer said. "It's part of the social psyche of America."

8 | The Training Track

By Winnie Hu

ORIGINALLY PUBLISHED IN OCTOBER 1999

*M*IAMI HERALD reporter Neil Reisner is coaxing us through the language of spreadsheets—medians, percentages, and, of course, errors. "It's mechanical, there's no math involved," he says reassuringly to the half-dozen journalists hunched over computers in the basement of Boston's Fairmont Copley Plaza Hotel.

As Reisner demonstrates how to find percentage change, my fingers haltingly inch toward the keyboard. I tap one key, then another, and another. With the third stroke, the carefully summed numbers vanish from my screen. I frantically pound more keys, hoping in vain to find the magical "undo" function. A young man sitting in front of me is doing the same thing. Instead, an error message flashes across our monitors.

"You have proved my theory about journalists," Reisner exclaims, fixing us with an exasperated look. "We have the attention span of fleas."

But an hour later, he still has our attention. We click and drag and type in long strings of formulas. I am learning, but I can't help feeling hurried. With little time and few resources to learn computer-assisted reporting in most newsrooms, journalists cram in what they can at training conferences like this one organized by the National Institute for Computer-Assisted Reporting (NICAR) and Investigative Reporters & Editors (IRE). Even then, these skills may well have to be learned again.

"I remember it right now," says one of my fellow students, Jay Reeves, an Associated Press reporter who runs a one-person bureau in Birmingham, Alabama. "If I went back next week and tried to use it, I could probably do it. In a month, I would get stumped."

The 1999 NICAR national conference in Boston drew 560 of us—the number swells almost every year—and its weeklong "boot camps," held mainly at the University of Missouri, have taken 752 journalists through statistics and databases since 1994. This in a business that a decade ago had barely heard the term "computer-assisted reporting."

The NICAR sessions ride a veritable wave of new training opportunities available to newspaper journalists these days, just as their popularity reflects a changing attitude in the industry about professional development in general. Indeed, as newspapers confront their complicated future, there have never been more training outlets or more journalists taking advantage of them.

On the other hand, there has never been more frustration. In an increasingly specialized and computerized world, training remains a low or nonexistent priority at too many papers—especially the smaller ones, which account for the vast majority of the nation's dailies. There are papers that do send their staffers to programs like the NICAR conference in Boston but then offer little in the way of follow-up training when they return. Some papers keep their training mostly in-house, with varying results. Others don't even do that. Every year, thousands of reporters and editors are still forced to burn vacation time or pay their own way if they want to learn new skills.

Even allowing for the undeniable progress, many journalists remain troubled by the catch-as-catch-can training situation.

"If we think that we are doing enough training, we are completely out of touch," says Bill Ostendorf, managing editor of visuals at the *Providence Journal,* who uses his vacation time to teach management, photo content, and design in other newsrooms. "Everywhere I go, people tell me over and over again: 'I feel incompetent.' Everybody."

NEWSROOM TRAINING: Gone are the days when it was considered a frill, like a company gym, or little more than a plum for a paper's stars. In the past decade, newspaper companies have begun to invest more heavily in training that better equips their journalists to cover a transforming world. Between 1988 and 1999, for instance, the *Washington Post* sent eighty-four staff members to intensive writing and editing seminars at the Poynter Institute for Media Studies in St. Petersburg, Florida. That works out to some seven journalists every year, and tens of thousands of dollars in tuition fees and travel expenses (not to mention the cost of their salaries while they attend). Over the same period, the *Philadelphia Inquirer* freed up thirty-four staff members to immerse themselves for a week in such topics as nuclear energy and public health at the Knight Center for Specialized Journalism at the University of Maryland.

Many more companies are taking advantage of one- and two-day training conferences that are within a few hours' drive of their papers. In April, Community Newspaper Company, the Fidelity subsidiary that owns four small dailies and eighty-seven weeklies in Massachusetts, sent eighty-eight journalists to the National Writers Workshop in Hartford, Connecticut.

The registration fees and hotel expenses came to more than $10,000. "In the community, we are a small newspaper, but in certain areas, like training and recruitment, it pays to be a bigger operation," says Vicki Ogden, Community's staff-development editor.

That recognition of training's importance has led to a surge in professional programs around the country. NICAR, for instance, is an initiative of IRE and Missouri's School of Journalism. Poynter and the American Press Institute are aggressively expanding their offerings and moving into online instruction. The Robert C. Maynard Institute for Journalism Education does management training and promotes more accurate coverage of minorities. The National Press Foundation is playing a bigger role. Specialized fellowships expose journalists to the rigors of law at Yale University, science at the Massachusetts Institute of Technology, and business at Columbia University. The Foundation for American Communications, known as FACS, offers short-term immersion in telecommunications, utility deregulation, and land-use issues. In June, twenty-five people enrolled in FACS's first "science institute" at the California Institute of Technology.

Still, the real training revolution is occurring in the newsroom itself. Where once "training" may have consisted of a frazzled editor barking out advice, now there are brown-bag lunches and elaborate "universities" that offer pointers on everything from databases to libel issues. Staff members are often required to learn. For instance, employees at the *Virginian-Pilot* in Norfolk and the *Greensboro News & Record* in North Carolina must plan for forty hours of training every year, says Jean Lamkin, who directed corporate training for Landmark Communications before moving to its human-resources division. "The company today will only survive if the employees are well trained and capable," she says. "We've got to do that to be competitive and achieve our strategic goals."

While the larger chains—Knight Ridder, Gannett, Newhouse—have promoted in-house training for years, many others are just getting started. And the sharpest turnaround can be seen at some companies not exactly known for throwing money around. Thomson's newspaper division has recently established formal training programs—even its own twelve-week school for fledgling reporters—in Oshkosh, Wisconsin. "Ten years ago, Thomson probably would not have had this kind of outreach," says Ray Carlsen, executive director of the Chicago-based Inland Press Association, which holds workshops around the country. "I think they just found out it's good business to train people. Unless you do, newspapers may find short-term profits and long-term erosion."

But many journalists agree with Providence's Bill Ostendorf that there is still not enough training. I heard that over and over again while taking part in his popular workshop on page design in March at a National Press Photographers Association (NPPA) conference in Baltimore. Many of the photojournalists had driven three or four hours to get there, on their own time.

Ostendorf's demeanor can be intimidating—more than once he snapped, "What were you thinking?" as he sized up rows of our page dummies taped to the wall—but his passion had an appreciative audience. At one point he made us raise our right hands and swear to take risks and keep learning new skills. "The thing I liked the best was the criticism," says Grant Currie, a photographer from the *Watertown Daily Times* in upstate New York. "Really constructive criticism is often negative, and people are unwilling to give a lot of it."

Journalists also tell me that what training there is remains too limited, effectively beyond the reach of whole groups of professionals, even entire newsrooms. Reporter Robin Lloyd says her paper, the *Pasadena Star-News* in California, seemed less interested in staff development than in getting seven to ten stories a week from everyone. "It would come out of our hide if we went to a conference," she recalls. "No one was going to pay the entry fee, the transportation, or comp the time. It was like pleading our case before the gods to even get vacation time to go to training. It was a sense of futility that we felt."

Lloyd, thirty-seven, had been at the MediaNews paper just two years when she quit to take a nine-month science fellowship at MIT. When her fellowship ended, she became a technology writer at CNN Interactive. *Star-News* editor Larry Wilson explains that he could not afford to leave her position open when he has only nine news reporters to start with. "We realize the importance of [training]," he says. "Ideally we would have more."

One of the first barometers of the training shortage was a 1993 Freedom Forum report, "No Train, No Gain: Continuing Education for Newspaper Journalists in the 1990s." The survey of 650 journalists at 123 daily and weekly papers found that nearly everyone said they wanted training, but few were actually getting it. Among the report's findings: "From the day a journalist enters the newspaper business, the training glass is mostly empty. Only 14 percent of the survey respondents say regular weekly or monthly seminars are available at their newspapers. Only 4 percent of the newspapers offer training in each of the seven basic skills surveyed." The report linked the scarcity of training opportunities to low newspaper quality and staff morale, and high employee turnover.

More recently, a needs analysis done for the Poynter Institute in 1998 showed that 53 percent of the one thousand journalists surveyed still receive fewer than twenty hours of training annually, says Poynter president James Naughton.

The training dearth is put into higher relief when newspaper practices are compared to other industries. According to a 1997 survey by the Inland Press Association and the International Newspaper Financial Executives, training expenditures for all divisions (not just editorial) accounted for between 0.84 and 1.05 percent of the payroll at the newspapers studied. That same year, companies in various other industries—ranging from health care to manufacturing to information technology—spent an average of 1.8 percent of their payroll on training. And at companies where training is a major priority, they dedicated 4.4 percent of their payroll to it, according to data from the American Society for Training and Development.

A participation survey of journalism development programs suggests that among newspaper companies, Knight Ridder is far and away the chief proponent of training, while other regular supporters include Times Mirror, Gannett, Newhouse, and the Associated Press. But such big chains as Community Newspaper Holdings, Thomson, Hollinger, Liberty, Media-News, Ogden, and Paxton—these seven alone hold a fourth of the nation's dailies, mostly smaller papers—are nowhere to be seen.

No matter the level of corporate support, this much is certain: Of the approximately 50,000 daily newspaper journalists around the country, just a fraction will get to take part in established training programs this year. Only 50 or so American journalists will get into the marquee, yearlong fellowships at Harvard, Stanford, Columbia, and the University of Michigan. API in Reston, Virginia, trains 1,000 to 1,500 journalists and business-side executives each year through its weeklong seminars. Poynter has increased its enrollment from newspapers and news services, but that number was only 530 in 1998 (still well up from 195 in 1988). Several thousand journalists will participate in programs like those of the Knight Center at the University of Maryland, FACS, NICAR, and IRE. And 3,000 to 5,000 more will attend two-day National Writers Workshops that Poynter co-sponsors every spring with eight newspapers around the country.

So what happens to everyone else?

Frankly, the answer depends on where they work. If it's a newspaper owned by, say, MediaNews or Donrey, there is probably little formal training available. At Knight Ridder and Times Mirror papers, besides their support of the external programs there are abundant opportunities to learn new skills right in the newsroom. But in-house training has its own limitations. Sure, in theory every reporter and editor can attend a paper's brown-bag lunch or two-hour session on copy editing for what it costs to send a handful of people to an outside seminar. But that rarely happens. Training editors acknowledge that on a regular basis their programs draw half the newsroom, and sometimes far less. Daily deadlines are unrelenting, and many reporters would rather skip a few hours of training than explain to editors why their copy isn't ready. It's a constant battle of priorities. "The people who need it the most are the ones you never see," says Adell Crowe, who runs training programs for *USA Today*.

The reality is that a great many journalists still do not receive any regular training—and they never will without the commitment of serious money by publishers and, increasingly, the newspaper chains. "We're not even in the adolescent phase of training," says Sandra Mims Rowe, editor of Portland's *Oregonian* and a longtime training advocate. "We're toddlers in this."

THE NEED FOR training and professional development seems to have less to do with the qualifications of individual journalists—far more have graduate degrees today than ever before—than with the complicated issues they must cover and the changing newsroom technology. "It's my clear impression that journalism school graduates and young people coming into newsrooms are smarter and better educated and have a clear sense of the world in which they live," says Bob Giles, director of the Freedom Forum's Media Studies Center in New York City. "That doesn't mean they're ready to be good journalists or that they know everything they need to know."

Journalists too easily make errors of fact or judgment, Giles says, when they don't know enough about the subjects they cover. And readers, also better educated than ever, often spot the goofs. "I think that newspaper editors have discovered that this is part of the credibility problem in which readers and key news sources lack trust in what they read in their daily newspapers," Giles maintains. In the past decade the Freedom Forum has published a series of reports that showed growing public distrust and dissatisfaction with the media's coverage of the military, physicians, science, religion, business, and the criminal-justice system.

Paul Davies learned the value of specialized training early in his career. While covering business for the *New Haven Register* in 1993, he found himself one day across the table from the CEO of Southern New England

Telephone, one of New Haven's largest employers. In retrospect, he says, he should have challenged some of the CEO's accounting of company finances. "I knew enough that it didn't sound right, but I didn't know enough to be able to really pinpoint it, and I think that's when it really hit me," he says. "If I'm going to be a business reporter, I've got to know what I'm talking about." Davies later quit to take a one-year Knight-Bagehot fellowship in economics and business reporting at Columbia. Although his editor wrote a letter supporting his application, Davies says the newspaper told him it couldn't guarantee a job for him afterward. He is now a business reporter for the *Philadelphia Daily News.*

Davies's case points up one of the inherent frustrations of newspaper training—that at most places there is no clear policy to ensure that reporters and editors get the development they need. "It's more hit or miss," says Del Brinkman, director of journalism programs for the John S. and James L. Knight Foundation in Miami, one of the leading funders of fellowships and other types of training. "They apply on their own—not necessarily with the encouragement of their employer. Too often it's the individual who feels the need for education." Adds Ted Pease, a communications professor at Utah State University who designed the "No Train, No Gain" survey questionnaire, "It's like turning a supertanker. It takes an awful lot to turn around a newsroom."

But, in interviews, many training advocates attest that the benefits are well worth the effort. Besides shoring up a newspaper's credibility, training can boost staff morale. Merv Aubespin, associate editor for development at Louisville's *Courier-Journal,* saw that happen with copy editors—a group once identified by the American Society of Newspaper Editors (ASNE) as the "Mount Everest of newsroom discontent." Four years ago, Aubespin and others organized a conference for thirty copy editors at the University of North Carolina at Chapel Hill that has since evolved into the American Copy Editors Society, a 1,200-member professional group that organizes its own training conference every year. "It became obvious what copy editors really needed was their own group to preach their own sermons," he says.

As Bill Ostendorf's workshops demonstrate, training also provides feedback in an industry notorious for not giving enough. Bradley Wilson, executive director of the NPPA, says the group's "Flying Short Course"— which every year makes five stops around the country—attracts more than 1,500 photographers who are hungry to talk about their work and trade ideas. About 85 percent of them pay their own way, Wilson points out. "Photographers have to put up with a lot of stuff and they don't have a good support network," he says. "Our profession is very bad at telling people, 'Hey, that's a good picture.' We just accept it."

The most compelling arguments for training are made by those who seek it out. Mike Hernandez, a photographer for the *Harrisburg Patriot News* in Pennsylvania, stopped going to NPPA conferences in 1991 because he felt he wasn't learning anything. But after eight years of shooting mostly routine assignments, he drove to the March conference in Baltimore. "I'm personally looking for something to make me better," he says. "I think I've reached a plateau, and I've been there for a long time. I'm looking—desperately looking—to get better somehow, so I thought I'd give this another chance." When Hernandez left the conference, he took away ten pages of notes on photo editing and layout.

UNLIKE DOCTORS, lawyers, and teachers, the journalist has no professional license, no requirement to take refresher classes to keep practicing. As a result, for generations there was no tradition of professional development beyond the newsroom walls. "The newspaper industry has always been a tremendous laggard when it comes to training," says *Oregonian* managing editor Jack Hart, who has researched what little early training existed. Newspaper executives established API in 1946, and a handful of fellowship programs like the Niemans have been around for decades, but there was little else. "When the rest of the economy was being transformed and upgrading, and other American industries were training to stay competitive, newspapers were still kind of snoozing along."

By the late 1970s, however, editors were scrambling to find ways to improve their products. ASNE introduced a contest to encourage good writing. At the same time, Gene Patterson, then editor of the *St. Petersburg Times*, recruited English professor Roy Peter Clark to consult with his staff. Other papers hired writing coaches of their own, launching a movement that laid the groundwork for training inside the newsroom.

Even so, many editors continued to view training suspiciously. Not without reason, they lamented the "fellowship syndrome"—in which good journalists were granted a year's leave only to depart not long afterward for more prestigious jobs. Then again, returning fellows often found little reason to stay. Bob Meyers was an assistant city editor at the *San Diego Union* in 1987 when he left for a yearlong fellowship to study public health. "I came back after a fellowship at Harvard—Harvard, hello it was Harvard—they put me on night rewrite," says Meyers. "It wasn't a demotion, but in my opinion it wasn't the best use of my talents." After that year, Meyers returned to Harvard to run the very same health-fellowship program. Now he is president of the National Press Foundation in Washington.

While there are notable exceptions, it was not until this decade that many newspapers committed the resources to undertake training in the newsroom. In part, this shift was forced by the dizzying technological advances that have transformed the industry. As newspapers moved to computer networks and pagination, a certain amount of training was required just to put out the newspaper every day. Later, database and spreadsheet training sprang from that. Sarah Cohen, former training director of IRE and NICAR and now a database editor at the *Washington Post,* says publishers have been more willing to pay for training when it involves technology. "We had tried over the years to do newsroom seminars on reporting, and a lot of places felt like, 'No, we've hired people who know how to be reporters already. They don't need training,'" she says. "But you bring in this new tool, and you can say, 'We'll train you on a computer,' but what we were really doing is training them how to be better reporters."

In addition, as society became more litigious, there were harassment and discrimination lawsuits to guard against. Another type of training was introduced into the newsroom. "I think newspapers train defensively," says Joe Grimm, who directs editorial development at the *Detroit Free Press.* Its three hundred journalists undergo mandatory sessions on diversity and sexual harassment. And certainly they're training for business reasons— the mounting competition from electronic media and alternative information outlets. Says John Lavine, director of NMC, the media-management center at Northwestern University, "At the end of the day, newspapers are based on brain power—they're based on how skilled, how smart and aware the staff is." By the same token, he says, "smart employees now recognize that investing in themselves is every bit as important as the company investing in them."

To oversee this training movement, newspapers created a new position —the training editor—to bridge the gap between the editorial and human-resources departments. Today there is a close network of newsroom trainers, educators, and supporters. "It's really like A.A. for trainers, it's a hand-holding experience," says Adell Crowe, who trains the 440-person news department at *USA Today.* "Some of my closest friends are through this group." Crowe and others brainstorm about how to reach journalists during a three-day conference—known as "train the trainers"—that the Freedom Forum sponsors each year. In June 1999, there were sixty-eight participants and a waiting list of twelve. "The idea is to give other trainers something to take back to their newspapers and use right away," says

Beverly Kees, editor and program director for the Freedom Forum's Pacific Coast Center. "It's one place you go where people are hurt if you don't steal their idea."

Mike Roberts unabashedly admits that he "borrowed" the idea for one of his latest workshops at the *Cincinnati Enquirer*. He invited a police officer to give a "Guns 101" primer that explained fifteen kinds of firearms. "It was a gun show for people that don't know much about guns and need to," Roberts says. "Knowing more about it can make your stories more precise." Roberts, the training editor since 1993, has also put his own ideas to work for the newsroom staff of 190. This year, he organized sessions for midlevel editors to help them with coaching, framing stories, and managing conflict. "These people have difficult jobs, and a lot of training beforehand has been aimed at reporters. They had been neglected," he says. Next year, he'll turn his attention to managers and department heads.

A NOTHER OF THE IRONIES about training is that the best-endowed papers traditionally spend the least amount of money on it, relatively speaking, although that is beginning to change. The *New York Times, Wall Street Journal,* and *USA Today*—to name just three examples—have rarely sent more than a half-dozen journalists to training conferences and fellowship programs in any given year. For instance, between 1988 and 1999, twenty-seven *Times* journalists attended Poynter seminars; *USA Today* had twenty-three, the *Wall Street Journal* just three. By comparison, the *Atlanta Journal and Constitution* sent sixty-one, the *Oregonian* sixty. Indeed, the 1997 Inland Press Association survey reveals that the largest newspapers as a group typically allocate the smallest percentage of their revenues to training. Among newspapers with a circulation between 360,800 and 696,000, just 0.2 percent of the revenue was spent on training. The smallest category of newspapers, those with between 8,000 and 9,500 circulation, spent an average of 0.46 percent of their revenue on training.

The discrepancy appears, in part, to be the latent sense among some journalists that training is for underachievers or apprentices. Yvonne Lamb, newsroom trainer for the *Washington Post,* remembers the lukewarm reception when she started organizing monthly seminars for local reporters in 1990. Executive editor Ben Bradlee headlined the first offering on ethics. "I had to overcome the feeling in the room that training was about remedial work," she recalls. "It took a slow buildup to get people to where they would come to a seminar on improving your writing." Today, *Post* reporters vie for twelve spots, twice a year, in an intensive five-day writing program. And brown-bag lunches with the likes of David Halberstam, Wendy Wasserstein, and Nora Ephron have packed the conference room.

When Crowe took over training at *USA Today* in 1992, she deliberately made her sessions "playful" because she was so desperate for participants. She bought candy for the copy desk, ran an occasional "spelling bee," and supplied popcorn for a movie about the First Amendment. "We used to be like the feel-good people," she says. "Well, now we're not doing that. Now it's much more job-specific, skill-specific." Crowe created USA Today University—known to the staff as USATU—a series of daily one-hour brown-bag lunches in the spring and fall. And more training is in the works.

Training programs are also evolving within the newsrooms of other industry leaders. This fall, the *New York Times* plans to start a "writing circle" for less experienced reporters that will be led by senior editor Bill Connolly. "I believe we learn best from our peers, with guidance," says Nancy Sharkey, the paper's former education editor who was tapped this year to promote staff development. "The *Times* has opposed a formal writing-coach program, since so many writing coaches wind up getting the whole paper written in their own voice." Since 1995, a series of seminars organized through the paper's "Deadline U" have brought together hundreds of staff writers and editors to discuss their craft; recent speakers have included Pulitzer Prize winners Rick Bragg, Isabel Wilkerson, and Jeff Gerth. Transcripts of some classes are posted on the Web. In addition, the *Times* has provided in-house Spanish lessons and offered seminars on press law, investigative and beat reporting, copy editing, and management.

But there are still holdouts. At the *Wall Street Journal,* assistant managing editor Carolyn Phillips says her paper's five hundred full-time news professionals join an environment where they learn on the job—or as she says, receive "training by osmosis" from their peers and bosses. "We actually still do believe the best training—the most enduring, critical training —is what's going on every day with every story." She acknowledges that the *Journal's* staff does not participate in many outside training and fellowship programs. "We are hiring extremely able journalistic talent to start with," she says. "Smaller papers are encountering a greater need to bolster hard skills than most big papers are—that's certainly still the case for the *Wall Street Journal.*"

At those smaller papers, meanwhile, editors concede the need for training; indeed, as Phillips suggests, they have the kind of green talent most in need of the basics. But they also plead practical problems that giants like the *Journal* don't have—mustering enough people to get tomorrow's paper out, for instance, or investing in journalists who will be moving on in a year or two. Perry Flippin, who directed training for Donrey from 1994 to 1998, used to spend several days at each property imparting his "practical, basic, shirtsleeve approach" to reporting, photography, and page design. But the crowd was always different when he returned. "We have a lot of turnover—most of our folks start low on the food chain and once they develop their skills, they move on," he says. "You never really catch up. About the time you think you've got one group trained, you've got to start over."

Other small papers have sent rising stars to API and Poynter only to have them snatched away by bigger papers. "It gets your back up even though it may not be anyone's fault," says Dennis Hetzel, editor and publisher of the *York Daily Record* in Pennsylvania. "Some of the conferences become recruiting tools for other newspapers that send people there. It's not enough to stop us from doing it, but it's frustrating."

Then there is the unprecedented turnover in newspaper ownership. When new principals arrive, training is precisely the kind of thing that gets frozen, or worse. Flippin lost his $200,000 annual training budget—not to mention his job—when Donrey recently pared itself from fifty-one dailies to just thirteen and decided there was no longer a need for a company trainer. "I'm going to make a pitch to reinstate" the position, says Flippin, now associate editor of Donrey's *Southwest Times Record* in Arkansas.

"Everybody's treading water because so many papers are being sold or swapped," says the Freedom Forum's Beverly Kees. "It's very hard on people."

Indeed, serious training—both in-house and outside the newsroom—requires serious cash, and most news companies have yet to show that kind of commitment. On the contrary, it is almost axiomatic among newspaper editors that training is one of the first things to go when the budget gets squeezed. During the recession of the early 1990s, many reporters and editors say they were told that there was not enough money for staff salaries, let alone conferences. "I mean, there were some really lean times in the early years," says the *Post*'s Yvonne Lamb. "People didn't go. Even for the big papers, we were a little better off, but there were lean years in the late '80s and early '90s."

The paucity of training dollars was one reason why outside training organizations and fellowship programs came to rely so heavily on philanthropic and media foundations. With few exceptions, they are still the largest benefactors, but news companies are also beginning to invest in programs. For instance, Times Mirror gave $20,000 to fund ten minority fellowships for a one-week management program sponsored by Oakland's Maynard Institute.

But several training organizations have turned to more lucrative sources. Bob Meyers says his National Press Foundation could not afford to offer its all-expense-paid seminars without the sponsorship of industry groups. In recent years, Visa, MCI, and State Farm have each paid between $35,000 and $50,000 to underwrite weeklong programs for journalists on electronic banking, telecommunications, and auto insurance. "Where else are we going to get the money? We are a pay-as-you-go foundation," Meyers says. Although newspaper companies do make donations, they don't begin to cover the foundation's $1.3 million annual budget.

Meyers says he meets with company officials beforehand to set ground rules. As sponsors, they are invited to a welcoming dinner for the journalists. And if the company has an expert, that person has the same opportunity to speak as everyone else—twenty minutes on the record, with questions. "You're not going to be able to propagandize them," Meyers tells the sponsors. "You're not going to be able to have fifteen flacks in the room, and your worst enemy may well be on the program." Meyers says his sponsors are not at all involved in designing the programs. Still, others caution that such arrangements can foster a public perception of undue influence on the media. "I mean, you could explain all you wanted to, all you're able to, but if the public believes that there is influence, that's all that matters," says the Media Studies Center's Giles. "It is that perception that is so dangerous."

IN SPITE OF—in some cases because of—all the management and money constraints, papers have become increasingly innovative in finding ways to train their staffs. At Community Newspaper Company (CNC), Vicki Ogden has helped centralize training for the 450 news staffers. Her monthly seminars at the corporate office in Needham, Massachusetts, draw as many as 50 journalists curious about municipal budgets, Internet searching, even the "wisdom of phone-in opinion lines." In May, she started a CNC University with sessions on time management, page design, copy editing, and libel law. "You can't farm out all your training, plus some of it isn't taught anywhere," Ogden says. "This is an opportunity to look at what our people do every day."

Media General, which owns the *Tampa Tribune* and the *Richmond Times-Dispatch,* stepped up training throughout the chain after acquiring twenty-one small dailies in Virginia, North Carolina, and Florida in 1995. "A lot of newsrooms were left alone and adrift, and people at these papers would tell me no one ever cared about the newsroom," says Tom Silvestri, the company's director of news synergy. In March, he organized a workshop on banking and finances led by two professors from the College of William and Mary. Twenty-four reporters and editors attended. Newspapers in Virginia and North Carolina have also sponsored their own one-day training sessions on reporting, editing, layout and design, government reporting, and photography.

Similarly, the Associated Press has made training a priority for its 2,300 editorial employees. A full-time training director spends about 40 percent of her time visiting the bureaus to conduct critiques. There are also trainers for the international desk and for computer-assisted reporting. Since 1994, AP has sent twenty-six journalists to NICAR's boot camps—the most of any news service or paper.

The *San Jose Mercury News'* three hundred journalists also participate in year-round training programs. Two writing coaches work with reporters during the week. Cross-training (in which an editor can work for several months as a reporter, or vice versa) is encouraged. Some years, four or five journalists are temporarily away on fellowships, their stipends often augmented by the paper. Every staff member's annual review includes a "professional development plan" that asks the journalist to list desired training. "The culture here in Silicon Valley is to be constantly learning," says Pat Thompson, an assistant managing editor. "There's a fast pace of change here, and I think people feel they have to learn to keep up."

Savvy editors also are partnering with universities, press associations, and established training organizations to take advantage of their expertise and resources. Last year, the *Oregonian* spent $35,000 for a five-day seminar in Portland that was taught by three faculty members from Poynter. Twenty-five editors and reporters met in a hotel conference room about fifteen miles from the newsroom. The training emphasized their newspaper's priorities: story development, newsroom diversity, and ethical decision making. "It was the best training we've done, and we do a lot of it," says editor Sandra Rowe. Similarly, the *Fort Worth Star-Telegram, Milwaukee Journal Sentinel, San Antonio Express-News,* and Fort Lauderdale's *Sun-Sentinel* have teamed up with the Maynard Institute to diversify news coverage at a time of shifting demographics in their communities. Maynard instructors come into the newsrooms to analyze news content and educate journalists about their newspaper's values. The "Total Community Coverage" programs cost from $2,500 for one workshop to $40,000 for training over several months. "It was a new idea to take training to newspapers," says Institute president Steve Montiel. "But I think the revolutionary part of it was not just training, but going in to examine the news values and practices. The long-term goal was to bring change there."

And the biggest changes in training are still to come. As computers and the Internet remake society, training has begun to leap from classrooms to chat rooms. Newspapers are signing up journalists for online courses that cost a fraction of traditional training programs. "It vastly increases the options," says Steven Ross, a Columbia associate professor who has taught an online computer-assisted reporting class for API. "It means you can get first-class training at even small newspapers."

API has spent nearly $1 million to develop online courses to supplement its residential programs for midlevel managers and executives. These online courses—the first half-dozen were unveiled in 1997—emphasize practical skills for younger journalists. Mary Lynn Martin, API's associate director for extended learning, says nearly four hundred reporters and editors log on every year. The courses run between three and five weeks, but typically require only an hour or two each day. In Ross's course, for example, students work on exercises, readings, and homework assignments on their own time. "We're teaching it to eleven people, and they're getting it. They're already doing stories or gathering data," Ross says. "If you learn spreadsheets in a day—and you can—you're not sleeping on it. It sticks to your mind better if you do a little over five days rather than cramming it in."

At Poynter, James Naughton says the staff is upgrading its Web site to "a teaching tool"—at a cost of $400,000—that will eventually offer reading materials from seminars and encourage e-mail exchanges with instructors. "If your news organization doesn't send you anywhere for training, at least while you're browsing you can find something of value here," says Naughton. Poynter holds controlling stock in the profitable *St. Petersburg Times*, and of late it has used some of the proceeds to make its residential seminars one of journalism's better bargains. As recently as 1995, Poynter charged $750 tuition for a one-week seminar plus $400 for a hotel room. Today that same seminar would cost just $350 total. Explains Naughton, "It's a mission at Poynter, it's not a business."

In many ways, then, newspaper training has gained an across-the-board level of respect that simply wasn't there ten or even five years ago. The NPPA's "Visual Edge" seminar, for instance, regularly draws three hundred photographers eager to learn all facets of digital photography. Gannett and the *Boston Globe* each donated $10,000 to NICAR's annual conference in March 1999.

On the other hand, long-term training—like the traditional fellowship —has become harder to justify. Despite the new emphasis on professional development, applications for the major fellowships seem to have peaked, with the number of applicants to prestigious programs at Stanford and Harvard leveling off. Several fellowship programs were even exploring alternatives. For the first time in 2000, Boyce Rensberger, director of the MIT program, was offering forty-eight journalists a "mini-fellowship" in science, each lasting a week. "There are many reporters who will never get the opportunity to take a whole year off," he says.

Others worry whether the new emphasis on training will survive the next economic downturn. "Training goes, and then newshole goes, and then jobs get frozen—but training is first," declares Giles. "You would hope that [newspaper executives] will have learned that it has a great value, but I've seen it happen too many times."

What may be different this time is that many journalists themselves have come to recognize the value of training and continuing education. From what I have seen, even if their newspapers forget, the journalists won't. That's why in Wilmington, Delaware, this year, more than five hundred of us took part in a National Writers Workshop.

This popular event was born out of desperation in 1992, during the height of the recession. John Walston, then managing editor of the *Wilmington News Journal,* scraped together a few thousand dollars for a bare-bones writing weekend. When best-selling author James Michener opened the conference by saying, "My fellow writers," that was enough to hook the 325 journalists who came that first year—most having paid their own way. "That's the beauty of it," Walston says. "It had nothing to do with companies or their budgets. We didn't market it to newspapers. We marketed it directly to journalists."

I felt that same spirit come alive at this year's Wilmington workshop, watching writer Ron Suskind prowl the auditorium stage, microphone in hand. "This is going to be group therapy," he promises his rapt audience. "We'll laugh, we'll cry, we'll hug."

Before he won that Pulitzer, Suskind tells us, before that job at the *Wall Street Journal* came along, he was just another underpaid, overworked guy on the beat. "We're journalists, we need to feel like we're special because we make so little money. What else are we going to think? We live next to lawyers, lobbyists, and doctors and they have additions on their houses— but no, no, no, we're in the high-fulfillment, discounted-pay profession," he says to appreciative laughter.

For eighty minutes Suskind holds forth like this—freely confessing his disappointments, but also testifying to many more joys. And in the end, he reminds us why we became journalists—not for money or bylines, but for stories that stir the heart.

"You'll have enough, and maybe you'll be interesting rather than rich," Suskind says. "You'll learn because what we do in our jobs—I call it 'living by other people'—it's hard to weigh and measure that stuff by scale, by salary and benefits, but it makes us better, I think, as people."

As Suskind tries to leave the stage, audience members surround him. I push my way to the front. They are asking for more stories, more advice, more understanding. Says Mike Harris, a sportswriter from Richmond, "You could tell he really, really cared about the business and the craft."

Another writer confides to me, "I feel like I've been to church."

Soon after the publication of this article, a recession led newspapers to redouble their cost cuts in an effort to satisfy the profit expectations of Wall Street. Besides cutting newshole and reducing the size of their staffs, newspaper companies also pulled back on their support and funding for training.

Training organizations such as Investigative Reporters and Editors began to notice that more journalists were having to pay their own way to training conferences. Their bosses even required many of them to take vacation days for the time spent away from work. Brant Houston, the head of IRE, wrote that one large newspaper "would not even allow reporters to take vacation days" to attend a training conference. "In another case," Houston said, "we were told that the feeling was: 'If a reporter can leave the newsroom for more than three days, then we probably don't need that reporter.'"

In a national survey conducted in 2002 for the John S. and James L. Knight Foundation, journalists cited the lack of training as their number one source of job dissatisfaction, ahead of pay and benefits. The survey said two-thirds of the nation's journalists received no regular skills training at all. Eighty percent of the news executives in the survey cited budget constraints as the major obstacle to better training.